HEALING
FOR THE
CITY

HEALING FOR THE CITY

Counseling in the Urban Setting

**CRAIG W. ELLISON &
EDWARD S. MAYNARD**

ZondervanPublishingHouse
Academic and Professional Books
Grand Rapids, Michigan

A Division of HarperCollins*Publishers*

Requests for information should be addressed to:
Zondervan Publishing House
Academic and Professional Books
1415 Lake Drive S.E.
Grand Rapids, Michigan 49506

Library of Congress Cataloging-in-Publication Data

Ellison, Craig W., 1944–
    Healing for the city : counseling for the urban setting / Craig W. Ellison, Edward S. Maynard.
      p.   cm.
    Includes bibliographical references.
    ISBN 0-310-54011-9
    1. City churches—United States. 2. Pastoral counseling—United States. 3. Minorities—Pastoral counseling of—United States. 4. Inner cities—United States—Psychological aspects. 5. City and town life—United States—Psychological aspects. 6. Church and social problems—United States. I. Maynard, Edward S. (Edward Samuel), 1930– . II. Title.
BV637.E44   1992   91-27078
235.5—dc20   CIP

Edited by Susan Lutz and Jan M. Ortiz
Cover designed by Lecy Design
Cover Photo Credits: Street Corner © Rob Sheppard / Frozen Images; Farmer's Market © Robert Friedman / Frozen Images, Inc.; Boston street © Steve Schneider / Frozen Images, Inc.; 5th Avenue, New York City © Michael G. Smith

Printed in the United States of America

91 92 93 94 95 96 / AK / 10 9 8 7 6 5 4 3 2 1

Contents

Preface

CRAIG W. ELLISON

IT ALL BEGAN in a diner in Queens, New York City. A lunch with Harvie Conn is always stimulating and that day in early June 1989 was no exception. Harvie asked me why there were no evangelical books on the counseling and family needs encountered in urban ministry. As I reflected on Harvie's question and did some research, I discovered that he was right.

I began thinking about the need, and soon realized that if I were to attempt such a book, I would need help to do it in the comprehensive way required to make it truly helpful to urban pastors, parachurch workers, laity, and Christian counselors. My thoughts went quickly to Ed Maynard, an insightful, experienced, and gracious Christian colleague with whom I'd developed a friendship several years before. Ed is a psychologist and cultural anthropologist. His training, warm Christian faith, fluency in Spanish, and experience as a Black American would combine with his counseling experience, I thought, to make him an outstanding co-author.

Later, there came another lunch in another New York City restaurant, this time with Ed. We signed on together for what has turned out to be a wonderful sixteen months of intellectual exchange, prayer, fellowship, and friendship. In the process, we have managed to co-author *Healing for the City: Counseling for the Urban Context* as well. With God's help, we have labored to produce a book that will help urban Christian helpers to be agents of healing in broken lives.

Early in the process, we received invaluable suggestions from urban workers I contacted at the Congress on World Evangelization in Manila. We want to especially thank Roy and Bonita Thompson (do all good ideas get exchanged over lunch?), Fletcher Tink, Glandion Carney, Fran Beckett, and Dave Cave for their important input, as I buttonholed them and asked, "What does a book on counseling for the city need to include?" These practitioners of urban ministry were generous in sharing their time and thoughts.

As the outline came together, we realized that we needed two authors with experience in counseling those from Asian and Hispanic backgrounds. We were most fortunate to be led to Siang-Yan Tan, Associate Professor of Psychology and Director of the Psy.D. Program at Fuller Theological Seminary Graduate School of Psychology, and to Luis Villareal, co-pastor of the New Life in Christ Neighborhood Church in Denver and a former psychiatric social worker and staff member with Youth for Christ. These two men have worked congenially with us to produce chapters with vital insights.

To make sure that we dealt with the kinds of problems most often faced by urban pastors and Christian workers, we sent a short survey to several people in New York City. We want to thank those respondents for sharing their thoughts with us.

As the book neared completion, we needed some formal evaluation from experienced pastors and workers. We want to thank Rev. Dan Ho, Senior Pastor of the Queens Christian Alliance Church, Rev. Paul Johansson, President of the New York School of Urban Ministry, Rev. Dr. Phil Joubert, Pastor of the New Light Missionary Church in Norwalk, Connecticut, and Luis Villareal for their insightful, challenging, helpful, and generous feedback. *Healing for the City* is a better and more sensitive book because of their contributions.

For her help and encouragement in the early stages of the manuscript, we want to thank Mrs. Melinda Sledge. We are especially grateful to Dr. James Sigountos for generously sharing his expertise with computer programming and word processing. Things would have been incredibly more difficult without his help.

We want to thank our wives, Sharon Ellison and Tina Maynard, for their prayers and encouragement as we moved through our literary pregnancy.

Finally, we want to thank Mike Smith for his strong support and continuing editorial leadership with regard to the publishing of practical materials promoting effective urban ministry. Mike's concern for books like *Healing for the City* spans a number of years. Urban workers can count him as a friend.

Preface

EDWARD S. MAYNARD

God is working in our lives and preparing us for his service even though we may be quite oblivious to it. Such was the case in the writing of this book. When I first decided to enter the field of psychology after years of teaching, I did not intend to specialize in the treatment of Christians. In 1978 Dr. Wyatt Tee Walker of Canaan Baptist Church in Harlem asked for volunteers to staff a counseling center to serve the church community. I became involved in that service and began to understand some of the problems that believers had and how to help them deal with those problems. Then I met Craig Ellison, an energetic, committed, and friendly brother in the Lord who had come to New York with a burden for urban ministry. We had many times of good fellowship and stimulating conversations over lunches in many parts of New York City. Craig is a gifted writer who encouraged me to accompany him in the writing of *Healing for the City*. Unbeknown to him, I had never collaborated with anyone before—even as a student I used to avoid study groups like the plague. As I hesitantly began to work with Craig, I found in him a wonderful colleague who is always encouraging and critical without condescension. It has been one of the most rewarding times of my life. The result is this book that we hand to you with the prayer that God will use it so that you too can help to "heal the brokenhearted."

SECTION ONE

Counseling in the City

Introduction

URBAN LIFE is a dazzling conundrum of contrasts. On the one hand, cities are symbols of human vigor, creativity, and vitality. There is a constant exchange of energy and ideas, a continuous interplay of thought and communication in urban centers. The city pulsates with people on the move. Its diversity presents a colorful and fascinating picture of the riches of humanity.

On the other hand, cities are contexts of brokenness. Urban dwellers live in a vortex of stress. Alcohol and drugs claim the allegiance and destroy the lives of millions. Physical and sexual assault shatter the well-being of countless children and women. Poverty deprives masses of people of basic resources for healthy living. Violence in the streets creates a pervasive climate of fear and mistrust. Intense competition and greed foster interpersonal isolation and distance.

There are two major temptations as one ministers in the city. One is to selectively focus on the bright side of the city, ignoring the brokenness of humanity. Churches and ministers who do this create insulated islands of cheery irrelevance. They have little interest in either acknowledging or trying to touch those who are in need.

The other temptation is to see only the dark side of the city, viewing it as a place filled with depraved, weird, and abnormal people—except for those in one's particular body of Christ. (And even some of those people are suspect!) With this attitude, outreach is much more probable, but it is likely to be done with overtones of paternalism. Those receiving ministry tend to be viewed as different, deficient, and even dangerous, when they should be seen as people—just like those within the body—who have made bad choices or had bad experiences that have left them struggling.

Healing for the City is a book about counseling urban dwellers in need, whether they are found inside or outside the church. Its focus is on the brokenness and problems of urban dwellers. We are not suggesting that all urban dwellers are burned out, sick, or generally abnormal. To the contrary. We are amazed at the resources and resilience of most urban dwellers, who handle the intensified stresses of urban life with a minimum of dysfunction. Nevertheless, the urban pastor, parachurch worker, and Christian counselor will be sought out by many who are unable to find healthy solutions to the psychospiritual needs and pain in their lives.

Healing for the City is written to provide practical guidelines for those called upon to counsel urban dwellers struggling with emotional, relational, and spiritual distress. It examines features of the urban environment and realities of urban, cross-cultural life that need to be understood if effective counseling is to be done. It looks at some of the most frequent counseling problems encountered in urban ministry. These problems are not unique to the urban setting, but in most cases are encountered more frequently. What is more, they are more likely to be wrapped together in a knot of multiple problems.

Healing for the City sees counseling as one of several important ministry interventions available to the urban church. While recognizing that some of the naturalistic assumptions of secular psychology are not compatible with an evangelical approach to helping, it chooses not to throw counseling out of the church. Counseling can bring about the healing of emotional and relational wounds when it is based on presuppositions compatible with biblical belief. Human beings are psychospiritual unities, and so we believe that biblically based counseling that selectively incorporates the best of contemporary professional counseling is a powerful form of urban ministry. We do not, however, feel that the primary role of the urban pastor is to counsel. We feel that parachurch workers, Christian counseling professionals, and peer counselors need to be trained to extend the healing ministry of the pastor. *Healing for the City* addresses all of these groups.

Chapter 1 presents an overview of the stresses that are unique to the urban environment or amplified by it. The experience of stress is viewed as a function of each person's perceptions. Each urban dweller does not experience the urban environment in the same way because of temperamental, familial, cultural, and environmental differences that shape each person's perceptions. Chapter 1 briefly describes major sources of urban stress, including overload, psychospiritual needs, personality styles, social-psychological factors, environmental realities, and poverty. It is important to know about stress because it creates internal pressure and pain that the urban dweller attempts to relieve in either constructive or destructive patterns. The urban counselor must be aware of stressors and of ways to help counselees reduce and manage the stress in their lives.

Chapter 2 provides a fundamental overview of the process of counseling. This is intended especially for those who have not had previous training. The chapter mentions the need for basic preparation that can be accomplished through courses, reading, and peer or professional consultation. It stresses the importance of the counselor as a person and suggests four qualities essential to effective counseling. Ultimate and immediate goals for counseling are surveyed and basic conditions crucial for healing are described. An overview of the process of counseling is presented with a specific problem-solving structure. Chapter 2 presents the underlying assumption of *Healing for the City*, which is that human beings are integrated systems. It suggests the approach of multimodal diagnosis as a helpful way to analyze and construct an intervention plan.

Chapter 3 examines issues that are particularly pertinent to the urban church or ministry setting. It suggests that Christian counseling and discipleship are compatible but not identical processes. Building on that concept, a case for lay counseling is presented, and suggestions are given for developing such a ministry. The place of preventive counseling through education in the church is explored, as is the relationship between counseling and preaching in the urban church. The responsibilities of the urban counselor for advocacy are examined. Finally, limitations and limits are given, along with guidelines for referral. A thorough set of endnotes supplements the chapter with helpful resourcing information.

Chapter 4 shows how counseling in the city must be contextualized. That is, it must be done with an awareness of the cultural influences that have influenced the counselee and will, therefore, have an impact on the counseling. The chapter presents several illustrations of the ways in which culture affects a person's view of his world, his problems, and his counselor. It suggests factors that the urban counselor must consider when working with people from different ethnic or cultural groups. In addition to cultural factors specific to a group, we have also examined the role of time and visible progress, language, and individualized versus group approaches. Finally, a self-assessment test of cultural sensitivity is given.

Chapter 5 deals with two of the most difficult and dynamic issues facing the urban counselor: racism and demonism. The chapter discusses the impact of racism upon the psychological, relational, and spiritual functioning of most minority people. A counselor must be sensitive to issues of race or risk losing the trust of the minority counselee and the opportunity to help him beyond a superficial level. Suggestions are made for dealing with racism in the process of counseling.

The second part of Chapter 5 addresses the realities of spiritual warfare in the city, and the possible role of the urban counselor. Because we view human beings as psychospiritual beings, and because we view the supernatural as real and potentially interactive with the natural, we believe that urban counselors must be prepared to deal with those who are demonized. Guidelines are given for this process. Urban ministers are warned not to engage in such warfare casually, but with caution and support. At the same time, we stress that the Almighty God is more powerful than the forces of evil. Urban counselors are cautioned not to spiritualize all counseling problems. They must soberly evaluate the interplay between the spiritual and psychological and choose an integrated path of intervention that emphasizes the psychological or spiritual in a way appropriate to the specific situation.

CHAPTER 1

Stress and Urban Life

WE LIVE IN a stress-filled world. In recent years we have begun to understand the tremendous costs of stress. These include rampant addictive behaviors, broken marriages, lowered job productivity, illness and soaring medical expenses, senseless violence, widespread depression, and emotional breakdown. People spend hundreds of millions of dollars each year on entertainment, recreation, biofeedback, therapists, drugs, vitamins, seminars, and books in their search for relief from stress.

Stress is not unique to city life but is magnified by it. City dwellers must wrestle with the special stressors of stimulus overload, constant change, crowding, noise, pollution, unpredictable transportation, cultural differences, homelessness, and drug infestation. Every day brings multiple demands into the urban dweller's life that require processing and adjustment. The sheer volume of information that greets a city dweller each day in the form of television, newspapers, magazines, leaflets, posters, and work materials creates stress. The need to be aware of and interact with large numbers of people, many of whom are different from oneself and some of whom are potentially threatening, brings significant stress to most city dwellers. People are often unaware that these realities are causing underlying stress in their lives.

At the same time, anonymity, isolation, and loneliness plague the lives of millions, bringing intense inner turmoil. Values that promote competitiveness and mistrust in the workplace, together with an almost desperate pursuit of wealth, comfort, luxury, and status, put many urban dwellers into a daily emotional drag race.

There is considerable agreement about some of the stress-related characteristics of big cities.[1] College students from a wide range of small, medium, and large places described big cities as being impersonal, as fostering feelings of confusion, and as being made up of people who are untrusting, while agreeing that the terms peaceful, safe, healthful, relaxed, close-knit, and sense of intimacy did *not* describe the big-city atmosphere. Cities are more complex and more stressful than small towns, but the degree of stress experienced by a given person depends on a number of factors.

Effective Christian counseling in the city must take stress into account. Not only does stress impact directly on well-being, but faulty attempts to cope with it may actually increase its negative effects. Christian counselors need to understand the nature and sources of stress for the individual city dweller, and learn ways to help him reduce and manage it. The result will be healthier people.

THE NATURE OF STRESS

What is stress? Dr. Hans Selye, the father of modern stress research and theory, has defined it as "the non-specific response of the body to any demand made."[2] Stress is the wear and tear caused by living life. We are constantly faced with demands on our body, mind, relationships, and spirit. These demands or stressors require responses, which place varying degrees of strain on our body and mind. We try to maintain a state of inner balance—what we are used to. Any stimulation, change, or perception of possible threat throws us out of balance. Stress is essentially the strain put on our minds and bodies when we try to recover our previous state of balance. It is a natural part of life.

Everyone who is alive experiences some stress. Problems develop when our lives are filled with more stress than we can handle without physical, emotional, relational, or spiritual breakdowns. When stress levels are not properly managed and we experience prolonged, excessive stress, we begin to disintegrate. Physical, emotional, relational, or spiritual breakdown eventually occurs.

The primary stress response is to prepare ourselves for fight or flight. When we feel threatened, a message is sent to our brain, various hormones are released, and sugar and fats are poured into our blood to prepare our body to actively struggle with the stressor. Often the thing that threatens us is not physical, but psychological: Our psyches are much more likely to be threatened than our lives. In the city, however, both kinds of stressors will often be present. The thing to remember is that whatever the stressor is, our bodies respond to it with an "alarm" response.

Although there is both good stress (eustress) and bad stress (distress) which, when accumulated, can result in breakdown, we will focus in this chapter on distress. When we mention stress, we are talking about distress.

Stress is physical or psychological tension in response to any stimulus that is perceived as potentially threatening to one's physical or emotional well-being. The key words are "perceived" and "threatening." What may be perceived as threatening by one person may not have the same effect on another. Some people see the city itself as highly threatening and do everything possible to stay away from it. Others love the city and seem to thrive on its diversity and energy. Some see racial and cultural differences as threats, while others celebrate those differences. Some see city streets as filled with danger, while others enjoy the activity. Ultimately, a "threat" is anything seen as a challenge to one's biological or emotional survival. Anything that might result in death, damage, devastation, or devaluation is a threat. Anything that promises the real possibility of pain is stressful. This suggests that the same situation may or may not produce stress, depending on whether or not a person perceives it as threatening.

Among the signs of stress are
- Constant fatigue;
- Increased irritability and quickness to anger;
- Frequent headaches or gastrointestinal problems;
- Trouble breathing;
- Feelings of being overwhelmed, pushed to the limit;
- Frequent mood swings;
- Lack of joy, flattening of emotions, depression;
- Racing thoughts;
- Difficulty concentrating, preoccupation;
- Insomnia or oversleeping;
- Muscle twitching, spasms, tightness;
- Spiritual flatness;
- Desire to run away;
- Increased mistrust;
- Paranoia.

Although these signs do not automatically indicate stress, the more of them that are present in a person's life, the greater the likelihood that the underlying problem is stress.

SOURCES OF STRESS

Overload

The very energy, color, and excitement that gives urban life its sense of vibrancy and anticipation ("somethin's always happenin'") also carries a price tag for many residents. Fast-paced city life often stretches people to their limits. The sheer volume of sights, sounds, people, information, and events that assault the urban dweller creates stress and requires creative attempts to cope. One's senses are bombarded daily with stimuli one must process and decide whether to heed or ignore. This experience is called stimulus overload.[3]

Stress researchers have found that as the number of life-event changes increases, physical and psychological disorders increase as well.[4] While there has been much criticism of these findings (due to apparent flaws in design and methodology), health and well-being do seem to suffer in overload situations. The degree to which something in the urban environment causes stress may reflect what one chooses to pay attention to when one's stimulus-processing capacity is overloaded.[5] Perceived helplessness or loss of personal control also seems to be a key element in the experience of stress.[6] For example, urban noise and crowding do not necessarily produce stress, depending upon adaptation and the degree of choice people feel they have over their environment. The complexity and novelty of the stimuli that need to be processed also seem to affect the amount of psychological and physical arousal produced.[7] High levels of input per se are not necessarily stressful, and may even be pleasing, depending in part on adaptation. For example, most initial encounters with the city leave non-urban dwellers feeling overwhelmed, while experienced urban dwellers may actually seek out greater and more novel stimulations.

The problem with overload is that it taxes our emotional and biological ability to determine whether or not each thing that reaches our senses is possibly threatening. If something is judged potentially dangerous, our body, mind, and emotions have to adapt. Substantial amounts of emotional energy are spent dealing with the stressors. The need to evaluate and adjust are at the heart of stress. Without some way to limit the number of potential threats (and thus our need to respond to them), people begin to break down.

The amount of breakdown will vary with different people, due to differences in the way each person interprets life events. Urban life is, of course, not uniform. There are differing amounts and intensities of stress, depending on *where* and *how* one lives in the city. In a sense, there are almost as many "cities" within a city as there are individuals! In general, however, the number of potential stressors (overload) is greater in cities than in non-urban situations. The amount of energy needed to "keep things together" is greater; if the demands of urban life exceed our processing capacity, we begin to "fall apart" to some degree.

In addition to the number of stressors, there are five other major classes of stressors that contribute to the build-up of urban stress. These are (1) psychospiritual needs, (2) personality styles, (3) social-psychological factors, (4) environmental factors, and (5) bioecological factors.

Psychospiritual Needs

Every human being living since the Fall[8] has struggled with deep inner needs for acceptance, belonging, equity, identity, security, significance, and transcendence. The interwoven dimensions of mind and spirit give rise to these psychospiritual or existential needs.

We each want to experience an inner sense of feeling okay (acceptance); of intimacy and attachment to one or more others (belonging); of physical, emotional, and spiritual safety (security); and of meaning and purpose for life that goes beyond the purely natural and connects with God (transcendence). Along with these experiences we'd also like to know that we matter and are valued (significance), and that life is fair (equity).

While urban life does not create these needs, it may deepen the deficits that we experience, depending upon the social-psychological and environmental experiences a person has. Experiences that reflect consistent caring, affirmation, and love help to meet our existential needs and provide us with a sense of *shalom* (well-being). Experiences that produce feelings of vulnerability, helplessness, invasion, and mistrust deepen our innate deficits and fill us with inner stress and pain.

Because human beings were not designed by God to experience the pain of psychospiritual deficits, we often compound our stress by trying to find relief from it. We search and scan; we stretch and strive and strain trying to find ways to meet our needs and alleviate stress. Attempts to meet the stress of existential deficits through lifestyles of affluence, appearance, achievement, or addiction will fail. Attempts to meet these needs through relational patterns based on power, manipulation, or emotional inequality will not work. Attempts to satisfy deficits of the soul through the diversions of entertainment, eating, and education will not do it. Perfectionism, workaholism, cynicism, and hedonism are coping attempts that only temporarily satisfy some of the deficits while deepening others.

Christian counselors must be able to help struggling people identify their key deficits (needs) and the way(s) they have tried to cope. They can then help them to find more constructive ways to live their lives and manage their stress. Perhaps the most powerful single source of inner healing comes when a hurting person is able to experience consistent, deep love. However, because we live in a fallen world that presents us with all kinds of opportunities to feel rejection, purposelessness, identity confusion, self-doubt, loneliness, anxiety, helplessness, victimization, and emptiness, we will never be completely free of psychospiritual stress. Because the city represents a greater concentration of psychologically and spiritually wounded (after-the-Fall) people, it also increases the likelihood that urban dwellers will experience pain and stress.

Personality Styles

In response to the stress of existential deficits (psychospiritual needs), each person begins to develop a characteristic coping pattern. This is based partly on observation of how "emotionally significant others" (especially parents) respond to stress, partly on rewards and punishments given by those important others, partly on what we're taught and told, and partly on our own trial and error.

Three personality styles that tend to intensify stress are (1) perfectionism, (2) nonassertiveness, and (3) a *type A* personality orientation.

Perfectionism increases stress because it pushes people to strive to be something more than what they are. They are seldom satisfied with themselves and their efforts. Their focus is on *what* they need to become rather than on *who* they are. Perfectionism creates stress because it refuses to give permission for people to relax and *be*. The perfectionist's life is bound up in "shoulds" and "oughts." Extreme competitiveness in the urban marketplace encourages perfectionism and its equally stressful companion, workaholism. Both patterns are rooted in dysfunctional family-of-origin patterns. They are each unsatisfactory attempts to meet deep psychospiritual needs. Because they bring temporary rewards of feeling in control, of admiration, superiority, and power, perfectionism and workaholism tend to become entrenched lifestyles. In reality, however, they amplify stress.

Nonassertiveness is expressed in either passive or aggressive patterns of interaction. These patterns are marked by difficulty in expressing one's thoughts and feelings constructively, by blaming oneself or others, by hierarchical or power-oriented relational styles, and by difficulty with close relationships. Passive people build up tremendous inner stress. Denial and suppression of real thoughts and feelings, people-pleasing ("I can't say no, what will people think?"), and fatalism all lead to this inner stress. Aggressive people create major stress in the lives of those around them. They also experience it themselves because of the mistrust, defensiveness, and alienation that reflect their style. The sheer number of people in cities who are competitively vying for space, status, and possessions encourages the nonassertive extremes of aggressiveness and passivity.

Type-A personalities are typified by the hard-driving, aggressive, competitive, time-urgent stereotype of the quintessential New Yorker. *Type As* are highly motivated to achieve and tend to be involved in several different activities at one time. Earlier thinking that automatically connected stress and *type A* personality has been revised, but research still suggests that *type A* individuals have a higher probability of heart attacks, ulcers, and hypertension.

Social-Psychological Factors

Among the most stress-generating social-psychological factors frequently intensified in urban life are (1) uncertainty, (2) isolation, and (3) dysfunctional family patterns.

Uncertainty is stress-producing because it requires us to focus energy and attention on survival. Mistrust, bred by experiences of betrayal or exploitation, feeds uncertainty, which makes our world unpredictable and keeps us in a constant state of "fight or flight." The word survival may refer to the maintenance of social status or to physical well-being. Crime may not only threaten physical survival and well-being, it also leaves its victims feeling vulnerable and helpless, uncertain about their ability to defend against painful invasion. A great part of the stress generated by drug-infested urban areas is due to the unpredictable and life-threatening behaviors and crimes of those who use drugs. Competition in the marketplace and unpredictable employers also often leave urban workers in a constant state of uncertainty and anxiety about the stability of their jobs and lives.

Isolation affects some urban dwellers more than others. Friendships seem to be harder to form in the city because of heightened mistrust, the need to select from a greater pool of possibilities, and role-focused relationships.[9] Certain groups of people such as the widowed and the urban elderly appear to experience the greatest amount of loneliness.[10] There is significantly less contact with neighbors, which produces loneliness, and increased casual or surface contact with people at work as community size increases, which also increases loneliness and isolation.[11]

However, when quality of friendships is focused on in terms of available social support, urbanites appear to be slightly better off.[12] It appears that while it's harder to make friends in the large city, once friendships are formed, they are as satisfying as in other locales. While fewer family members tend to be mentioned, those who are tend to be seen as friends and not just as family. Friendships are usually more spatially spread out in larger communities and seem to require more energy and planning in order to establish and maintain them—adding at least some stress. Exceptions to spatial spreading can frequently be found in tightly knit ethnic and new-immigrant communities, and among those in lower-class neighborhoods. On the other hand, the very poorest urban dwellers tend to be among the most transitional and therefore isolated.

Dysfunctional family life includes out-of-wedlock births, broken marriages, blended families, single-parent families, alcoholism, domestic abuse, and assorted other addictions that mar the family life of millions of urban dwellers. Each of these dysfunctional patterns creates special stresses and strains on parents and children.

Single-parent families must cope with the stress of inadequate resources (approximately 60 percent of all single mothers live below the poverty level), as well as find the extra energy required to parent alone. Children in single-parent families are less likely to have their emotional needs sufficiently met, in general, due to the increased demands on the remaining parent and the pain released when a parent exits in cases of divorce. Blended families that witness a succession of "fathers" and half-siblings experience identity confusion and underlying anxiety about bonding and security. Even in more stable blended families, there are extraordinary relational strains as issues of rules, roles, rights, and responsibility have to be negotiated.

The dysfunctional dynamics of alcoholism tend to create deep insecurity, shame, and rage in "victimized" family members. Adult children of alcoholics typically have trouble forming and maintaining trusting, intimate relationships. Domestic abuse unleashes tremendous fear and turmoil. Addictions create chaotic climates of instability, mistrust, rejection, and anger due to the addict's exploitation of family members.

Environmental Factors

Although stress research has typically focused on the duration of stress and on major stress-producing events, more recent studies have been concerned with the impact of daily hassles.[13] These recurrent, comparatively minor irritants may include commuting, work demands, nonresponsive bureaucracies, and the impersonal treatment of personal concerns, pollution, health care, and poverty.

Commuting between home and work creates stress in several ways. Unpredictable train breakdowns, street repairs, accidents, and freeway delays make it difficult for urban dwellers to plan their days with confidence. Attempts to avoid such delays lead many to leave home earlier and earlier in the morning and to return home later and later at night. The amount of energy needed to cope with the delays or the long hours drains a person's reserves of coping energy. The commute also lessens the time available for spiritual and emotional renewal, further decreasing the store of available energy and making individuals more susceptible to potential stressors. When the commuter finally makes it home, he often does not feel like relating to family members. He is often irritated, and pulls away from them. This ends up creating more stress because a number of our psychospiritual needs require interpersonal involvement for satisfaction. As we have already seen, the failure to constructively meet psychospiritual needs leads to a further build-up of inner stress.

Work demands are frequently daily hassles as well. When an urban dweller believes that affluence and achievement will satisfy his underlying psychospiritual needs, intense inner stress may be generated. For example, Sean is a very bright, unmarried investment counselor who makes over $80,000 a year. But he nevertheless finds himself under immense self-generated pressure to produce more so that he can protect and enhance his status and security. At the other extreme, Joe is an unskilled laborer who is at the mercy of impersonal economic forces and the totalitarian demands of exploitative employers. In the middle are the millions of Marys and Jims, white collar workers, who are subjected to multiple, arbitrary work demands in highly competitive work environments.

Nonresponsive bureaucracies and impersonal treatment of personal concerns generate stress because they leave urban dwellers feeling insignificant and helpless. Even agencies that are supposed to help those in need frequently leave their clients feeling victimized and diminished. It is stressful when you do not know how you will be treated or whether your needs will receive careful consideration. The build-up of pain that results from being belittled and ignored often leads to apathy and fatalism on the one hand or rage and destructiveness on the other. A history of being devalued can lead to a reciprocal pattern of uncaring behavior. One cannot help but wonder if horrendous acts of violence such as the "wilding" attacks by juvenile gangs are, in part, attempts by those who have been regarded as insignificant and irrelevant to feel significant and powerful.

It has been our counseling experience that the combination of heavy work demands, lengthy commuting, and impersonal treatment contributes heavily to the formation of addictive behaviors involving alcohol, drugs, sex, overeating, and even too much television viewing. Tom, for example, who is married and a sincere Christian as well as being a successful young photographer found himself trapped in an intense addiction to pornographic magazines, videos, and prostitutes. Bill is an energetic computer programmer in his thirties who has struggled with homosexuality since he was a teenager. Since becoming a Christian, he has abstained from most sexual activity, although he has occasionally failed. Both men began to be freed from their sexual addictions when they realized that they were most susceptible to sexual temptation when the daily hassles of life intensified. Their addictions were a destructive, unconscious attempt to relieve stress.

Bioecological Factors

In 1976, forty-three major cities in the United States had unhealthy air quality.[14] Simply breathing the air in cities like New York is equivalent to smoking two packs of cigarettes per day.[15] Pollution fosters stress as a result of its negative impact upon both physical and emotional well-being. It costs six billion dollars a year to treat pollution-impacted respiratory diseases, according to the U.S. Public Health Service. Burning eyes, headaches, dizziness, and allergy-like sinus problems diminish the quality of life. Higher levels of air pollution have been found to be associated with psychiatric emergencies[16] and hospital admissions.[17] Students subjected to unpleasant but nontoxic air in laboratory experiments reported feeling more anxious, fatigued, and aggressive, and less able to concentrate.[18] Bad odors have been found to lower performance on complex tasks and reduce persistence at difficult problem-solving tasks.[19] The need to curtail exercise because of heavy urban pollution eliminates an important way to reduce tension and stress as well.

Finally, poverty introduces and magnifies stress at several critical points. Prenatal conditions are typically worse for the poor, resulting in children being born with biological and intellectual impairments that lessen their ability to cope with stress. Significant numbers of obstetricians, family physicians, and nurse-midwives are limiting their practices among women with high risk pregnancies. These often include low-income women who are likely to smoke and have poor diets during their pregnancies. Addicted babies of addicts (if they live) suffer inordinately from stress on many fronts. General medical care for the poor is inferior, increasing the probability of biologically-induced stress and decreasing adaptive energy supplies.

Poverty creates additional stress due to the daily struggle for physical survival. A high percentage of poor families are fragmented, unstable, and fatherless. The poor lack resources for more healthy living environments and are far more likely to be exploited and victimized. A recent survey by Partnership for the Homeless, a nonprofit New York group that operates a system of homeless shelters, indicates that the dramatic four-year trend (1984–1988) of fast-growing numbers of homeless families with children has stabilized. Nevertheless, 31 percent of the homeless are families with children. Overall, homelessness may affect as many as 2 million people in the U.S. and many more in major cities such as Manila, Bogota, and Mexico City. Even for those poor people with homes, there is no money for the kinds of stress-reducing comforts that greater affluence brings. One of the amazing realities of the city is how *well* many who are poor do cope by finding strength in their relationships with God and through their extended family units.

SUMMARY

Healing for the city must address the sources of stress and its damaging effects on urban dwellers. Often the most destructive effects of stress are due to faulty coping patterns that actually accentuate it. In any case, the experience of stress varies from person to person, so counseling must help each individual discover primary sources of stress and shape appropriate stress-reduction strategies. This intervention may be primarily psycho-spiritual in focus, or consist of practical advocacy efforts aimed at changes in environmental conditions. The objective is not to completely remove stress, but to help urban dwellers manage it so that they can function in the healthiest way possible. Urban dwellers who constructively relieve stress, will be free for more positive spiritual, emotional, relational, and physical life patterns. They will also have energy for greater ministry involvement and a more dynamic Christian experience. We will consider a variety of counseling strategies for stress reduction and management in Section 3.

NOTES

[1]E. Krupat, *People in Cities* (New York: Cambridge Univ. Press, 1985), 38–43.
[2]Hans Selye, "The Stress Concept Today," in I. L. Kutash, L. B. Schlesinger & Associates, eds., *Handbook on Stress and Anxiety* (San Francisco: Jossey-Bass, 1980).
[3]S. Milgram, "The Experience of Living in Cities," *Science* 167 (1970): 1461–68.

[4]T. W. Miller, ed., *Stressful Life Events*, Monograph 4 (Madison, Conn.: International Univ. Press, 1989).

[5]S. Cohen, "Environmental Load and the Allocation of Attention," in A. Baum, J. E. Singer, and S. Valino, eds., *Advances in Environmental Psychology*, Vol. 1 (Hillsdale, N.J.: Erlbaum, 1978).

[6]O. Tanner, *Stress* (New York: Time-Life Books, 1976).

[7]D. M. Geller, "Responses to Urban Stimuli: A Balanced Approach," *Journal of Social Issues* 36 (3) (1980): 86–100.

[8]Genesis 2–3.

[9]K. A. Franck, "Friends and Strangers: The Social Experience of Living in Urban and Nonurban Settings," *Journal of Social Issues* 3 (1980): 52–71.

[10]H. Lopata, "Loneliness: Forms and Components," *Social Problems* 17 (1969): 248–61.

[11]W. Key, "Rural-Urban Social Participation," in S. Fava, ed., *Urbanism in World Perspectives* (New York: Crowell, 1968).

[12]C. Fischer, *To Dwell Among Friends: Personal Networks in Town and City* (Chicago: Univ. of Chicago Press, 1982).

[13]A. Delongis, J. C. Coyne, G. Dakof, S. Folkman, and R. S. Lazarus, "Relationship of Daily Hassles, Uplifts and Major Life Events to Health Status," *Health Psychology* 1 (1982): 119–36.

[14]U.S. President's Council on Environmental Quality, Environmental Protection Agency. Washington, D.C.: U.S. Government Printing Office, 1978.

[15]J. Rotton, "The Psyhcological Effects of Air Pollution," unpublished manuscript (Florida International Univ., 1978).

[16]J. Rotton and J. Frey, "Air Pollution, Weather and Psychiatric Emergencies: A Constructive Replication," paper presented at the American Psychological Association Convention (Washington, D.C.: 1982).

[17]N. Strahilevitz, A. Strahilevitz, and J. E. Miller, "Air Pollution and the Admission Rate of Psychiatric Patients," *American Journal of Psychiatry* 136 (1978): 206–7.

[18]J. Rotton, "Affective Cognitive Consequences of Malodorous Pollution," *Basic and Applied Social Psychology* 4 (1983): 171–91.

J. Rotton, J. Frey, R. Barry, M. Milligan, M. Fitzpatrick, "The Air Pollution Experience and Physical Agression," *Journal of Applied Social Psychology* 9 (1979): 397–412.

[19]Ibid.

CHAPTER 2

The Nature of Counseling

COUNSELING HAS BEEN defined as "a process by which a person is assisted to behave in a more rewarding manner."[1] As a process, it takes place over a period of time and promotes healing, comfort, clarification, and reconciliation. People who seek counseling have usually attempted to change some behavior that is not, in the final analysis, rewarding to them. However, their attempts have been unsuccessful and so they come to counseling with aspirations and anxieties, hoping for a helper who will relieve their distress and help them replace it with something more rewarding.

The three basic elements in counseling are the counselee (the person in pain desiring to be healed), the counselor (the helper who listens), and the negative experience, or that which causes pain and distress. The counselee identifies the negative experience and is helped to choose a path that is more satisfactory. Those seeking help are so-called experts on the problem; they have been living with it for weeks, months, and often years. Now they want release. The counselor must, therefore, carefully listen and help the counselees spell out their needs. Counselors assist individuals to identify and achieve goals that they have selected in response to the difficulties they are experiencing. The counselor provides an atmosphere of acceptance and genuine caring to facilitate the process.

PREPARATION FOR COUNSELING

Aside from the formal preparation for counseling, an individual may prepare to do effective counseling by following some important guidelines. One of these guidelines is to recognize that the counselor is the most important instrument used in counseling. It is, therefore, imperative that counselors, preparing to help others, take a very honest look at themselves. This should be an ongoing process. The counselor needs to be aware of personal thoughts and feelings and the impact they have on the counselees.

Having done an honest self-assessment, the counselor will want to consult current books that examine the specific issues he (or she) will encounter as a counselor. A list of such books begins on page 323. There is no one book that has all of the answers. The counselor will need to acquire a library of references to use as the need arises. (The thirty-volume Resources for Christian Counseling Series, published by Word, is an excellent source of practical counseling guidelines for a wide variety of problems from an evangelical perspective.) In addition to books there are a number of journals that can be very helpful to the counselor (see p. 330). These journals describe techniques that other therapists have found useful, and they also report on research that may shed light on some of your cases.

Some counselors have also found that peer supervision can be extremely helpful. In peer supervision, several counselors with similar education and preparation in counseling get together to discuss their counseling cases. One advantage of this approach is that the therapist presenting the case gets fresh insights from the other counselors. Peer supervision is most effective if the group is mixed in terms of gender and ethnicity. For example, a female therapist may spot something regarding a female counselee that a male counselor has totally overlooked. As a variation on peer supervision, several pastors may want to organize a monthly counseling consultation with a professional therapist. In any case, to be an effective counselor, one must always be learning. Workshops and seminars are extremely helpful to the beginning counselor, and even experienced counselors periodically attend them to upgrade their skills. We have used the term *counseling practice* in this book, for that is what it is. In a sense, we are always practicing because we never get to the point where we know it all.

THE COUNSELOR

Research shows that the counselor's personality is the most crucial factor in counseling.[2] While effective counselors are not limited to one personality type, certain qualities have been found to be essential to effective counseling. Fortunately, for the person who reacts to the counselor even before any counseling takes place, these are characteristics that can be developed. In addition to the belief that the most significant resource a counselor brings to the relationship is herself; the most significant variable is that the counselor understands herself.[3] However, the therapist is superior to any theory, no matter how elegantly postulated.

The counselor must be genuine. The counselee must sense that the counselor respects him and is genuinely concerned about him as a person. This need is heightened in the urban setting. There, counselees have often experienced disrespect and denigration in their dealings with "professionals" of all kinds: teachers, doctors, lawyers, and others.

Closely connected to genuineness is empathy. Empathy is the ability to place oneself in another person's position.[4] A Native American proverb states that one person should not criticize another until he has walked a mile in the other's moccasins. One can only convey one's understanding of the counselee's problem through this basic quality of empathic understanding. Though you can never completely understand the counselee's predicament, you must come as close as you possibly can. Avoid saying things like "I know *exactly* what you are going through." This is especially important in cross-cultural counseling situations. A white counselor from a middle-class background does not know *exactly* what a poor minority person is experiencing, nor does an African American counselor automatically know what a recent Asian or Hispanic immigrant is experiencing.

The key to empathic understanding is to identify a personal experience that approximates the counselee's experience. In cross-cultural counseling, it is also imperative that the counselor read about the cultures of his counselees. The counseling process is greatly enhanced if you can refer to some aspect of the counselee's cultural experience. One enhancement will be the building of rapport with the individual. Because of rapport the counselee will feel an affinity with the therapist, paving the way for effective counseling to take place.

Another essential quality is unconditional positive regard.[5] However sordid a tale the counselee tells you, he is to be treated as a person worthy of your respect. We must "look again" (the literal meaning of respect) at our counselees and let them feel that although we may not agree with everything they are telling us, we do have positive regard for them as persons.[6]

Treating a counselee with unconditional positive regard means that the therapist must be nonjudgmental. He will be faced with every human problem imaginable, including attempted suicide, rape, incest, drug addiction, and spouse abuse. In Galatians 6:1, Paul makes it clear that there is no evil, no matter how gross, whose seeds are not lurking in our own hearts. This does not mean that the therapist agrees with the behavior, but to be effective, he must understand how the person came to be in this predicament. It is a great relief to the counselee to be able to unburden himself in an atmosphere of acceptance. Once his trust has been earned, the counselee can be confronted about the negative behavior.

Finally, the counselor must be a stable, dependable person. The urban dweller has invariably experienced many disappointments and frustrations. He needs an individual who will bring some stability into his life. A simple matter such as keeping appointments at the time and place agreed upon is an example. Beyond that, the counselor must present himself as an individual on whom the counselee can depend. For example, a forty-five-year-old client whose father had deserted the family when he was a young boy was visibly upset when the therapist was late for an appointment, having been unavoidably detained. It took much of that session to reassure the counselee that the therapist did indeed care and would always be there for him if at all possible.

GOALS OF COUNSELING

Someone has facetiously said that if we do not set goals, we might end up someplace we did not intend to go. This is certainly true in counseling. In counseling we have in mind both immediate and long-term goals.[7] The long-term goals are the more abstract and difficult ones to define even when we know exactly what they are. They include removing symptoms, restoring earlier levels of functioning, freeing the person to reach his potential, and helping him find personal meaning and values. These goals, though very important, can be attained only after more immediate goals are reached.

Immediate goals include (1) helping the person do what is in his best interest, (2) the reduction of emotional distress, (3) increased self-knowledge, and (4) improved relations with others. The order in which these aims or goals are listed is not always important. However, sometimes the counselor may find that emotional distress must be reduced before any other goal can be addressed. The individual may feel he is "going to burst" if he does not get certain feelings "off his chest." The counselor must be sensitive to this need. This can be done by saying something as simple as, "Tell me more about the argument you had with your boss." Without any other stimulus and in a permissive environment, the counselee usually feels free to vent his anger and frustration.

Helping the counselee to do what is in his best interest is one of the earliest goals of counseling. God asked Cain, "If thou doest well, wilt thou not be accepted?" (Gen. 4:7 KJV). When the counselor helps the counselee do the right thing, that right thing should always be in line with the Word of God. Most often what we find in the counseling of Christians is that their lives are out of sync with God. The work of the counselor involves persuasion and the skillful use of the Scriptures to gently move the counselee toward this goal of conformity with God's design for human functioning.

The reduction of emotional distress is the second goal of counseling. It is sometimes difficult to identify the source of the distress, but as we allow the counselee to express his feelings, it will normally become apparent. Creating a warm and nonthreatening environment permits the individual to express his distress freely. It may be necessary to permit him to release his feelings in terms that may be, strictly speaking, unchristian, but this is needed if the release of anger and stress is to come.

A third goal in counseling is increased self-knowledge. The counselor will often need to raise issues with the counselee that had previously been outside his or her present level of awareness. These unconscious feelings may surface in dreams that the individual relates to the counselor. This happened in the case of one young woman who was unaware that she had a crush on her boss. Unconsciously she was acting in a seductive manner, and that was causing a strain in their relationship. When she related a dream in which they were romantically involved, the therapist was able to point out that this was her unconscious wish. She had not been aware of this feeling previously.

The last of the immediate goals is the improvement of interpersonal relations. Most problems that individuals bring to a counselor involve the impairment of relations with others. Whether the problems are related to past or current relations, they are causing problems for the counselee *now*. Most of the time, the poor relationships are with "significant others"—the counselee's parents, siblings, and other loved ones. It may be important for the other party to be brought into the counseling process. When this is possible, the therapist is able to observe the interaction directly and more accurately.

This list of immediate goals is not meant to be exhaustive, but most counselors find them useful in assisting counselees to move toward specific long-term goals.

HEALING AND THE COUNSELING PROCESS

Healing, as it relates to counseling, is not cure. It is not the total removal of pain. Rather, it involves the reduction of and the healthy management of the hurts in one's life. Through comfort, clarification, challenge, caring, and constructive insight, a person is helped out of brokenness toward wholeness.

Basic Conditions

For real healing of hurting people to take place, the therapist must be aware of the process by which counseling is carried out. *How* will I help to heal this person who is asking me for help? While the specific counseling method may vary, there are three essential conditions: (1) acceptance, (2) reassurance, and (3) confidentiality.

Acceptance is the most important precondition in an urban healing ministry. A poor or minority person has undoubtedly experienced rejection in many ways. If she is rejected yet again, no effective counseling can take place. The urban counselor should expect his counselees to test him to see if he is going to reject them. Some counselees will approach the therapist in an apparently hostile manner. This is a defense against being hurt again and it may be especially true if the counselee is a member of a minority group and the therapist is not. Some counselees will openly question the ability of the therapist to understand them because of the cross-cultural issue. The counselor must convey respect to the counselee and communicate that there is help.

It is not so easy for the counselor to deal with behaviors that are totally wrong from a biblical perspective. For example, a poor minority female may ask for counseling because she is pregnant with her fifth child and is considering an abortion. To immediately condemn such an unscriptural decision would be to lose the counselee. The counselor can be empathic toward her, holding all that she tells him in strictest confidence. This encourages feelings of safety and reliance. The counselee is now ready to hear the strategies that can be employed to deal with the problem.

Reassurance is the second basic condition for helping hurting people. The wounded individual must feel that although his situation is causing him a great deal of pain, it is not hopeless. Most often people come to us asking for help, while they are fully persuaded in their heart of hearts that nothing *can* help. The counselor must, within the bleak picture painted before him, find a ray of hope. Otherwise, the counselee will have no reason to continue counseling.

Confidentiality is the third condition and is of the utmost importance. The counselee must absolutely know that what he shares will remain with the counselor and will go no further. This is probably more important in the urban setting than almost anywhere else. Because counselees may have been betrayed by schools, police, and other agencies that are supposed to be helpful, it is absolutely critical for the urban counselor to clearly promise and deliver confidentiality. Exceptions should be communicated at the outset of counseling. Cases of confidentiality would normally include cases in which the counselee appears to be a danger to himself or others, in which there is suspected child abuse, and in which the counselee gives his informed consent. In church settings where the counselor is also the pastor, care must be taken to inform congregant-counselees about the church's views on confidentiality and church discipline.

Overview of Helping

Robert R. Carkhuff has written a useful book entitled *The Art of Helping: An Introduction to Life Skills.*[8] In it he lays out a four-step process for counseling problems that are not clear-cut. These include: (1) attending, (2) responding, (3) initiating, and (4) communicating.

Carkhuff likens the counseling process to the developmental or child-rearing process. The parent responds to the needs of the child and initiates a plan to satisfy those needs. The child who has had his needs met by nurturing parents will become a nurturing person. In the counseling process, the therapist takes the stance of a nurturing parent who is ready to respond to the counselee's needs and initiate steps to help him. In the urban context, this developmental approach is especially important since the counselee may not have had nurturing, caring parents. The attitude that the counselor assumes will be crucial to the success of the therapy.

The first step in helping is to explore where the person is in relation to where he wants to be. The counselor must identify with the person and as Carkhuff puts it, "filter the helpee's experience through his own."[9] A thirty-five-year-old man experiences headaches, upset stomach, and other somatic symptoms every Monday morning before going to work. As the counselor explores this, he finds that this man thoroughly loathes his work. Where he is, then, is that his misery relates to a job that he intensely dislikes. The next step is to take constructive action—get from where he is to where he wants to be. In this case, he maps out a plan of action either to change jobs within his field or, if appropriate, get retrained for another field.

Attending

Just as a parent attends to her child's need for food, security, and the like, so you must attend to the counselee's needs. That is, you need to pay attention—position yourself physically to attend—face the person and remove barriers. If there is a desk, come from behind the desk and sit about five feet away, facing the individual. You should use discretion, of course, and if the counseling is cross-gender, you must remove any hint of sexual intention. Eliminate any interruptions, including telephone calls and uninvited visitors. Maintain eye contact, even if the person is looking at the floor. Be ready to engage his eyes whenever possible.

Let the person know you are listening. Respond to his pain verbally. "That must be very painful for you," or "I understand," or even a mere murmur are all appropriate responses. Avoid making judgmental remarks such as, "Didn't you know better than that?" There will be time for confrontation later if that is indicated. Right at first the task is to attend (pay strict attention) to your counselee. Repeat key phrases to her in your own words to be sure that you understand her. This also lets her know that you are listening. Listen for a theme; the counselee will often tell you the problem in several different ways. Pick up the theme and repeat it: "It sounds as if you have had it with that job."

Responding

The process of attending involves both the context and the "feeling tone." Allow yourself to experience as closely as you can what the client is feeling. When you respond, you are responding to where he is emotionally. We have referred earlier to empathic understanding, and it is an absolute necessity at this point. "You're really angry at your wife for putting you down like that in front of other people." Be prepared sometimes for denial; he may not be at the point where he can admit his anger. You can then say, "I thought I detected anger in your voice when you talked about what she said at the church supper." You may want to call attention to his posture, or his clenched fists, or his clenched teeth as he related the incident, which can help him get in touch with his feelings. By responding, then, you are reacting to his feelings so that he can explore the areas that are causing him difficulty. When he has done that, he is ready for the initiating phase.

Initiating

This stage takes the counselee beyond where he is. Carkhuff calls this stage *additive empathy*. The counselee who experienced physical discomfort before going to work was helped to see where he was. He got in touch with his feelings and he should now be ready to make a move to get out of his rut.

The counselee will tell you in various ways that he is ready. He may say, "But what do I do?" The real message is, "I know where I am, I know how I feel about it, and now I'm ready to move." Be sure that he is committed to where he needs to be. At strategic points, try to personalize the issue: "You are disgusted with this job and you want to make a move." However, he may not be quite ready to "make a move," in which case you may have to confront him, going back to the "feeling tone" of his dislike for the job. Check to see if he is at the point where he wants to be. If he has really understood where he is and where he needs to be, he will be ready to act.

The task now is to establish a problem-solving technique. Richard Vaughan,[10] a noted pastoral counselor, has suggested the following seven steps:

1. Define the problem.
   2. Establish the goals. What does the person hope to achieve?

3. Establish possible courses of action the counselee could take to solve the problem.

4. Evaluate the pros and cons of each course of action, based on its value to the overall goals of counseling, the likelihood of success, and the person's Christian faith and values.

5. Get the counselee to decide on one course of action.

6. Devise a plan to implement this course of action.

7. Arrange for the person to report on his progress in implementing the chosen course of action.

Vaughan makes three points about this scheme. First, there is overlap in these steps. They are not separate and discrete. Second, this outline is not meant to be followed slavishly. The steps should be viewed as general guidelines. Finally, this procedure should be seen as a collaborative effort involving the therapist and the counselee. The following case will illustrate how this strategy operates.

An urban pastor is asked to provide counseling for a problem that has arisen in the church's Christian school. An eighth grade girl has been caught with drugs in her school bag. She is a very bright student who recently arrived in the city school from Jamaica. She plays in the orchestra and her services are needed at the upcoming graduation. The school is small and the news that she was found with drugs has spread through the student body like a prairie fire.

The central problem to be solved is: What should be done with this girl? She is a new arrival in this country. Further investigation reveals that she was safeguarding the drugs for a boyfriend who did not attend the school. The student has felt rejected by her mother and craves attention. She kept the drugs for her boyfriend, fearing that he would leave her if she did not.

What does the pastor hope to achieve? He wants to help the girl, who appears penitent and has asked for forgiveness, yet he must also establish the fact that the possession of drugs is absolutely forbidden.

There are at least three courses of action open to the pastor. First, he can expel the student. Second, he can suspend her for a semester, which means she would not graduate. She would then be ineligible for admission to a special high school for gifted students for which she qualifies. Third, he can bar her from participation in the graduation exercises, call the Parent-Teachers Association together, and apprise them of the case, and can then tell the PTA that he will, if they agree, let the student continue in school.

Evaluation of the possible courses of action (step 4) is crucial. The third option was selected, which is step 5. The plan of action (step 6) is outlined within the choice selected. The pastor's decision turned out to be successful in that he was able to help the student understand that drugs were forbidden. He was also able to engage the PTA in a way he had not done before.

In this example, we saw how the process of counseling functions with a clear, focused problem. But there are times when the problem is not at all clear. The counselee may seek counseling because he "feels depressed" or her "marriage is not fulfilling." These issues require a different approach. When confronted with vague, unfocused complaints, you, the counselor, must probe carefully to determine the nature of the problem. You might ask such questions as "What do you feel is promoting your depression?" – "What is there about your marriage that bothers you?" – "Have there been any changes in your life lately?" Continue to reflect back the counselee's responses and probe until she can give you some specific issues to examine. Ask for concrete examples, such as "Can you give me an example of what happens at work that seems to be associated with your headaches?"

Communicating

In this phase the therapist selectively rewards healthy behavior and selectively extinguishes unhealthy behavior. This can only happen after completing the first three steps of attending, responding, and initiating. There is now a basis for communicating *conditional regard*; that is, we do not accept the person at less than they can be. Because of the relationship of acceptance that has been established, the counselor can now confront the counselee about self-defeating behavior and discrepancies with positive therapeutic outcomes.

These are four specific counseling steps for problems that are not clearly focused. They are not totally discrete, but flow one into the other. The therapist need not spend more time than is necessary at any one point. If the counselee is ready, help him to move on to the next point.

HUMAN BEINGS AS SYSTEMS

To understand the counselee and promote healing, we need a conceptual framework. Human beings are unique creations and the capstone of God's creation. It is said only of mankind that God "breathed into his nostrils the breath of life and man became a living soul." One of the important meanings of *nephesh* (soul) is an "entire person."[11] Thus, God's will for human beings is that they be whole, unified beings. Paul confirms this concept of wholeness or unity of the body, soul, and spirit in 1 Thessalonians 5:23, when he prays that their "whole spirit and soul and body be preserved . . . ." The word Paul uses for "whole" is *holokeros*, which means complete in every part.

The Christian counselor recognizes that the counselee is troubled because the unity God intended for human beings has become disturbed within him. The overarching purpose of counseling is to restore the wholeness that God intended through the healing power of God's Spirit.

Human beings, after all, have been created in the image of God. It is of note that God's name as creator is Elohim, the plural of Eloah, which indicates the unity of divine persons. In creation, the Godhead functions as one. C. I. Scofield aptly points out that we "can never divide the Essence."[12] Humanity is God's crowning creation and was brought into being by the Godhead, thus attesting to our central importance to God. Just as the triune God is unified, so humanity should be unified—an integrated system of body, soul, and spirit.

The intended nature of human beings is, from God's standpoint, whole and entire. We counselors need to remember that as we deal with our counselees. Elijah, after he raised the widow's son (1 Kings 17:21), said that "the soul (*nephesh*) of the child came into him again and he revived." Here soul is translated "life-soul." Human beings are to have their life-souls revived.

If one part of the system is affected, the whole system goes with it. Cain's sin in murdering his brother affected his visage. God asked him why his countenance (*panim*) had fallen. The shame and guilt he was experiencing showed on his face. The system in Cain's case was affected negatively by his misdeed. God told him that if he did well he would be accepted or, as John Darby translates it, "his countenance would look up (*sehyath*)."[13] Literally, he would be *elated* or have a good conscience. Another meaning of *sehyath* is restoration.[14] The peace (*shalom*) that God intended for humanity to enjoy would be restored.

As the therapist holds in mind the view of humanity that God had at creation, he will be effective as he counsels. He will recognize the imbalance that has come into the system and seek to help the individual to restore it.

HEALING AS MULTIMODAL

One useful model that is compatible with the view that human beings are systems is the *multimodal* approach devised by A. A. Lazarus.[15] Counselors and psychotherapists often stress the diagnosis of the individual when they attach a label such as obsessive-compulsive behavior or hysterical personality. Lazarus suggests that these labels do not necessarily lead to more effective treatment because they are not precise enough. He proposes that the therapist use what he calls the BASIC ID. This is an acronym and what follows explores this concept. (It is not, by the way, a Freudian approach.)

B stands for the *behavior* that the individual exhibits. The counselor needs to know which behaviors are the most problematic and which behaviors would bring satisfaction and well-being to the counselee.

A stands for *affect*. What feelings affect or are troubling to the counselee? Are these feelings persistent and chronic, or are they recent and intense? What impact do they have on the person's level of functioning?

S refers to physical *sensations* such as seeing, hearing, smelling, tasting, and touching. The therapist should ask about sensations that may be uncomfortable and may interfere with normal behavior.

I represents *images*. Here it is important to inquire how the person sees himself. What is his body image? What is her self-image? Moreover, how do these images influence behavior? A woman who perceives herself to be unattractive might be withdrawn and hesitant to interact with others. Other mental imagery that is anxiety-producing, fear-arousing, or obsessive in character should be noted as well. Memories that are still impacting a person's self-image and choices should be uncovered.

C is for *cognition*, which includes the controlling beliefs and values of the individual and how his thoughts affect his emotions, behaviors, and relationships. In the example cited earlier, the woman who sees herself as unattractive might also believe that "no man would want her."

I stands for *interpersonal*, which includes the important people in the counselee's life and his relationship to them. Included here are significant expectations, conflicts, and misunderstandings, as well as any deficient social skills.

D is for *drugs* in a very broad sense, in that it includes the licit and illicit drugs the person may be taking, as well as the general health and biological well-being of the individual.

Clearly, any of the above areas might be more dominant in one individual than in others. For example, the area D—the abuse of drugs or alcohol—may present itself as the most prominent feature of an individual's functioning. And if this is so, this aspect of his life affects every other. As one twenty-seven-year-old heroin addict stated when asked if he was married, "Who would want a junkie?" Area D or drugs was his most prominent problem area, and it affected his cognition as well. Further questioning uncovered the fact that his interpersonal relations were seriously affected by his drug abuse. The purpose of multimodal diagnosis is to get, in Lazarus' terms, "a thorough and holistic understanding of the person and his/her social environment."[16] With that understanding the healing process can begin.

The multimodal system must not be thought of as a mechanical checklist. At each step, along with the attempt to understand the counselee, the therapist must convey a sense of genuine caring. Ultimately, the process of healing begins after the multimodal diagnosis has been completed and the seven aspects of the counselee's personality (BASIC ID) have been taken into account. Interventions should be specific and aimed at particular problems or themes identified in the multimodal profile.

The Christian counselor must also give consideration to spiritual issues that are either underlying or actively contributing to the person's functioning in the seven dimensions of the BASIC ID. Spiritual assessment may also reveal certain strengths that can be utilized in the healing process (for example, that the person has very strong faith). In addition to less formal analyses of the spiritual dimension there are instruments such as the Spiritual Well-Being Scale,[17] that have been shown to be related to a variety of measures of physical, psychological, and relational well-being.[18]

The following case is an example of the multimodal method of counseling, typical of the cases one finds in an urban setting.

Case Study

Ms. B. W. came for counseling after she had been fired from her job for embezzlement. She had not, in fact, stolen money from her company, but had often borrowed money and had replaced it at a later time. However, before she could replace the last amount borrowed, the company audited the books. She confessed her misdeed and was fired from the company.

Ms. B. W. is a thirty-four-year-old woman, who looks older because of obesity. She was pleasant during the initial interview. Open and honest with her answers, she had been reared in Georgia by her unmarried mother. She attended college in North Carolina but had to leave after her sophomore year because she had become pregnant. Seeking better employment opportunities, Ms. B. W. left North Carolina for New York. There she met and married her husband, a janitor. Using the BASIC ID, Ms. B.W.'s profile is as follows:

Behavior: Acceptance of the role of criminal; married to a man whose intellectual level is beneath hers; living in substandard housing.

Affect: Fear, depression, discouragement.

Sensations: False hunger; eats to ease anxiety.

Imagery: Poor self-image.

Cognition: "Everybody knows I'm a criminal."

Interpersonal: Afraid to form relationships for fear that her "secret" will come out.

Drug-Biology: Overeats, obese, does not exercise.

Spiritual: She attended Sunday School as a girl and considers herself a Christian, but her religious commitment is not related to her ethics.

Completing the multimodal assessment, the therapist must answer this question: "What is the principal issue in this person's life?" Or in Lazarus' terms, "What is the major modality that is affected?"

In this case the therapist began with *behavior*, which appeared to be where B. W. was having most of her difficulties because of her belief that she was a criminal even though there had never been a trial nor a conviction. The therapist confronted B. W. with the irrationality of these thoughts and in addition stressed "thought stopping," which was a relatively easy procedure to learn. All B. W. had to do when she began thinking of herself as a criminal was to immediately think "Stop!" And because she was a Christian, it was effective to remind B. W. of the completeness of divine forgiveness. These techniques were also instrumental in dealing with her impaired cognition, in which she felt that "everyone knew she was a criminal." (It should be pointed out at this point that the therapist will often find that the steps in the BASIC ID overlap.)

The issue of *affect* was tied to her concern that, given her history, she would never get another job. The therapist, however, encouraged her to seek jobs even if she was repeatedly turned down. When she followed this strategy, she was able to get a menial factory job that she disliked. The therapist then addressed the fact that she had two years of college and should consider returning to her studies. She did so, earned a B.A., and went on to do graduate study.

The issues of *imagery* and *interpersonal* resolved themselves when B. W. returned to college. After her first semester, she recognized that she functioned well and received good grades. This improved her self-image and she formed some satisfying friendships.

The *drug/biology* component was not resolved. Although she attempted to lose weight, she found it very difficult.

The BASIC ID provides the therapist with a direction in which to assist the counselee. How badly does the counselee want to change? This question must be addressed as part of the assessment since the extent to which the technique will work depends on the extent to which the counselee is motivated. In the case of Ms. B. W., she had hit rock bottom and therefore was highly motivated to make some changes in her life.

FORMAL AND INFORMAL COUNSELING

Formal counseling is that which takes place at a time and place that has been prearranged between the therapist and the counselee, and is the ideal. Often, however, the urban pastor will find himself in crisis intervention (informal counseling) situations that arise quite spontaneously. These crises most often include rape, spouse abuse, incarceration of a family member, crime victimization, and burnouts (fires).

Crisis intervention counseling is unique. It is usually time-limited, most often lasting from one to six weeks. Those involved usually feel overwhelmingly confused and helpless and if the issue is not resolved, it will return. In cases of spouse abuse, for example, the abuser must be dealt with sharply or he will do it again. There is, therefore, a need for formal counseling in some cases.[19]

Crisis intervention is needed to bring about immediate relief for the counselee, but the counselor must determine if long-term counseling is also needed. A church worker brought a twelve-year-old rape victim in for counseling. After one session the counselor arranged for specialized rape counseling, but the church worker did not take the girl because "she was doing fine." A few weeks later, however, the girl attempted suicide—very often a delayed reaction to a crisis situation such as this.

The immediate goals of crisis intervention are: (1) to relieve distress, especially anxiety, confusion, and hopelessness; (2) to restore the counselee's functioning; (3) to help him find existing resources to assist him in the difficulty; (4) to understand the relationship between the crisis and past problems; and (5) to develop new attitudes and coping behavior that might be useful in future crises.[20] (Very often, as noted earlier, what appears to be a crisis is the result of previously unresolved difficulties. For example, a man suffering from manic-depressive illness was constantly causing problems for his family because he refused to take his medication. He would become abusive and the police would have to be called.)

SUMMARY

Human beings are God's special and unique creation, but as a result of the Fall, a host of physical and social ills have followed. The urban dweller appears to be more often the victim. The therapist is in a key position to help the counselee work through these problems and become a whole person again, and to be a healer, certain basic principles must be mastered. Most of all, however, the counselor must be a genuine, caring person who is committed to seeing individuals set free to grow.

NOTES

[1]J. D. Daniel and S. Eisenberg, *The Counseling Process* (Chicago: Rand-McNally, 1973).

[2]J. C. Hansen, R. R. Stevic, and R. W. Warner, *Counseling: Theory and Process* (Boston: Allyn and Bacon, 1972).

[3]R. R. Carkhuff, *The Art of Helping: An Introduction to Life Skills* (Amherst, Mass.: Human Resources, 1973).

[4]B. N. Ard, *Counseling and Psychotherapy: Classics on Theory and Issues* (Palo Alto: Science and Behavior, 1966).

[5]Ibid.

[6]E. Fromm, *The Art of Loving: An Equiry Into the Nature of Love* (New York: Harper and Brothers, 1956).

[7]S. J. Korchin, *Clinical Psychology: Principles of Intervention in the Clinic and Community* (New York: Basic Books, 1976).

[8]Carkhuff, *The Art of Helping*.

[9]Ibid.

[10]R. Vaughan, *Basic Skills for Christian Counselors: An Introduction for Pastoral Ministers* (New York: Paulist, 1987).

[11]L. R. Harris, L. G. Archer, and B. K. Waltke, *Theological Wordbook of the Old Testament* (Chicago: Moody Press, 1980).

[12]C. I. Scofield, *The New Scofield Reference Bible* (New York: Oxford Univ. Press, 1967).

[13]J. N. Darby, *The Holy Scriptures: A New Translation from the Original Languages* (Lancing, Sussex: Kingston Bible Trust, 1975).

[14]Harris, Archer and Waltke, *Theological Wordbook of the Old Testament*.

[15]A. A. Lazarus, *The Practice of Multimodal Therapy: Systematic, Comprehensive and Effective Psychotherapy* (New York: McGraw-Hill, 1981).

[16]Ibid.

[17]Craig W. Ellison, "Spiritual Well-Being: Conceptualization and Measurement," *Journal of Psychology and Theology* 11 (1983), 330–40; R. K. Bufford, R. F. Paloutzian, and C. W. Ellison, "Norms for the Spiritual Well-Being Scale." *Journal of Psychology and Theology* 19 (1991), in press.

[18]C. W. Ellison, "Toward an Integrative Measure of Health and Well-being," *Journal of Psychology and Theology* 19 (1991), in press.

[19]Korchin, *Clinical Psychology*.

[20]Ibid.

CHAPTER 3

Counseling in the Urban Church

CHURCHES AND PARACHURCH settings offer a variety of healing intervention possibilities that traditional professional counseling does not. In this chapter we will answer such questions as: Are counseling and discipleship related? What is the possible role of the laity? Are preaching and counseling complementary or conflicting? What can the urban church do in the way of preventive counseling? What are the limitations of the counselor?

COUNSELING AND DISCIPLESHIP

At first glance, counseling and discipleship do not seem to be closely related.[1] Counseling has to do with helping people straighten out the emotional and relational distortions of their lives when they are unable to find constructive ways to cope with pain. They are usually experiencing intense negative emotions or emotional numbing and they are trying to clarify confusion, find comfort, or somehow bring about changes in their experience of life.

Discipleship, on the other hand, has to do with the development of a person from spiritual infancy to spiritual adulthood. It is a process of spiritual parenting and spiritual formation that we usually do not view in terms of pain and crisis, but in terms of growth.

When we look more closely, however, the differences between counseling and discipleship may not be as discrete as they appear. Ministry in the urban setting presents us with the reality of suffering—a reality that the suburban church has not had to face to the same degree. The subject of suffering has been downplayed in Western evangelical theology because most of evangelical theology has been developed by nonurban, middle-class theologians who have not experienced suffering to the same degree as many of the urban and the poor.

The Bible teaches that suffering is an unavoidable part of the believer's life. Acknowledging pain and constructively processing it are part of what it means to become a disciple of Jesus Christ. Not only did Jesus suffer intensely and unfairly, but so did almost all of the early apostles. Thus, becoming a disciple of Christ necessitates learning how to be a healthy person in the context of post-Fall disintegration, disorder, and distress.

Perhaps one of the more subtle obstacles in our ability to see the link between counseling and discipleship is our tendency to blame the victim. This is especially true in relation to the urban poor and those with emotional problems. While we may grant that discipleship has to include a consideration of suffering, we tend to see the suffering of Jesus and the apostles as externally-generated, unavoidable, and thoroughly spiritual in nature. However, we view people with emotional and relational or distress that stems from the disruptions of urban stress and poverty, negatively. Their suffering appears to be due to their failure to cope with life and their irresponsibility or bad choices. Their pain is not apparently spiritual, so it does not have anything to do with discipleship—or so we may think.

If, however, we view the spirit and soul as tightly intertwined parts of the person, the picture changes. We begin to see the pain of life as a product of the Fall—something Satan destructively capitalizes upon. Learning to live with the pain of life in constructive ways is part of psychospiritual growth and maturity. This growth may need to be helped by counseling, which is essential component of discipleship in a context of suffering.

Christian counseling and discipleship in the city, then, are compatible processes. Both are concerned with helping people grow into a maturity that is able to weather the inevitable storms of life. Both involve a model or mentor whose words and viewpoints have an impact on the counselee-disciple, providing a growth alternative to faulty or less-mature life patterns. Both are nurturing relationships that encourage a focus on truth and accountability. Both involve *un*learning faulty patterns and learning new, healthy patterns. Both encourage the experience of *shalom* through the internalization and implementation of God's guidelines for wholeness and holiness. Both promote the ultimate well-being of people who best reflect the qualities of Jesus in their lives.

When we view counseling and discipleship as compatible components of growth and maturation we are able to accept people *as* they are and *where* they are from the beginning. As we see the relationship with counseling, we are better able to incorporate the weaknesses and problems of real life into discipling. At the same time we are enabled to see counseling as a psychospiritual enterprise, not as something strangely detached from spiritual struggle and growth. We are also able to see counseling in broader terms of growth toward maturity rather than merely as a cure of disease, and to incorporate preventive forms of counseling into our practice. Counseling is not restricted to curative and corrective intervention when we view it as a part of discipleship.

COUNSELING AND THE LAITY

At the heart of healing is love. Love is expressed in attitudes and actions that communicate acceptance, respect, validation, value, perceived potential (hope), appreciation, constructive correction, and affirmation. Clearly, these expressions are not limited to professional or pastoral counselors. Indeed, they are simply the earmarks of *koinonia* —a caring Christian community. Therefore, an active counseling role for the laity is implied by this view of counseling and discipleship.

Scripture makes it plain that the interaction of believers is to be characterized by the kind of dynamics experienced in therapy. For example, Colossians 3:12-14 commands believers,

> as God's chosen people, holy and dearly loved, clothe yourselves with compassion, kindness, humility, gentleness, and patience. Bear with each other and forgive whatever grievances you may have against one another. Forgive as the Lord forgave you. And over all these virtues put on love, which binds them all together in perfect unity.

As we experience healthy interaction with others in a climate of caring, we promote emotional and relational healing.

Beyond this "usual" form of mutual counseling, there is a place for laity who are given additional training as intentional counselors or people helpers.[2] Christian caregivers[3] within the Christian community, with the acquisition of helping skills, are able to build on and deepen ongoing relationships. Siang-Yang Tan[4] describes three models of lay-counseling ministry: (1) the "informal, spontaneous" model, which assumes that lay counseling should occur in relationships already present in the structures of the church and that require only some basic caring-skills training; (2) the "informal, organized" model, which assumes counseling should be well-supervised but should occur mostly in informal settings; (3) the "formal, organized" model, which assumes that the counseling should be done formally through a structured lay counseling center in a local church.

Whichever approach is used, lay counseling must be put into the context of the multifaceted mission of the church.[5] It must not be elevated above other ministries or have any elitist attitudes associated with it. Those selected for training become pastoral-care associates for the pastor.

Selection

Selection of participants is vitally important. The pastor, together with his director of lay counseling and a professional Christian counselor (if not the director), should screen interested people. A church does not have to have a large number of lay counselors in order to have a greatly amplified ministry of pastoral care. Generally speaking, a ratio of approximately one lay counselor per twenty-five congregants is ample. In a church of 100 regular attendees, that means four lay counselors would be a significant and adequate addition to the pastor. Among the criteria used for selection are the following:

- *Emotional stability.* The lay counselor should not be characterized by frequent or significant mood swings, or suffer from a serious psychological disorder herself. She should be dependable and trustworthy, and have appropriate relational boundaries (neither too close and involved nor too distant and detached).
- *Good interpersonal relations.* The lay counselor should enjoy relating to people, be sensitive to needs, and be perceived as approachable and genuine.
- *Biblical grounding and spiritual maturity.* The counselor must not be a spiritual novice but should give evidence of spiritual maturity. He should be well-grounded in biblical truth and show some ability to apply it practically.

Inventories such as the Spiritual Well-Being Scale, the Religious Status Interview, the Character Assessment Scale, and the Spiritual Maturity Index may be helpful for the evaluation of this dimension.[6]

- *Interest in helping others.* Do not drag people into this ministry out of an appeal to their duty to care. Consider those who want to be involved but be sure they are thoroughly screened. There are many reasons for wanting to counsel; not all of them are healthy.

- *Trustworthiness.* Is the prospective counselor able to keep confidences? Personal information obtained through counseling must not be shared with others. Sharing with a supervisor is acceptable as long as the person being helped understands that. Loose lips are unwanted equipment for counseling.

- *Nonjudgmental attitude.* The lay counselor must be able to look beyond the dysfunctions and disorders that are revealed and love with Christ's love. A critical and harsh counselor will do irreparable damage to those who have allowed themselves to be vulnerable.

- *Commitment.* The prospective counselor should be committed to thorough training and to being a caregiver for a designated period of time. Many church offices are held for two to three years. We encourage a similar length of commitment for the lay counselor.

Other criteria might include age, sex, education, ethnic and cultural background, availability, teachability, and spiritual gifts.[7]

Training

Once interested persons have been interviewed and selected they should be trained. We encourage approximately forty hours (twenty weeks, two hours per week) of direct training. In addition, specific reading should be assigned. Lay counselor training needs to include the following basic ingredients:

- *Knowledge of human development.* Know the most common life tasks associated with various times of life.[8] These tasks provide the dynamic for personal growth and point out potential pitfalls to growth. Since people mature differently depending on how well they handle the tasks of personal growth, the failure to adequately negotiate these challenges leads to some level of social-emotional crippling and subsequent difficulty in handling life.

● *Knowledge of dysfunctional behaviors.* Which behaviors are unhealthy? How can the counselor identify self-defeating and pathological patterns of thinking, feeling, and acting? It is helpful for lay counselors to be aware of the diagnostic categories that professional counselors use so that they can refer clients with more chronic and severe disturbances to professional counselors. Table 3-1 lists the major classes of disorder identified in the *Diagnostic and Statistical Manual (DSM III-R)* of the American Psychiatric Association.

TABLE 3-1
Summary of DSM III-R Diagnostic Categories

Disorders Usually Evident in Infancy,
     Childhood, or Adolescence
Organic Mental Syndromes and Disorders
Psychoactive Substance Use Disorders
Schizophrenia
Mood Disorders
Anxiety Disorders
Somatoform Disorders
Dissociative Disorders
Sexual Disorders
Sleep Disorders
Factitious Disorders
Impulse Control Disorders Not Elsewhere Classified
Adjustment Disorders
Psychological Factors Affecting Physical Condition
Personality Disorders
Conditions Not Attributable to a Mental Disorder

● *Knowledge of common problems.* What are the problems lay counselors are most likely to encounter? What should they do to help those who display specific patterns? Lay counselors need specific training in how to deal with addictions (chemicals, sex, gambling, lying), adult children of alcoholics, the empty-nest syndrome, retirement, depression, domestic abuse (including sexual abuse of children), interpersonal conflict resolution, life purpose, marital problems, parenting problems, premarital counseling, stress, crisis pregnancies, and victimization.

- *Approaches to helping.* Lay counselors should be exposed to various models of Christian counseling[9] as well as to general models of helping.[10] Videotapes are helpful in bridging the theory-practice gap.[11]
- *Skills training.* Lay counselors should practice role playing, communicating nonverbally, probing, empathy, summarizing, and reflection.[12] Triads are very useful in these kinds of role-playing situations. For example, in the first round, person A counsels person B and person C observes. In the second go around the dynamics change and person B counsels person C while person A observes. Finally, person C counsels person A while person B observes. Each counselor-in-training gets a chance to "be" the other person and if each shares a problem, it makes the skills training very real.

One of the most well-known and systematic training programs for caregiving laity (and pastors) is Stephen Ministries.[13] Stephen Ministries has Leader's Training Courses (LTC) each summer in St. Louis, Los Angeles, Berkeley (Calif.) and Baltimore, as well as one-day Introductory Workshops at various locations throughout the country. The typical Leader's Training Course of Study involves sixty-two hours of in-class training sessions over a twelve day period. In addition to lectures there are small group discussions and skills-practice sessions. Each congregation typically sends its pastor and one or more lay leaders and these people return to their congregations and train lay counselors. Topics typically addressed in the training sessions include the art of listening, approaches to psychotherapy, crisis theory and intervention, how and where to find helpers, practicing the first helping contact, referral, building a leadership team, ministering to depressed people, sexuality, and a variety of more specialized topics.

Another approach to training is a one year, part-time course (Certificate in Christian Counseling) offered through Ontario Bible College in Toronto, Ontario, Canada. The program is specifically for the training of pastors and laity and combines theory, practical-skills training, and discussion and analysis of audio and video tapes.[14]

Best Fit

The third guideline for developing a lay counselor program is to match the interests and backgrounds of each trained counselor with people having certain kinds of problems. (This assumes a "formal, organized" approach utilizing an initial screening interview and the assignment of counselor-counselee pairs.)

In less formally organized models, lay counselors need to know what they can and cannot handle. There needs to be an established procedure for referring a counselee to another lay counselor (or a professional) if the first counselor does not feel qualified to handle a specific problem.

Commissioning

Many churches have special commissioning services for those called by the Lord to professional ministry and missions. These services, or moments within services, recognize and affirm God's calling of the person(s) to a particular expression of ministry, and commit the church to uphold them prayerfully and monetarily. An annual commissioning of lay counselors helps them recognize their responsibility to God, and helps the congregation realize the importance of a caring ministry within the church.

Supervision

A trained pastoral-staff person or professional counselor should meet monthly with lay counselors to discuss concerns and difficulties and provide continuing in-service training for the counselors. In order to make these meetings relevant counselors can be asked to submit, for discussion, brief vignettes of problem cases (with names and details altered sufficiently to maintain confidentiality).

In addition to these monthly sessions, lay counselors should have regular access to the designated supervisor for individual assistance. An annual retreat is also an excellent opportunity for review and evaluation, as well as for renewal and affirmation.

PREVENTIVE COUNSELING THROUGH EDUCATION

An important part of preventive counseling and discipleship is the life-education program provided by the urban church.

Premarital, marital, and family instruction aids people in establishing realistic expectations and proper relational patterns. Such education provides information and models that are able to motivate and guide couples needing changes in their relationships.

Premarital education and counseling needs to focus especially on expectations for marriage, clarification of basic values, principles for effective communication, conflict resolution and negotiation, relational styles, financial management, sexuality, and family-of-origin patterns. Special attention should be paid to such family-of-origin dysfunctions as alcohol or drug abuse and physical or sexual abuse since these factors frequently contribute to emotional and relational problems within marriage. The methods that the couple plans to use to promote the spiritual development of their family must be considered as well, if spirituality is to be more than an individualized, weekend religious exercise.

Premarital education effectively conducted in the Sunday School by scheduling it regularly as a marriage-and-family-life component of junior high, high school, and college age classes gives everyone some biblically-based education on this critical dimension of Christian life before they are married. It also lessens the likelihood that the intensity of a romantic relationship will override the couple's ability to respond to the training. A small church that has few engaged couples at any given time can use this format to provide valuable preparation within the broader group.

In addition to the more generalized framework just suggested, the pastor should require at least four to six premarital counseling sessions before he preforms a marriage ceremony for anyone. The urban church must stand strong against the easy-marriage-easy-divorce mentality of our society. There is something wrong when we allow people to spend more time and energy on the wedding than on building a strong foundation for the marriage.

A premarital diagnostic assessment is very helpful and perhaps the most useful and popular instrument in use today is the Prepare Inventory,[15] which asks the couple to evaluate their attitudes and feelings toward thirteen relationship dimensions vital to marriage. The couple's responses to the 125 items are profiled in a convenient format for the counselor who gives feedback to the couple about their strengths and areas for growth.

Feedback that focuses on a particular couple's relationship is one of the advantages of the Prepare Inventory. The counselor is then able to focus on that couple's unique patterns. Another advantage is that it provides a structure the couple can use to systematically discuss key dimensions of their relationship, and to specifically work through potential problem areas. It can also easily incorporate any biblical input on marriage that a pastor may want to include. Finally, it gives the couple "objective" feedback on the state of their relationship and may help them to see that they should *not* get married. I have had several couples make this difficult decision (much to my relief) as a result of the feedback they received from the Prepare Inventory and the premarital counseling process.

The Prepare Inventory already used by approximately 200,000 couples is available in English, Japanese, and Spanish editions. It is also available for use in small-group situations, which might be needed in larger urban churches where the pastor is conducting numerous weddings and finds it impossible to offer more than two or three sessions of private counseling for individual couples.

It is also critical that the church offer marriage and family-life education. Couples relate to one another in marriage largely on the basis of what they have observed and experienced in their own families. Fewer and fewer people are growing up in healthy families and negative influences such as alcoholism and sexual abuse are often everyday experiences. One author has estimated that there are over 5.5 million born again adult children of alcoholics in the United States.[16] It is also of interest to note that incidences of abuse occur at almost the same rate in the Christian church as they do throughout society,[17] which means that 38 percent of all women have been sexually abused before reaching age eighteen. This statistic rises to an alarming 54 percent if noncontact experiences such as exhibitionism are included.[18] In 75 percent of all child sexual-abuse cases, the perpetrator is someone the child knows and loves. (Even as I write, I am counseling two families in which the fathers—Bible-believing Christians—have been involved in emotionally shattering incestuous relationships.)

These kinds of experiences are part of the secret emotional lives and relationships of thousands of people in our urban evangelical churches. Dysfunctional family experiences during childhood negatively affect the ability of adults to develop trusting, intimate, nurturing, secure, and healthy marital and parental relationships. Beyond the more blatant traumatic effect of alcoholism and abuse is the impact divorce and single parenting have on a child's ability to model healthy, emotionally intimate relationships as an adult. Recent evidence suggests that teens and adults whose parents divorced when they were small have significantly more immature and promiscuous sexual patterns than do children from intact families.

Marriage and family-life education needs to be provided through sermons, marriage and family-life films (such as the Focus on the Family[19] series), retreats and seminars (which can be held inexpensively right at the church), and the regular Christian education and Sunday School program. Such education must be realistic and candid, not hidden behind spiritualized platitudes and euphemisms. It needs to include material specifically aimed at Christian marriage and family life,[20] while at the same time utilizing more general information on communication, conflict, intimacy, and sexuality that is helpful to and compatible with Christian faith and practice. There are a growing number of informational resources available and appropriate for church use.[21] (Some are not specifically Christian but are "Christian-friendly.")

Urban-life education also needs to provide information and support for divorce recovery and single parenting. Over a million divorces a year in the United States during the 1980s have made divorce a way of life for 59 percent of all children born to the baby boom generation. Sex education and teen pregnancy-prevention education should be incorporated into junior- and senior-high Sunday-school programs. All teens should have the opportunity to have private counseling sessions in conjunction with these classes.

Finally, family-life education needs to include parenting issues. Unless trained to parent, one is most likely to repeat the patterns observed and experienced during childhood. For many, those patterns were less than ideal. Parent education needs to examine such critical concerns as values, multi-generational patterns of dysfunction, use of television, and assertive discipline. Parents need to learn how to build a child's self-esteem, and how to respect their children and behave consistently toward them. They need to learn how to help their children accept cultural and ethnic differences, and, in addition, parents need to learn how to set realistic yet flexible goals for the intellectual, moral, social, physical, emotional, and spiritual development of their children, and to develop methods for achieving their goals.

COUNSELING AND PREACHING

The relationship between preaching and counseling has been an uneasy one for many pastors. On one end of the spectrum are those pastors who argue that, if they preach well, there will be no need for counseling. On the other end are those who are so enamored by counseling that their ministry is focused almost exclusively on it—whatever preaching is done resembles group therapy. Harry Emerson Fosdick, for example, saw preaching as an act of pastoral counseling. What he saw as deficiencies in both expository and topical types of sermons led him to develop the "counseling sermon."[22]

A more balanced view sees the preaching-counseling relationship as complementary; neither one should be absorbed by the other. Highly effective preaching should be *expected* to regularly stimulate self-examination and changes in the way life is viewed. It should motivate and cause people to seek counseling in order to implement a message into their own lives. Both preaching and counseling are tools for shaping mature followers of Christ.[23]

Counseling deepens preaching because the speaker-counselor is forced to come to grips with the real-life struggles of the people in the pew. God's Word is a living Word for living people; preaching that detaches the Word from the nitty-gritty of life deadens it. Preaching must be theological, but the application of it must also be practical or it will fail to touch broken lives. Counseling must be theologically based or it will not adequately address the needs people have. Excellent preaching and effective counseling work together: they both produce hope, stir motivation to change, comfort the distressed, provide information and guidance, and release healing grace. They are both part of God's design for human wholeness and holiness (in our opinion, emotional wholeness and spiritual holiness are thoroughly interwoven), though the form and emphasis of communication is different for each. Preaching emphasizes speaking; counseling emphasizes listening. Preaching is preacher-oriented; counseling is parishioner-oriented. Preaching is frequently cognitive in focus; counseling is more emotionally focused. Preaching is unidirectional in delivery; counseling is interactive. Preaching is proclamational; counseling is dialogic. Preaching is generalized; counseling is individualized.

Preaching and counseling are powerful agents for growth when jointly dedicated to the goal of disciple-making. If a pastor is compassionate in his preaching style and personal interactions, congregants will feel safe enough to reveal their weaknesses in counseling and will be helped to personally apply grace and truth so that they can grow in psychospiritual maturity.

COUNSELING AND ADVOCACY

An individualized, medical model of pathology and healing is the foundation of classic psychotherapy. Counselors using this model focus on "What's wrong *inside* this troubled person?" Treatment focuses on encouraging the *individual* to make changes. With the rise of family therapy in the past fifteen years, attention has shifted to the impact interlocking dysfunctional systems have on a person. This systemic emphasis thrust interpersonal factors into dynamic prominence because they are seen as more critical in analysis and treatment than are individual variables. There has been such an emphasis on the system in the family-therapy field that several recent books have begged therapists not to forget the individual!

Before the systemic approach of family therapy became popular, community psychology, begun in the 1960s, has encouraged mental health practitioners to have a broad focus. Community-psychology approaches weigh the impact broader environmental, sociological, and political influences have on the origins and maintenance of emotional and relational problems. Therapeutic intervention *on behalf of* the suffering has brought about changes in the larger societal systems that tend to promote dysfunction and distress. Thus, rather than simply trying to get the individual to adjust to the system, community psychology suggests that therapy should try to change the pathology in the system itself.[24]

Because we do not view human beings as existing in a vacuum (where all problems would be self-generated), the role of advocate, taken on by the counselor in an urban setting, seems both legitimate and essential. After all, should not Christian counselors be working to change social-welfare policies that promote the disintegration of poorer families? Should not Christian counselors be advocates for improved prenatal care and nutrition that would reduce the high rates of neurological impairment and the high rates of infant mortality in minority groups? Should not Christian counselors, recognizing that the chances for out-of-wedlock births, drug addiction, fragmented families, and abusive parenting increase when teens drop out of school, be advocates for the education of minority and poor children (40 percent of whom do not graduate from high school)? Should not Christian counselors be pressuring junior and senior high schools to offer quality instruction on marriage and family life, combining book knowledge with real-life examples? Should not Christian counselors, recognizing that nonaction insures that despair will become even more deeply entrenched in thousands of families and hundreds of thousands of future adults, be actively involved in promoting safe, humane, and healthy housing policies for homeless families? Extremely high levels of anxiety, depression, demoralization, distress, danger, uncertainty, and insecurity all combine to assault the emotional well-being of the homeless.[25] And, should not Christian counselors be advocating programs aimed at preventing alcohol and drug abuse?

We certainly have an example of advocacy in the person of Jesus Christ. Scripture makes it clear that Jesus is our advocate now, that he speaks on our behalf and entered into suffering for our sake.[26] When Christ walked on this earth he challenged the prevailing social-religious-legal system directly and indirectly, advocating justice and systemic change on behalf of the sick and oppressed. As a result, he did not win any "Best-Loved-Citizen" awards from the power brokers. Instead, his advocacy took him to Calvary, and "by his wounds we are healed." [27] The cost was great for him and it is great for counselor-advocates, but the healing that comes is even greater.

LIMITATIONS AND LIMITS

The typical urban pastor must be a generalist to properly lead and manage the local church. It is inadvisable for the average pastor to specialize in counseling because of limits on his time and energy. His ministry will be far more fruitful if he emphasizes preaching, accepts a limited number of short-term counselees (we recommend no more than six to eight hours of counseling per week with a maximum of eight sessions per person or couple), wisely uses referrals for longer-term counseling, and encourages self-help groups to deal with eating disorders, adult children of alcoholics, and single parents.

However, for most of us it is difficult to accept the fact that we are limited and even more difficult to establish boundaries in the face of pressing needs. Being needed is a powerful elixir for most of us; it speaks to our deep needs for worth, identity, significance, and purpose. For some reason we feel strong and healthy ourselves if we are able to help those who are not coping with life as well as we are. Helping others gives us the feeling that we are vitally important, but we can easily develop a hero or messiah complex and see ourselves as almost indispensable rescuers of the emotionally and relationally needy.

The messiah complex is unhealthy and is rooted in a deeply felt need to take responsibility for the plight of others, to remove pain, and to make things right. It is based on an equally unhealthy inner belief that one's own needs are secondary and selfish— taking care of one's self is egocentric and bad.[28] Attempting to earn a sense of worth by external actions, allowing others to determine the choices one makes, overachievement, attraction to those with similar experiences, difficulty in establishing intimate relationships, isolation and loneliness, endless activity, and attempts to "do it all" are characteristics of the person with a messiah complex.[29]

Not only does this "messiah" ultimately drive himself into the ground, burned-out by his workaholism, but he frequently ends up hurting others. If he is a pleaser messiah, his helping will tend to block honest communication of feelings. Rescuer messiahs tend to encourage feelings of helplessness in others. Crusader types transmit anger if those they are trying to help do not totally commit themselves to a master plan, which denies legitimate needs and is often unrealistically demanding. Givers try to control others through gift giving; those receiving help are given the message that they are not capable of caring for themselves. Protector messiahs damage others by inappropriately withholding truth on the one hand or revealing too much information on the other. The counselor messiah is deeply dependent on those being counseled and tends to make others dependent on him. Counselees become entrapped and unable to genuinely grow.[30]

Genuine and effective helping, then, must be based on a counselor's recognition of his own limitations. Counselees must not be used, even subtly, by the counselor to meet his own inner needs—otherwise, counseling becomes exploitive and destructive. A limit on the number of hours one counsels and the number of counseling sessions one has with a specific counselee provides important safeguards. An accountable consulting relationship with another person who understands the messiah trap is also especially helpful and that person in turn can help you work through your own unresolved psychospiritual needs.

A messiah complex is a trap the counselor often falls into and one, along with sex, that must be avoided.[31] If a counselor has not worked through his own unresolved inner struggles, if he spends inordinate amounts of time in helping relationships and not enough time with his family or friends, he is setting himself up for a problem. Invariably, some counselee at some time will idealize the counselor (transference) and will want to be sexually involved with this apparent tower of sensitivity, affirmation, supportiveness, and strength. (Sexual involvement is often the way in which an immature person expresses the need for acceptance, belonging, or significance.) It is critical that the counselor recognize such sexual acting out as immature, unhealthy, and dangerous behavior and that the counselor confront it. By addressing sexual acting out clinically, by taking the overtures out, and by examining its faultiness and damaging consequences, the sex trap can be avoided. If sexual acting out continues, the counselor should gently but firmly terminate the counseling relationship.

At the same time, counselors must be aware of their own emotional and sexual needs, and recognize counter-transference if it occurs. Counter-transference takes place when the counselor projects unresolved emotions onto a counselee. This leads the counselor to initiate unhealthy and inappropriate expressions toward the counselee. One form of inappropriate expression is seduction. There is absolutely no legitimate biblical or professional reason for flirting, for sexual innuendos, for sexual touching, or for sexual intercourse between counselor and counselee. Any such activities are exploitative of the counselee for the counselor's sinful and selfish purposes. If a counselor is tempted in this area, he needs to confess it before God, seek a consultation with a professional Christian counselor to "air it out" and gain proper perspective, and most likely end the counseling relationship. In the case of referral, the counselor should carefully communicate that he has sensed a therapeutic impasse and that he believes another counselor would be better able to help. Care should be taken to avoid the impression that the counselee is the problem, that the counselee's situation is hopeless, or that the counselor is rejecting the counselee.

To minimize the danger of falling into sexual traps, several simple precautions should be taken. These should be regarded as nonnegotiable laws for the counselor. First, there should be no touching of a counselee of the opposite sex except for a possible handshake as the person leaves the office. Same sex touching should be done very judiciously especially in the case of gay counselees. In any case, a pat on the arm or shoulder, or a handshake should be the limit in all cases. Second, the counselor must avoid high-risk situations, such as opposite-sex counseling alone in one's office at night, or house calls for opposite-sex counseling. Third, it is wise to do your counseling in settings where another person, such as a staff member or a spouse, is readily available to intervene. Such an arrangement is also helpful for situations that may involve physical aggression on the part of the counselee. Finally, nonprofessional counselors may wish to limit their counseling to same-sex counselees, although the result may be a loss of therapeutic impact in some situations.

REFERRAL

Referral is not to be limited just to situations involving intense counselee transference or counselor counter-transference. Due to limitations in one's training and knowledge, limitations in schedule, and decisions not to deal with certain problems, the counselor may wish to refer. Pastors and paraprofessional counselors are not usually equipped to deal with chronic affective and personality disorders. Unless you are a professionally trained therapist or have been specifically trained to handle difficult cases, it is usually best to refer those who are psychotic and clinically depressed, those who have borderline personality problems, those who are active drug addicts, those who are sexually or physically abusive, those who are phobic, and those who have learning disabilities. Referrals should also be made in cases where the counselee is involved in severe domestic abuse situations or is suffering from eating disorders (anorexia nervosa, bulimia).[32]

It is simply not possible for a pastor to know how to address all of the problems presented to him. It is far better for him to select a limited number of problem areas (marriage and family, stress management, nonchemical addictions, spiritual struggles, adult children of alcoholics, codependency, grief counseling, and parenting difficulties) in which to become knowledgeable and experienced and refer people with other kinds of problems.

Pastors and other nonprofessional counselors should become acquainted with professional therapists who are potential referral resources in the city. We recommend that pastors and ministry personnel gather written information about the clinics and professionals that seem most compatible with their ministry. Then invite the professional therapists for lunch to discuss counseling philosophy, counseling-faith integration, training, backgrounds, referral procedures, and their preferred working relationship with the pastor. It is appropriate to explicitly assess the therapist's attitude toward Christian faith, values, and practices. If the therapist is a Christian, ask questions to determine how his or her Christian faith is integrated with therapy.[33]

NOTES

[1]For a more complete discussion, see Craig W. Ellison, "Counseling and Discipleship" in Roger Greenway, ed., *Discipling the City*, 2d ed. (Grand Rapids: Baker, forthcoming).

[2]Gary Collins, *How to Be a People Helper* (Santa Ana, Calif.: Vision House, 1976).

[3]Kenneth C. Haugk, *Christian Caregiving: A Way of Life* (Minneapolis: Augsburg, 1984).

[4]Siang-Yang Tan, "Lay Christian Counseling: Present Status and Future Directions." Invited paper presented at the International Congress on Christian Counseling, Lay Counseling Track, Atlanta, Ga. (November 1988). Requests for reprints should be sent to Dr. Tan, Graduate School of Psychology, Fuller Theological Seminary, 180 N. Oakland Ave., Pasadena, CA, 91101.

[5]Rodger Bufford and R. E. Buckler, "Counseling in the Church: A Proposed Strategy for Ministering to Mental Health Needs in the Church," *Journal of Psychology and Christianity* 6 (2) (1987): 21–29.

[6]Craig W. Ellison, "Spiritual Well-Being: Conceptualization and Measurement," *Journal of Psychology and Theology* 11 (4) (1983): 330–40;

H. Newton Malony, "The Clinical Assessment of Optimal Religious Functioning," *Review of Religious Research* 30 (1) (1986): 3–17;

Paul F. Schmidt, *Manual for Use of the Character Assessment Scale*, 2d ed. (Shelbyville, Ky.: Institute for Character Development, 1983);

Craig W. Ellison, "Spiritual Maturity Index." Unpublished thirty-item index of evangelically-oriented expressions of spiritual maturity;

Craig W. Ellison, "Toward a Measure of Health and Well-Being," *Journal of Psychology and Theology* 19 (1) (1991): 35–48.

[7]See Siang-Yang Tan, *Lay Counseling: Equipping Christians for a Helping Ministry* (Grand Rapids: Zondervan, 1990) for a thorough discussion of selection criteria and all other aspects of establishing a lay counseling ministry.

[8]One theoretical approach that has been widely accepted in Western society as a way to organize the social-emotional process and crises of development is the eight ages of man proposed by Erik Erikson, *Childhood and Society*, 2d ed. (New York: W. W. Norton & Co., 1963).

[9]For example:

William Backus, *Telling the Truth to Troubled People* (Minneapolis: Bethany House, 1985);

John D. Carter and Bruce Narramore, *The Integration of Psychology and Theology* (Grand Rapids: Zondervan, 1979);

Gary R. Collins, *Christian Counseling: A Comprehensive Guide*, revised ed. (Dallas, Tex.: Word, 1988);

Gary R. Collins, *Psychology and Theology: Prospects for Integration* (Nashville, Tenn.: Abingdon, 1981);

Also, the thirty-volume Resources for Christian Counseling Series edited by Gary R. Collins and published by Word is an outstanding resource. Series volumes deal with a wide variety of counseling topics including eating disorders, depression, family violence and abuse, crisis counseling, guilt, unplanned pragnancy, self-control problems, substance abuse, homosexuality, the demonic, anger, marriage, children, and adult children of alcoholics.

In addition, Gary Collins will be the Series Editor for a new series, Contemporary Christian Counseling, also to be published by Word.

Lawrence Crabb, *Effective Biblical Counseling* (Grand Rapids: Zondervan, 1977); Roger F. Hurding, *The Tree of Healing: Psychological and Bibilical Foundations for Counseling and Pastoral Care* (Grand Rapids: Zondervan, 1985); William T. Kirwan, *Biblical Concepts for Christian Counseling* (Grand Rapids: Baker, 1984).

[10]One of the best for beginners is Gerald Egan's *The Skilled Helper*, 4th ed. (Monterey, Calif.: Brooks/Cole, 1990). It is practical and focused on problem solving. Vaughn and Lazarus's approaches, mentioned in chapter 2, are also very helpful.

[11]For example, tapes are available through Menninger Video Productions (Topeka, Kansas); Research Press Video Catalogue (Champaign, Ill.); Christian Marriage Enrichment (1913 E. 17th St., Suite 118, Santa Ana, CA).

[12]Egan's companion workbook, *Exercises in Helping Skills*, 4th ed. (Monterey, Calif.: Brooks/Cole, 1990), is an excellent skills awareness and training guide to use with triads focusing on real life problems of the trainees.

[13]Stephen Ministries, 1325 Bolard, St. Louis, MO, 63117, is a not-for-profit religious and educational organization working transdenominationally and internationally. (Telephone: 314-645-5511.) Another organization that regularly provides biblical and clinical counselor training for laity is the Dayspring Institute, Inc., in Concord, California.

[14]Siang-Yang Tan, "Training Paraprofessional Christian Counselors," *Journal of Pastoral Care*, vol. XL, no. 4 (December 1986): 296–304.

[15]Information on the Prepare Inventory and the counselor training workshop required to use it may be obtained by writing Prepare-Enrich, Inc., P.O. Box 190, Minneapolis, MN, 55440, or by calling 800-331-1661. Training workshops are regularly held throughout the United States, Australia, Japan, and other locations.

[16]Sandra D. Wilson, *Counseling Adult Children of Alcoholics* (Dallas: Word, 1989).

[17]Maxine Hancock and Karen B. Mains, *Child Sexual Abuse* (Wheaton, Ill.: Harold Shaw, 1987).

[18]Ibid., 11–12.

[19]Dr. James Dobson's Focus on the Family (Pomona, CA, 91799) has a toll-free number (800-A-FAMILY) available six days a week to order a wide variety of films, books, cassettes, magazines, and videos. It should be noted, however, that these films are not specifically tuned to urban, cross-cultural, or lower income family life and may not be fully appropriate for many urban-center churches.

[20]An outstanding example of this is the "What Makes A Christian Family Christian?" video and workbook series by David and Karen Mains. The series of four video presentations and eight workbook sessions was designed to be used easily by intact families or single parents. The series focuses on practical, creative ways to enhance the *Christian* dimension of Christian family life.

[21]Among the best resources available are Christian Marriage Enrichment, 1913 E. 17th St., Suite 118, Santa Ana, CA, 92701 (H. Norman Wright); Focus on the Family (see footnote #19); International Marriage Encounter, 955 Lake Drive, St. Paul, MN, 55120; Research Press, 2612 North Mattis Ave., Champaign, IL, 61821.

[22]Donald Capps, *Pastoral Counseling and Preaching: A Quest for an Integrated Ministry* (Philidelphia: Westminster, 1980).

[23]I like this term for disciple as introduced by Gordon MacDonald in *Forging a Real World Faith* (Nashville, Tenn.: Oliver Nelson, 1989).

[24]See Erich Fromm, *The Sane Society* (Greenwich, Conn.: Fawcett Publications, Inc., 1955) for an early, trenchant analysis of Western civilization as a fundamentally sick system which promotes insanity and dysfunctional behavior.

[25]William R. Breakey, "Homeless Men and Women," *Division of Child, Youth and Family Services Newsletter*, American Psychological Association, Div. 37, vol. 12, no. 4 (Fall 1989).

[26]1 John 2:1.

[27]Isaiah 53:5.

[28]Carmen R. Berry, *When Helping You Is Hurting Me: Escaping the Messiah Trap* (San Francisco: Harper & Row, 1988).

[29]Ibid., 32–40.

[30]Ibid., 56–69.

[31]See Jerry Edelwich with Archie Brodsky, *Sexual Dilemmas for the Helping Professional* (New York: Brunner/Mazel, 1982).

[32]The *Diagnostic and Statistic Manual-3R* (DSM-3R), published by the American Psychiatric Association and available in training book form through several publishers of psychological literature such as Brunner/Mazel, Inc. (New York), gives helpful and definitive information for identifying these and other recognized psychological disorders.

[33]Among the best nationwide referral resources for professional Christian counselors, social workers, psychologists, and psychiatrists in the United States are:

(a) Focus on the Family, 801 Corporate Center Drive, Pomona, CA, 91799, (800) 232-6459;

(b) Christian Association for Psychological Studies, Dr. Robert R. King, Jr. (Exec. Dir.), P.O. Box 628, Blue Jay, CA, 92317, (714) 337-5117;

(c) Family Research Council of America, Inc., Gary L. Bauer (President), 601 Pennsylvania Ave. N.W., Suite 901, Washington, D.C., 20004, (202) 393-2100;

(d) National Association of Christians in Social Work, P.O. Box 90, St. Davids, PA, 19087;

(e) Minirth-Meier Clinic, 2100 North Collins Blvd., Richardson, TX, 75080; (214) 669-1733;

(f) The Professional Association of Christian Counselors and Therapists, Dr. Samuel R. McElroy (President), P.O. Box 5839, Rockville, MD, 20855-0839, (301) 948-6441;

(g) Rapha (Christ-centered in-hospital psychiatric units), Box 580355, Houston, TX, 77258, (800) 227-2657 nationwide;

(h) CoNET Referral Network, Christian Counseling Services, 515 Woodland St., P.O. Box 60383, Nashville, TN, 37206, (615) 254-8341;

(i) The American Board of Christian Psychology, P.O. Box 1273, Copperas Cove, TX, 76522, (817) 542-4581;

(j) The American Associaiton of Christian Counselors, P.O. Box 55712, Jackson, MS, 39216-1712, (601) 981-2180;

(k) United Assocation of Christian Counselors, International, 3837 Walnut St., Harrisburg, PA, 17109, (717) 652-7688;

(l) American Board of Christian Psychology, 950 First St., South, Suite 201, Winter Haven, FL, 33880, (813) 294-1385.

CHAPTER 4

Contextualized Counseling

CITIES ARE MUCH more culturally diverse than either the suburban or rural sections of a country. Because diverse racial, linguistic, and ethnic groups are competing for the same resources and space, cities have frequently become arenas of interethnic conflict, suspicion, and unfulfilled aspirations.

Interethnic conflict occurs when two or more different groups come into contact and one views the other as an intruder. Differences breed suspicion, which results in verbal and sometimes physical conflict—or death. A case in point is the Yusef Hawkins incident in Brooklyn, New York. Hawkins and his friends crossed an invisible line into a white section of the borough to buy a used car. They were mistaken for other African Americans reputed to have come to "make trouble." Hawkins, a young black man, was killed by a gang of white youths.

The instigator of the attack on Yusef Hawkins was an unemployed high-school dropout, which upholds the theory that those most likely to perpetrate violence against members of another ethnic group usually see that group as competing for limited resources. It is these limited resources that affect the issue of unfulfilled aspirations. The perpetrator has very few options for advancement open to him.[1] Albeit, the victim often has even fewer options than the perpetrator because upon coming to the city seeking a better life, he finds that his hopes are thwarted by financial difficulties, exploitation, and racial and ethnic hostility.

People who seek the guidance of the urban minister or counselor may come from different backgrounds, especially in multicultural congregations. Not only might the counselee differ ethnically and economically, he probably has had experiences that make it difficult to treat him. For example, if he is a minority person, he is likely to have been labeled "second-class person," with all of the implications of that label. His schooling has probably been inadequate because of poorly trained teachers who often view the children they teach as impossible to teach. In addition to the second-class person label a minority inner-city child picks up, the label "culturally deprived" has also been placed on him from the first day of school.

In 1962, F. Reissman published *The Culturally Deprived Child* in which the cultural-deprivation school of thought became popular.[2] This book, though well-intentioned, gave intellectual backing to an attitude held by middle-class white educators that poor minority children were unable to learn. This misconception came about because the children lacked proper stimuli—books and toys—as well as actively involved parents. Thus, they were poorly taught and the result was a so-called self-fulfilling prophecy—a poorly educated person unable to compete in mainstream society. Thus, the counselee not only differs in culture from the counselor, but typically he and his culture are seen as inferior. This is part of the "baggage" that the urban counselee often brings with him to the counseling process. He seeks opportunity but instead is literally and figuratively betrayed, belittled, and brutalized by the city.

> Jose is a thirty-year-old unemployed Puerto Rican man who was referred for counseling by his pastor because of his inability to hold a job and provide for his wife and three children. He was born in New York to a mother and an abusive alcoholic father who had migrated from Puerto Rico in 1948 in search of work. Jose attended public school in East Harlem but graduated from high school with inadequate academic skills. He was clearly a bright man, but he often became frustrated with the boring, repetitious factory jobs he was able to get and often quit in disgust. Before long, Jose entered the welfare cycle, which supported his family. Due to his battered self-esteem, his mental health deteriorated rapidly.

CULTURE AND COUNSELING

Each person who appears in the counselor's office brings with him a particular cultural apparatus that affects the way counseling is processed. Culture is that all-encompassing set of boundaries, expectations, morals, and mores that shapes our lives, guides our behavior, and gives us our values and beliefs. Every human being is a product of his culture. That culture is responsible for the language he speaks, the colors he prefers, and even his response to pain, among a host of other behaviors.[3]

The very process of counseling is either supported by or sabotaged by the culture from which a person comes, especially in the case of women. For example, a Puerto Rican woman being counseled by a white male is likely to experience great opposition from her husband, who resents the fact that each week she is sitting alone in a room with another man. In another classic example of a cultural clash a Hmong tribesman physically abused his wife, a waitress, for smiling at the patrons in the restaurant where she worked. In Hmong culture a virtuous wife does not smile at any man except her husband. In American culture the Hmong wife was expected to be pleasant to the patrons of the restaurant; in fact, her job and that part of her family's livelihood depended on it. Yet there was a cultural prohibition against smiling at other men.[4] The counselor's task was to help the husband understand the differences in cultures that contributed to his family's tension.

One of the cultural issues that the urban counselor may have to contend with is the notion held by African American and Hispanic people that anyone who goes for counseling is "crazy." This point will be discussed more fully later, but it is important to mention it here because it is a significant cultural barrier to effective pastoral and professional counseling in these cultures. This is not to say that counseling does not go on in every culture, because it does. It just is not called counseling nor is it conducted in the same manner. Other cultures have "indigenous" counselors who perform their function in culturally appropriate ways.

A case in point is the strong belief among Puerto Ricans that mental illness is caused by evil spirits. People often go to the "spiritualist medium" for help.[5] One expression of the belief in evil spirits is the religion of *Santería*—an intermingling of Catholicism and African animism—especially strong among the Cubans and Puerto Ricans. The practitioners of *Santería* listen to *los santéros* ("counselors") who purportedly help people with their problems. In *Santería* the Catholic saints are transformed into African gods such as Shango and Elegua and there are *los bablowos* (priests) who divine the future, as well as those who undertake cures such as *Osanyin*. Each practitioner and *santéro* has his or her own god. The people present offerings to a particular god in order to obtain certain favors.[6] The Christian counselor needs to be aware of these "other counselors" within the Puerto Rican community as he ministers to those who come to him because even those Puerto Ricans who accept Christ feel a pull to return to the familiar folk treatments.

In the African-American community, the minister performs the counseling function. For those who are not religiously inclined, the barber, hairdresser, or bartender may be the "counselor" to whom they turn. What makes these indigenous counselors preferable is their accessibility to and participation in the counselee's culture. The counselee usually feels more comfortable with someone who participates in her culture because she feels that she does not have to explain as much to a counselor who is part of her culture. Indigenous counselors also have intricate knowledge of emotionally important symbols, of which language is but one. However, it is important to note that the counselor and counselee, though of the same ethnic group, may still encounter important cultural differences. Social class, for example, can be a significant barrier to communication. Therefore, the counselor should be very careful about making generalizations because of the significant subcultural issues that lie within any given ethnic group.

Bearing this in mind, there are, nevertheless, significant cultural issues in the inner city that have an impact on a counseling ministry. Because blacks, Hispanics, and Asians are the predominant groups inhabiting our inner cities, our discussion will focus on them.

Since the time of their arrival, blacks have had a history of oppression in the United States, which influenced the African-American personality. For many, life has been a constant struggle to overcome adversity. A saying heard in the African American community is, "A dark man born of a dark woman is bound to see dark days." It will be especially important for the nonblack counselor to know this history and establish credibility with her counselee. A white counselor, after all, represents the oppressors and there may be manifestations of resentment with which to deal. The most effective way to deal with resentment is to meet it head on. Point out the racial difference, but do not accept a denial of "It doesn't matter" at face value. As the counseling proceeds, point out where the issue of race itself or the differences in language may be impeding the counseling. A nonblack counselor must listen carefully and not assume she understands everything a black counselee may be saying or doing.

All too often, minority counseling has focused on deficits, but it is crucial to note that minorities have had to be strong to survive the prejudice and discrimination perpetrated against them. Indeed this strength should be pointed out to the counselee so that he feels empowered to make changes in his life for the better. At the same time, it must be acknowledged that blacks and other minorities sometimes unfairly blame racial discrimination for their difficulties. The counselor must be alert to occasions when the counselee is using racism as a cop-out.

Hispanics, historically exploited for their labor, form a large economically and socially depressed group. The Hispanic's self-image has been radically lowered, which is manifested in higher high-school dropout rates, leaving members of this ethnic group clustered at the bottom of the economic ladder. A common counseling problem among Hispanics is disrupted relationships within the family. Language has had considerable impact; the children learning the dominant language (English) that gives them an advantage over their parents. In the country of origin, the father was an authority figure. Now he finds himself dwarfed by his children, who know English—he does not—and diminished by his wife—she often earns more.

Migration is a complicated issue and presents a host of problems for Hispanics. Their experience is one of being uprooted and placed in an alien culture.

> Maria is an eighteen-year-old young woman who emigrated from Mexico with her uncle and two brothers. Her uncle tries to be helpful, but she says that she longs for her mother or some older female in whom she may confide. Her brothers have all but abandoned her; both are living with other women and have left her to fend for herself. The women in the church who would like to help her are unable to do so because of Maria's limited English and their limited Spanish.

There are three qualities necessary for the effective counseling of Hispanics: (1) personableness; (2) skill at labeling a problem; and (3) the ability to raise the counselee's expectation for change.[7]

One of the important features of Hispanic culture is personalism, referring to the supreme importance Hispanics place on personal relationships. One reason Hispanics feel alienated when they migrate to large industrial areas is because of the lack of personal relationships.[8] Hispanics, then, judge the counselor according to his personal qualities as opposed to his professional expertise or theoretical orientation.[9] Therefore, the counselor must be perceived as being authentic, honest, and available.

Problems must have labels that are easily understood by the Hispanic counselee if counseling is to be effective. The counselee may need to use Spanish words to get a handle on the label the counselor uses to identify a given behavior. For example, the word *susto* means a feeling of apathy, restlessness, and withdrawal caused by some fright or trauma.[10] As the counselor works with Hispanic counselees, he should build up a vocabulary of such terms, the meanings of which the Hispanic counselee is more than willing to share. In any case, note 19 at the end of this chapter also contains a list of the terms and their meanings.

Asians and their use of counseling have not been studied extensively. This is primarily because they use counseling very sparingly, usually only when the situation is so grave that it can no longer be handled at home.

> A twenty-six-year-old Chinese man was taken to a veteran's hospital with delusions and hallucinations. He had recently been discharged from the army, but believed a soldier with whom he had had a dispute was flying in a helicopter over Chinatown trying to harm him. However, the man was taken to the hospital not because of delusions and hallucinations, but because he had taken burning incense and placed it on the back of his neck, causing severe burns. At no time did his parents visit him in the hospital.

Asians are viewed as quiet people who have no problems.[11] Mental illness is perceived as a thing of shame in the Asian community. Hence, in Chinese and Japanese cultures it is not desirable to express feelings or discuss personal problems with strangers.[12] Thus, the counselor needs to be patient and allow the counselee to gradually open up. He must exercise extreme caution in issues involving the parents of an Asian counselee because Asian children tend to deify their parents and never criticize them. He might even find it necessary to allow the counselee to write out his thoughts for the counselor to read.

The most recent Asian immigrants to the United States are from southeast Asia. They are primarily Vietnamese and Cambodians, who have experienced some of the most inhuman treatment known to man. Some suffer flashbacks from their horrifying war experiences and need a great deal of supportive counseling for post-traumatic stress. Yet these immigrants have strong family ties and the children are, in the main, very obedient and very good students.

Native Americans have probably been the most mistreated group in American society. Over 50 percent now live in cities though in the past many were literally herded onto reservations where the housing conditions were and continue to be poor and the education substandard. Even though many have excelled, often Native Americans have poor self-images because of discrimination. They have high rates of alcohol abuse and commit suicide at a rate much higher than the general population. This has implications for their emotions, aspirations, and motivation. One direction counseling may take, therefore, is to help the Native American deal with problems of victimization and negative self-image.

There is a common theme that runs through the lives of minority and poor people. They suffer disadvantages from the dominant society, are often exploited, and frequently struggle with a negative self-image. People may not have identical reactions to the treatment they have suffered, but the discriminatory conditions to which they have been subjected produces similar results. The counselor who is sensitive to the history of minorities and the poor will be equipped to do a better job of counseling.

CONCEPTS OF TIME AND VISIBLE PROGRESS

The concept of time is especially crucial in urban counseling because poor, ethnic minorities often wish to see immediate results. These are people who have frequently been deprived of physical necessities and have learned to seek immediate gratification to survive. One of the reasons that drug use is so prevalent in the inner city is that people seek a quick solution to their problems.

Very often the counselee will want to know two things: (1) how long the counseling will take and (2) how they are progressing. A study was conducted on two types of counseling—time-limited counseling as contrasted with time-unlimited counseling. The clients involved in time-limited counseling (an average of eighteen sessions) showed better progress than did those involved in time-unlimited counseling (an average of thirty-seven sessions),[13] the results of which were confirmed in a follow-up study.[14]

Length of time, then, is a factor, and the evidence suggests that more time spent in counseling does not necessarily improve the outcome. One way to handle the time issue when the counselee raises it is to say, "We will terminate when the issue that you came in with is resolved. You will be the best judge of that." And usually it works out that way. Counselees will typically say that they are feeling better and that the issue that brought them to counseling in the first place is not bothering them the way it was.

In addition, the urban counselee must be reassured that she is making progress or she will probably drop out of counseling. She will often ask: "Is this working? Am I wasting my time and money?" It is important to reflect this question back to the counselee: "What do you think?" The counselor may also refer to the issue that brought the person to counseling. For example, "Are you able to stand up to your boss now?" might be asked of one who came because of lack of assertiveness. A young man addicted to pornography raised those same questions and the counselor asked, "Can you walk past the newsstand where you used to buy pornographic magazines without buying one?" The point is to let the counselee assess his or her own progress.

Most often the decision to terminate counseling is mutual, but occasionally there will be disagreement. Usually this happens when the counselee wants to stop before she has achieved her goal. The counselor should encourage her to realize that they are not finished.

> Suzanne, a thirty-four-year-old woman, was married to a homosexual man who had decided he did not wish to continue the marriage. Suzanne refused to accept the fact that the marriage was ending; she was sure that there was something she could do. In the meantime, she did not work regularly, ate poorly, and was emaciated. She called her husband at his office so often that he was in danger of losing his job.

She left counseling to try to get back a man who obviously had no interest in her. Continued counseling could have helped her deal with the real need to get on with her life.

Termination of counseling can be a traumatic experience. The counselee may have formed a very close bond with the counselor and it is not uncommon for the counselee to begin to exhibit maladaptive behavior as a way of continuing the relationship. One way to deal with the problem of termination is to let the counselee know you understand how difficult termination is for him. It helps to reassure the counselee that you will be glad to see him anytime. This is usually enough to satisfy termination anxiety.

PSYCHOLOGICAL DYSFUNCTION AND CULTURE

It is almost axiomatic to state that poor and minority people living in urban ghettos have had to adapt to the lifestyle to which they have been consigned. They have had to develop a set of coping skills in order to survive, but all too often the term pathological has been applied to those skills. For example, a black person who has been victimized by discrimination and develops an attitude of mistrust is often diagnosed as paranoid when, in actual fact, this is exactly what has kept him alive. He has had to adopt this attitude of suspicion and distrust to preserve his life in a hostile world.

Similarly, Puerto Ricans have been accused by author Oscar Lewis of participating in a culture of poverty. He asserts in *La Vida* that the culture of poverty gives way to a "weak ego structure, orality and the confusion of sexual identification, all reflecting maternal deprivation; a strong present-time orientation with little disposition to defer gratification and plan for the future."[15] This reflects a judgmental assessment that does not hold up under scrutiny.

Substance abuse is a major problem in the United States in general but it plagues the inner city. One major factor contributing to high levels of urban substance abuse is the amount of stress and inner tension produced by the culture.[16] All too often, the stresses generated by poverty, racism, and limited opportunity lead to the use of mind-altering chemicals as a means of temporary escape.

Over thirty years ago researchers demonstrated that mental illness was related to population density (the number of persons per unit of space).[17] Albeit, those who *perceive* their living conditions as crowded and do not prefer this situation are the ones adversely affected. Since crowding is an integral part of urban living and poverty an ever-present reality, it is no surprise that great numbers of urban people struggle with mental distress. What is important to recognize is that mental distress is not necessarily an issue of ethnicity. Rather, it is due to the environmental conditions to which members of an ethnic group are often relegated.

Another major difficulty in the urban center is suicidal behavior. We use the term suicidal behavior rather than suicide because urban ethnic minorities not only commit overt suicide, they also engage in behaviors that, while not overtly suicidal, are ultimately self-destructive. Life seems so totally bleak and the possibility for positive change so minimal that they may either take their lives or engage in behaviors (such as drinking and driving, drug abuse, or violence) that eventually lead to their destruction. Another form of self-destructive behavior is the failure to observe basic health habits. Blacks, especially males, smoke cigarettes and use alcohol—a lethal combination—to a higher degree than do whites. Health professionals report that blacks often fail to take prescribed medication and do not keep doctor appointments.

In light of this, counseling must be short-term, action-oriented, and offer visible results to be effective. Simple, reinforcing behavioral "homework" assignments may be helpful, depending on the counselee's motivation and the counselor's ability to generate interesting assignments.

The urban counselor needs to be prepared to confront substance abuse, mental illness, and suicidal behavior when they surface in counselees. Minorities often live lives devoid of hope, which leads to despair and to maladaptive behavior of many kinds. The counselor must convince his counselees that there is hope; that their Creator loves them even if, at the moment, they do not love themselves.

LANGUAGE ISSUES IN COUNSELING

The spoken word is the major medium for carrying on counseling. The language patterns one uses may present a problem when working with minority urban people. In the United States, minority people often use "non-standard English which is usually not understood by the counselor who is from a different ethnic group and class."[18] Black counselees, for example, may speak "Black English," which tends to use words that are contradictory in meaning to standard English. ("Man, that was a bad gig." The word "bad" here is opposite in meaning to standard English.) Black English sentences also tend to be somewhat shorter and the use of nonverbal cues more pronounced.

Counselees from Hispanic backgrounds typically use Spanish words from time to time even if their English is quite good. This applies even to those born in the United States of Spanish-speaking parents. There are certain Spanish words that carry much more emotional meaning for the counselee than can be expressed in English. Actually this is true of any primary or "heart" language.[19]

Since language is central to the counseling process, the counselor needs to learn as much as he can about his counselee's particular dialect, vernacular (in the case of Black English), or language. The fact that the counselor is making an effort to understand the counselee goes a long way toward building rapport. The counselor does not need to be afraid to ask the meaning of a given word or phrase. It is far better to do that than to proceed as if you understand something when you do not.

A word of caution is in order, though, with respect to language. The counselee may use the fact that the counselor "doesn't understand me" to resist the counseling process. It is not a simple matter to determine when communication is the problem and when the counselee simply does not want to come to grips with the issue at hand. The counselor will need to remove any true barriers to communication, but this can be done if the counselor is sensitive to the problem and is willing to learn from the counselee.

INDIVIDUALIZED VS. GROUP APPROACHES

Most often we understand counseling to be a one-to-one relationship and, indeed, it often is conducted that way. There are situations, however, in which the counselor may find it useful to conduct group counseling.

Group and family treatment is included in this chapter because the difficulties faced by urban minority counselees are rarely isolated phenomena. Normally, their difficulties are at least partially rooted in their interaction with significant others. It is much more effective for the counselor to personally observe and directly intervene in the counselee's social world than to deal with him in isolation. As much as possible, relatives and friends who seem to be emotionally involved in the person's problems should be brought into counseling. Participation in groups that are not made up of relatives and friends may also be helpful in identifying and correcting faulty perceptions and interaction patterns. These are self-help groups and are advantageous because the participants see that they are not alone in their struggles with a particular problem; they find encouragement from others who understand, and they see new potential and avenues for change.

Group approaches to counseling have a relatively long history. In 1905, Dr. Joseph Hershey Pratt, a Boston internist, started group counseling with tubercular patients.[20] He found that these patients expressed feelings about their illness that would not have been possible outside a group setting. Since then many other groups, including self-help groups of all kinds have sprung up; some of them, such as Alcoholics Anonymous, have been very effective. Many groups patterned after the A. A. model have been organized in recent years—Gamblers Anonymous, Overeaters Anonymous, Adult Children of Alcoholics, Sexaholics Anonymous, Parents Without Partners, Narcotics Anonymous, Rape Survivors, Battered Women's Support, Cancer Support, Incest Survivors Anonymous, TOUCH (AIDS support), and Bereavement Support. The key to many of these self-help groups seems to be the mutual support that an individual gets from those with similar difficulties.

While self-help groups have been remarkably effective, a word of caution is in order for believers who take part—the overcoming of the addiction must be seen for what it is. To avoid using God's name, Alcoholics Anonymous, substituted the term Higher Power. But, Christians need to understand the reality of the presence of God in the person of the Holy Spirit and the counselee who has been able to overcome his addiction through the self-help group must also be discipled by the local assembly. It is in the local church that spiritual growth takes place. In addition, the person may need the services of a professional counselor to deal with issues in her life that cannot be handled either by the self-help group or by the church.

> A young pastor became addicted to pornography and found a self-help group that helped him to overcome it. He realized after he was free that he needed to understand the forces in his life that caused the addiction in the first place. Through the counsel of a Christian, and with his wife at his side, he was able to uncover and resolve several childhood conflicts.

The counseling also greatly improved his relationship with his wife. The self-help group was effective in helping him to overcome the sexual addiction, but he needed professional help to resolve the underlying problems that led to the addiction in the first place.

Typically, group treatment differs significantly from self-help group treatment in the area of leadership. Group treatment involves a group leader—usually the counselor. It is the responsibility of the counselor to set the ground rules. The emphasis of group treatment is on the system or group processes, as opposed to the individual in one-on-one counseling.

Group treatment is also economical. The counselor is able to see many more counselees if she has groups than if she limits her practice to individual counseling. Group treatment is not meant to completely take the place of individual counseling, but it is a possible form of treatment under certain circumstances and for very specific individuals.

Group treatment is most effective when the individuals in the group have some traits or problems in common. The urban Christian worker may find that a group of troubled teenagers would make a viable group. Teens tend to band together in any case and thus can be very effectively counseled together. Often inner-city youngsters feel that the problems they face are unique to them; group counseling can help them see that others are struggling with similar issues. They will also see that there may be more than one solution to their problems. The inner-city youngster in a group-counseling situation learns to be supportive and at the same time learns to ask for support (the latter being difficult because they often have received little nurturance and neither know how to give it nor ask for support).

Group counseling, however, is not suitable for everyone. Those who should not be counseled in a group setting include psychotic persons who may be disruptive, suicidal persons, those with other severe problems, and finally, those who are completely self-absorbed. These people do not usually make good candidates, but once the members have been chosen, the actual arrangements can be made.

Group counseling is at its best when carried on with six to eight members. Sometimes you may be able to effectively handle up to twelve, but more than twelve makes the group unwieldy and permits shy members to hide and avoid dealing with their own issues. There are two types of counseling groups: closed and open. A closed group does not permit new people to join the group once it has been formed. An open group allows new members at any time. The counselor must be sensitive to the nature and needs of the group. For example, a group that has formed and is dealing with very intimate issues may best remain closed to new members.

Chairs should be arranged in a circle so that each member can see the other members as well as the counselor. At the first meeting of the group, the counselor should set the ground rules. If it is an open group, she will have to repeat them for each new member who joins. A cardinal rule in group counseling is that there is to be absolute confidentiality. This must be strictly enforced or the group will not function well, if at all. It must be stressed at the outset that the purpose of the group is to be helpful for each member. The members are free to be critical, but never destructive.

The leader of the group has the responsibility to facilitate the counseling process, to be on the alert for potentially destructive behavior, and to intervene where necessary. The counselor is much less direct in group counseling than in individual counseling. A typical session might go like this:

Joe: I went looking for a job again this week, but I couldn't find anything in my line.

Mary: In your line? You have been out of work for three months. You have a wife and three young children and you're holding out for something in your line!

Jim: I think what Mary is saying is that you should take anything at this point to meet your obligations while you look for something in your field.

Susan: Joe, I think that some of the arguments that you have been having with your wife might be related to your wife's feelings that you are not being responsible.

Counselor: Joe, how do you feel about what Mary, Jim, and Susan have said?

Notice that the counselor does not intervene until she feels that her input is needed. While the members of the group were making valid points, they did not give Joe a chance to respond. Thus, the counselor provides that chance for him. Intervention is only needed if and when the group is not progressing optimally.

FAMILY COUNSELING

For many years, counseling was based on the *intrapsychic* view of human behavior.[21] That is, it was assumed that the difficulties an individual experienced had to do with forces within his or her psychological makeup. Family counseling asserts that one can only understand the individual in the family context in which he is embedded.[22] Family therapy sees the family as a system, much like the systems of the human body in which each organ functions to make the system work. Any malfunction in any part of the system affects the entire system. When this occurs, the family attempts to get the system working again, even if what they do is labeled as being dysfunctional.

It is important for the urban counselor to recognize that many of the problems that appear to be individually based are actually rooted in dysfunctional-family dynamics. Often the family will come in because of the misbehavior of one member. Family counselors call him the identified patient (I. P.); he is labeled as the cause of the problem. The patient, however, is reacting to the imbalances and troubles within the family system. Therefore, the counselor needs to involve as many of the family members as possible in order to observe family dynamics. All family members should be present at every session if at all possible. (The counselor should not be surprised if the member who is causing the disruption refuses to attend.) It is important when doing family counseling to get as complete a history of the family as possible (e.g., date of marriage, ages, economic status, significant relatives). After that the counselor can suggest ways to deal with the problems within the family, thus clearing up the individual's dysfunction.

> An inner city Italian family brought their nine-year-old son for treatment because he was disruptive in school. Probing by the counselor revealed that the child had been born out of wedlock and raised by his mother alone. The mother married again when the child was seven years old. The new husband was from a strict Italian family and had been raised to obey rules without questioning. He attempted to force this type of behavior on his stepson. The young boy, not able to rebel against this type of autocratic behavior at home, acted out his anger at school. The counselor pointed out the cause of the family disruption and they then were able to begin functioning more smoothly together.

Family treatment is effective because it gives the counselor the opportunity to *observe* the dynamics of family interaction rather than just hear about it from an individual counselee. Intervention is done with the whole family present so that each member is affected by it.

Marriage counseling is a special form of family counseling.[23] Often marriages are in trouble because each member of the union brings emotional baggage into the marriage. The husband has a set of expectations about the wife based on his relationship with his mother; the wife likewise has expectations about the husband based on her relationship with her father. When these expectations do not mesh, the task of the counselor is to bring these differences into the open and help the couple work out realistic solutions. Again, as in family therapy, the counselor has the opportunity to observe the interaction between the husband and wife and point out where they are hurting each other.

Family and marriage counseling have very definite advantages. The counselor must be sensitive to the interactive behavior of the family or couple. This requires skill and sensitivity that can only come as the counselor gains experience in this type of counseling.

SUMMARY

One of the salient features of the city is its diverse ethnic mix. Industrialization has drawn people from various parts of the country and the world to the urban center. Therefore, the urban Christian counselor must become familiar with the cultures of those he serves.

The Christian counselor must also be aware of several other elements unique to urban counseling. One of these is the perception that inner-city people have of time and the consequent need for urban dwellers to see visible progress. Another is that there are certain psychological difficulties that appear to cluster within certain groups—be aware that these difficulties have cultural roots. Yet another unique element is language and the barriers involved with its use. Even those who speak English use it in ways that are bound up with the culture. It is imperative that the counselor be sufficiently conversant with those language styles to build a bridge to the counselee. In addition to his knowledge of his counselees' cultural backgrounds, the counselor needs to be aware of some effective counseling strategies. One of these is group counseling. It is useful for working with several counselees at once and also provides a vehicle to help them improve their interpersonal skills.

SELF-ASSESSMENT TEST OF
CULTURAL SENSITIVITY

Below are a series of questions followed by boxes in which
you place an "x" to indicate whether you do this "very well," "not
at all well," or somewhere in between.

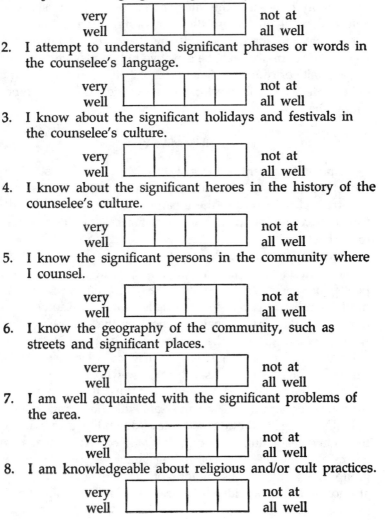

1. I speak the language (foreign) of my counselee.

    very   not at
    well   all well

2. I attempt to understand significant phrases or words in
    the counselee's language.

    very   not at
    well   all well

3. I know about the significant holidays and festivals in
    the counselee's culture.

    very   not at
    well   all well

4. I know about the significant heroes in the history of the
    counselee's culture.

    very   not at
    well   all well

5. I know the significant persons in the community where
    I counsel.

    very   not at
    well   all well

6. I know the geography of the community, such as
    streets and significant places.

    very   not at
    well   all well

7. I am well acquainted with the significant problems of
    the area.

    very   not at
    well   all well

8. I am knowledgeable about religious and/or cult practices.

    very   not at
    well   all well

9. I am able to adjust my vocabulary to that of the counselee.

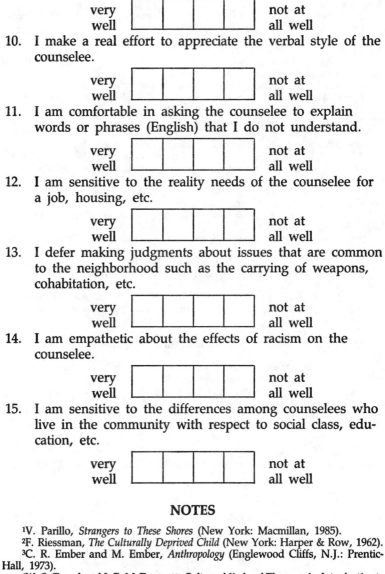

very well | | | | | not at all well

10. I make a real effort to appreciate the verbal style of the counselee.

very well | | | | | not at all well

11. I am comfortable in asking the counselee to explain words or phrases (English) that I do not understand.

very well | | | | | not at all well

12. I am sensitive to the reality needs of the counselee for a job, housing, etc.

very well | | | | | not at all well

13. I defer making judgments about issues that are common to the neighborhood such as the carrying of weapons, cohabitation, etc.

very well | | | | | not at all well

14. I am empathetic about the effects of racism on the counselee.

very well | | | | | not at all well

15. I am sensitive to the differences among counselees who live in the community with respect to social class, education, etc.

very well | | | | | not at all well

NOTES

[1]V. Parillo, *Strangers to These Shores* (New York: Macmillan, 1985).

[2]F. Riessman, *The Culturally Deprived Child* (New York: Harper & Row, 1962).

[3]C. R. Ember and M. Ember, *Anthropology* (Englewood Cliffs, N.J.: Prentic-Hall, 1973).

[4]W. S. Tsend and J. F. McDermott, *Culture, Mind and Therapy: An Introduction to Cultural Psychiatry* (New York: Brunner-Mazel, 1981).

[5]E. Mumford, "Puerto Rican Perspectives on Mental Illness," *Mount Sinai Journal of Medicine* 40 (1973), 6.

[6]M. Gonzalez-Wippler, *Santeria: African Magic in Latin America* (New York: The Julian Press, 1973).

[7]A. J. Marsella and P. B. Pedersen, *Cross Cultural Counseling and Psychotherapy* (New York: Pergamon, 1981).

[8]J. Fitzpatrick, *Puerto Rican Americans: The Meaning of Migration to the Mainland* (Englewood Cliffs, N.J.: Prentice-Hall, 1987).

[9]Marsella and Pedersen, *Cross Cultural Counseling and Psychotherapy.*

[10]Ibid.

[11]F. X. Acosta, J. Yamamoto, and L. A. Evans, *Effective Psychotherapy With Low Income and Minority Patients* (New York: Plenum, 1982).

[12]Marsella and Pedersen, *Cross Cultural Counseling and Psychotherapy.*

[13]W. E. Henry and J. M. Shlien, "Affective Complexity and Psychotherapy: Some Comparisons on Time Limited and Untime Limited Treatment," *Journal of Projective Techniques* (1958): 22, 153–62.

[14]J. M. Shlien, H. H. Mosak, and R. Driekurs, "Effect of Time Limits: Effects of Two Psycho-Therapies," *Journal of Counseling Psychology* (1962): 9, 31–34.

[15]O. Lewis, "The Culture of Poverty," *Scientific American* (1966): 215, 19–25.

[16]J. C. Coleman, *Abnormal Psycholoty and Modern Life* (Glenview, Fla.: Scott, Foresman and Co., 1976).

[17]R. L. Atkinson, R. C. Atkinson, and E. R. Hilgard, *Introduction to Psychology* (New York: Harcourt Brace Jovanovich, 1983).

[18]D. W. Sue, *Counseling the Culturally Different: Theory and Practice* (New York: John Wiley and Sons, 1981).

[19]Some additional examples of Spanish phrases that frequently occur are the following:

Me siento mal. (I feel bad or terrible.)

Yo no puedo mas. (I feel as though I can't go on any longer; I can't take it any longer.)

Usted sabe? (Do you know or understand? . . . This is often expressed by counselees in order to get feedback. In some cases the person is asking if you are understanding them.)

Ay, yo no se. (I don't understand what is happening.)

Entonces. . . (And then. . . this is used when the counselee is about to change the subject.)

[20]S. J. Korchin, *Modern Clinical Psychology: Principles of Intervention in the Clinic and Community* (New York: Basic Books, 1976).

[21]M. McGoldrick, J. K. Pearce, and J. Giordano, *Ethnicity and Family Therapy* (New York: Guilford, 1983).

[22]Ibid.

[23]Korchin, *Modern Clinical Psychology.*

CHAPTER 5

Confronting Evil

RACISM

RACISM IS AN INVENTION of sinful mankind. It is not inborn, nor is it genetically inherited. Racism is taught and handed down from generation to generation. Small children know nothing of the social meaning of racial differences. They can be observed playing together, knowing that there are differences in skin color but attributing nothing negative to that difference.

All persons have been created in the image of God; there was no mention of race at all with respect to the creation of human beings. In Acts 17:26, Paul states unequivocally that "from one man he made every nation of men, that they should inhabit the whole earth." Peter's experience on the housetop was intended by God to correct his ethnocentrism, "Do not call anything impure that God has made clean" (Acts 10:15). In Acts 13:1, the Spirit of God makes clear that all are to be included in the church and among those mentioned in the church at Antioch was Simeon who was called Niger, an African. So, it is clear from Scripture that the idea of preference on any level is abhorrent to God.

The Bible states that "anyone who hates his brother is a murderer, and you know that no murderer has eternal life in him" (1 John 3:15). The fact that racist attitudes may lead to hatred and to murder has been amply attested to in human history. Between 1870 and 1955 there were 11,020 *documented* lynchings of black people in the United States. We underscore documented lynchings because the addition of those lynchings that were not officially recorded would multiply the number three or four times.[1] In 1943 in Los Angeles, Mexican Americans were murdered in the infamous "Zoot Suit" riots, on the basis of race only. The murder of six million Jews during the Holocaust is another horrifying example of prejudice.

Before discussing the effects of racism, we need to make the point that racism affects the racist as well. Studies have shown that racist whites are people with low self-esteem who need to denigrate others to feel good about themselves.[2] Further research shows that they also have less positive mental health than those who are not racist.[3] To be a racist one must have a serious personality disorder. That is not to say that the effects of racism are the same for the racist as for the victim, but the point is that both are affected.

The Effects of Racism

Institutional Racism

Racism affects every aspect of the minority person's life. For this reason it has been called "institutional racism." Both prejudice (the racist attitude) and discrimination (the racist acts) touch the minority person in his school, job, neighborhood, and everywhere else he may find himself. It even enters into his unconscious life in the form of dreams.

> A nine-year-old black boy dreamed that he was playing in the park with a white boy. His white friend invited him to his house for milk and cookies, but upon their arrival, the white mother told her son that he could not bring his black friend into the house.

The earliest study on the effects of racism on the black-American psyche was done fifty years ago. For this study, two black psychologists placed black dolls and white dolls in a room and then asked black girls to choose the prettiest doll. Most of the girls chose the white doll.[4] As can be seen from the results of this study, one of the most detrimental effects of racism is low self-esteem, and one of the main reasons for poor self-esteem is the denigration so many minority people experience very early in life. This manifests itself in lowered aspiration so that minority people do not attempt to enter arenas they consider the preserve of whites. Nowhere is this more evident than in education. However, the institutionalized racism that is pervasive in this society infects minority children even before they enter school. The child grows up thinking that there is something "bad" about him. A fourth grade class in a predominantly Hispanic neighborhood told their new teacher that it was "bad" to speak Spanish. Thus, minorities, especially blacks and Hispanics, are dropping out of high school at a rate approaching 70 percent.[5] The drop-out problem has implications for the whole community—there are few positive role models, minorities are underrepresented in the professions, and the cycle of poverty is repeated.

The media do not help matters any. They generally portray minority people in a negative light, reinforcing the idea that their culture is devalued. The media play up the misdeeds of minorities. Recently, a white Bostonian reported that a black man had shot his wife through their car window as they drove through a black neighborhood.[6] This was widely reported in the news with everyone believing the white man's story—until the fact that the man himself had shot his own wife came to light. Yet the positive achievements and altruistic actions of minorities are seldom reported. History books have, until recently, completely omitted minority contributions to society and culture. Arthur A. Schomburg, for whom a library in New York City is named, amassed his large collection of books by and about people of African descent as a result of being told by his teacher in Puerto Rico that his people (blacks) have no history.

The urban counselor has a dual task as he treats the issue of low self-esteem in his minority counselees. The first is prevention and the second is treatment.

Too often we wait for symptoms to appear and then attempt to treat the illness instead of preventing the problem in the first place. The minority child can and should be "inoculated" against inevitable racial insults he will receive, before they come. There are a host of books available for children portraying minorities in a positive light that counselors can use in their "inoculation programs."[7] Almost all of the books emphasize the racism against which the main character has had to struggle. This bibliotherapy can be an effective antidote to the low self-esteem so prevalent among minority people. The counselor can work with the children in groups, having them read and discuss appropriate books. The children can act out the lives of the people whose stories they have read and they can draw pictures about their books. The children should be counseled that prejudice and discrimination are not their fault because the most destructive effect of racism is that the minority person internalizes the racism—he begins to believe that there is something "wrong" with him and thus begins the slide into low self-esteem.

A young black boy was kept after school by his teacher, also black, because he was not working up to his capacity. When asked by the teacher why he did not do better he replied, "What's the use? I'll only be a janitor when I grow up anyhow."

The tragedy of this story is that the pupil did not see that his black teacher was not a janitor. The boy's poor self-esteem blinded him to the obvious. The purpose of preventive counseling is to disallow this internalization process before it starts.

The treatment of low self-esteem is much more difficult than its prevention because the behavioral, cognitive, and emotional effects become "stamped" into the individual. As a result, behavior will often be self-destructive and include such things as excessive alcohol or drug use, abusive behavior toward others, and chronic unemployment. Cognition blames others for lack of advancement, and thinks that success is impossible. The emotional effects include feelings of worthlessness, hopelessness ("It doesn't matter how hard I try, I never get anywhere"), rage, and depression.

Again bibliotherapy may be used to correct negative beliefs such as, "Blacks (Hispanics, Asians) can't get a fair shake in this society." The counselor needs to be familiar with the literature about the given ethnic group in order to suggest readings to correct these misconceptions. (See Resources: For Further Reading.) If dealing with a believer, the book with the greatest impact is the Word of God, which is replete with references to God's view of the worth of his creatures.

The Christian counselor will need to challenge the mistaken cognitions for what they are: misconceptions. Have the counselee look at his mistaken conceptions realistically. You may have to point out that racism exists, but that there are those who have overcome. The counselee needs to see where he is using racism as an excuse for inaction.

It will be obvious that behavior, cognitions, and affect, though presented by Lazarus in his Multimodal Model as discrete, are systemically intertwined. As you deal with the self-destructive behavior, you will also challenge false beliefs and impact negative emotions.

Anger

A common reaction to racism is anger. The minority person feels that his goals have been constantly blocked by the society that prohibits him from reaching his potential, and his frustration leads to anger.[8] Two black psychiatrists have gone further in describing the African-American's reaction to racism and have called it "black rage."[9] This rage is a result of the relentless racism that invades every aspect of the minority person's life. As noted earlier, it even pursues him into his dreams. Even the simplest needs of the minority person are often tinged with racism. For example,

> A well-dressed professional man of Puerto Rican descent was attempting to get a cab one bone-chilling winter night. He stood on a busy corner and watched whites hail cabs successfully while he waved and whistled in vain. Then one taxicab slowed down, but when the driver realized the potential fare's ethnicity he began to drive away. Enraged, the man kicked the side of the cab.

This case illustrates the daily insults minorities endure and the deleterious psychological results of those insults. For the minority person nothing is simple. His life is a constant battle to maintain his sanity in a racist society. Even though much of the literature about minority anger centers around low-income individuals, we need to be concerned about the plight of the middle- and upper-income minorities as well. There is probably no frustration greater than that experienced by minority people who have done everything society has dictated for success only to find that doors are still slammed in their faces.

Anger in response to racism is frequently turned inward on the self. The minority person irrationally believes that he is at fault and he begins to believe the racist fiction that he is in a certain social position because he just does not want to better himself. These beliefs turn into anger and the result can be depression or self-destruction. Both reactions are part of the same psychological dynamic. The depressed person feels that he is worthless and can do nothing right. The self-destructive person, feeling worthless, cares little about himself and seeks to destroy himself. The incidence of self-destructive behaviors such as alcoholism, drug addiction, and automobile accidents is very high in the black community. The incidence of the ultimate self-destructive behavior—suicide—is also fairly high, but while blacks generally do not commit suicide as often as whites, the rate of suicide is equal between blacks and whites for the age range of twenty to thirty-five.[10] Then there is anger that expresses itself in aggressive behavior, to which we now turn.

Intra-racial violence (labeled blacks murdering blacks) occurs at a much higher rate among African Americans than among any other ethnic groups.[11] One of the theories as to why this occurs is that this type of violence is a function of displaced aggression. The rage that the African American feels toward whites cannot be directly expressed because of the severe reprisals that would follow, so he then vents his anger toward a less threatening object, his fellow black.[12]

The inner city counselor will come face-to-face with black people's anger (self-deprecation and depression or aggressive behavior). Treatment of these types of anger in counseling is much more difficult to outline. The counselor should, first of all, let the counselee know that he is free to verbally express legitimate anger and second that he (the counselor) is aware of the source of the anger. We made a point of emphasizing the role of empathy in chapter 2. This is crucial in the treatment of African Americans. However, it might be much more difficult to get Asians to express anger since, as we pointed out, it is culturally forbidden, especially among the Chinese.

The next step is to see in what area of the BASIC ID (explained in chapter 2) the anger is manifesting itself, and begin the treatment from there.

> A twenty-year-old oriental male sat in the counseling room with balled fists and spoke through clenched teeth. He had come for counseling in response to difficulty he was having in regard to his relationship with a white girlfriend. She found him to be too passive and lacking in demonstrative affection. His father was angry that he was seeing a white woman. He soon lost interest in school and as a result received poor grades.

In this example, anger was primarily expressed through behavior. The young man manifested his anger in a way that would hurt both his father and the young woman. Scholastic achievement is very highly prized in Chinese culture and thus he chose to act out in that area. Because his girlfriend was also a high achiever, he was able to get back at both the girlfriend and the father.

In another case, anger and frustration were focused in the Drug/Biology area.

> A thirty-five-year-old black social worker was denied a promotion in her agency while a less qualified white social worker was given the position. The black social worker began to develop a number of somatic symptoms, including headaches and heart palpitations. Obviously, her anger and frustration were focused in the Drug/Biology area.

In both these cases, the counseling approach began with the way in which the counselee expressed the underlying problem. The Chinese youth needed to be shown that he was indeed angry. (The Chinese tend to be unaware of their feelings because their culture does not allow open expression.) The social worker was counseled to be more assertive and to speak to her supervisor, which she did. (She did not get the job but felt better for being able to confront the racism involved in the denial of that promotion. She was given the next promotion available.)

There is within minority people a reservoir of strength—a strength that has carried them through years of adversity at the hands of racist societies. The history of race relations is a sordid one. The settlement of the western United States involved the slaughter of thousands of Native Americans; the settlement of Australia cost many of the indigenous people their lives; the "final solution" in Nazi Germany culminated in the genocide of Jews. It is estimated that as many as 50 million Africans were captured during the ignoble era of slavery. However, in each case, the victims have survived and in many cases have triumphed over their circumstances. We need to tap into this strength and not dwell on the negatives in our counseling of minorities.

> A young black actor came for counseling because, in spite of some clear success, he was hesitant to move on in his career. He wanted to move into directing, but felt stymied.

As the counseling proceeded, it appeared that the actor had a stereotypic image of what a black person could do, that is, only acting. He did not visualize himself going further. The counselor helped him to see the irrational limitations he was putting on himself, but, more importantly, to use the strengths he had already exhibited in getting to the point where he was.

In the field of minority counseling there is a so-called deficit model,[13] which is akin to "blaming the victim." In the deficit model, emphasis is placed on what the minority person does not have. It emphasizes the purported cultural deprivation of father absence rather than capitalizing on strengths such as resourcefulness and perseverance in the face of tremendous odds. In the literature on minorities there are numerous examples of men and women who have risen from abject circumstances to great accomplishments. This type of literature may be used to great advantage with minority clients.

In the blaming-the-victim scenario, the minority person, rather than the discriminatory society, is seen as being responsible.[14] Often the counselee must be made to see that she is caught up in a blame-the-victim scenario. The counselor needs to point out to the counselee that while she is not responsible for the discrimination that placed her where she is, she is responsible for extricating herself from the psychological bonds that hold her there.

Racism and Christianity

The urban counselor may be called upon to deal with an aspect of racism that is especially painful for Christian minorities. That is racism *within the evangelical Christian community.* The Word of God is replete with references to the love that believers should have for one another, without regard to social status. "My brothers, as believers in our glorious Lord Jesus Christ, don't show favoritism" (James 2:1). James goes on to say that the rich should not be given preference over the poor in the church. John makes this point in stronger terms, "We know that we have passed from death to life, because we love our brothers. Anyone who does not love remains in death" (1 John 3:14). John makes the love of the brethren a test of the genuineness of the work of God in the soul.

Dr. Howard Jones, in his book, *White Questions To a Black Christian,* gives a number of poignant examples of racism. In all of these cases, he expresses the pain of being discriminated against by professing believers.[15]

> A young black female college student was a sincere believer seeking to follow the Lord's leading in her life. She went away to college and did not know where to go for fellowship. However, she heard about a Bible-believing church and went to Sunday services, but as she entered the church, she received the "hate stares" that every black person is familiar with. After the services she attempted to be friendly, only to be coldly brushed off. This discrimination by whites who professed to be born-

again believers was painful and her eyes welled up with tears as she recounted it.

In counseling people who have been hurt by this type of racism, the counselor needs to patiently allow the expression of anger and hurt without censorship. One method that has been used successfully for getting the counselee to express how they feel about discrimination is the "empty chair" method. The counselor places an empty chair in front of the counselee and asks her to imagine that the racist person is sitting in it. The individual should be instructed to say what she is feeling to the person represented by the empty chair.

After allowing the counselee to ventilate in this way, the counselor should use the Bible to help the person see the way God views her. Guided imagery with respect to her relationship to the Lord and how he has accepted her without regard to her race may be helpful. (Guided imagery is done by having the person close her eyes and go back in her mind to the scene that you want her to recall. Move into it slowly, and ask her to recall as much detail as she can—colors, smells, sounds, etc. You may then ask her to picture Jesus interacting with her to bring about comfort, acceptance, and healing.) Those who have been wounded by racism need to forgive the racist and release their hurt feelings to the Lord. This may take several sessions. When the counselee is ready to forgive, pray with her over the issue.

Racism is the most destructive element with which minority people have to cope. It is both overt and subtle. It is perhaps more subtle in our times when the overt trappings of racism, such as discrimination laws, have been outlawed. Nevertheless, racism is crippling. It constricts. It has a way of culturally conditioning minorities to accept its tenets. Minority people must see that God created them in his image with no inherent inferiority whatsoever, and that he sees them as having equal value with all mankind. This is the job of the Christian counselor in an urban setting.

THE DEMONIC AND DELIVERANCE[16]

One of the most difficult problems facing the urban pastor and Christian counselor is that of demonization. Many people congregate in cities and bring with them influences that scripturally come under the heading of the demonic. A very common demonic influence is that of the fortuneteller or gypsy, as they are sometimes called. We know from Scripture that the believer is not

to become involved with such people, but unfortunately they
sometimes do.

> A Christian man had been afflicted with epilepsy for many
> years and even with medical help his condition declined. In
> desperation his wife persuaded him to go to a gypsy who
> "prescribed" bizarre rituals involving the killing of pigeons and
> the placing of the blood on various parts of the man's body. At
> some point the matter came to the attention of the church and
> the couple was counseled about the serious nature of their
> actions.

The outcome was that the "prescription" did absolutely no good,
the epilepsy grew worse, and the man died. Among the issues in
this case is the accessibility of demonic agents in the urban
environment and the ignorance of some believers about the
danger involved.

An Old Testament example of the demonic is found in
1 Samuel. King Saul, seeking guidance for battle, went to a
medium and requested that the spirit of Samuel, who had been
dead for some time, be brought back (28:7). Scripture says that,
previous to this incident, "the Spirit of the LORD had departed
from Saul, and an evil spirit from the LORD tormented him"
(16:14). It is questionable whether Saul considered beforehand the
seriousness of what he was about to do—especially when he had
just previously expelled "the mediums and spiritists from the
land" (28:3). He was desperate. The result was a lost kingdom and
the loss of his life.

The most dramatic New Testament example is that of the man
named Legion (Mark 5:1-20). Scripture says that he was "possessed by the legion of demons" (v. 15). The man's bizarre
behavior and the plea to "torment me not" (v. 7 KJV) are clear
evidences that this was not a case of mental illness, but of demon
possession.

It is not always simple to differentiate between mental illness
and demon possession, but we will attempt to make a differential
diagnosis later in the chapter.

Some question whether there is such a phenomenon as
demon possession, but Scripture makes it clear that it is possible
for a person to a demoniac. One of the signs of demonization is
fantastic strength on the part of the one under demonic control.

> An urban pastor reported that he was counseling a woman who
> he suspected was possessed. In the course of counseling, the
> woman sprang out of her chair, screamed incoherently, and

threw the pastor's desk, which weighed at least two hundred pounds, across the room.

Another sign of demonization is that of evil commands given by demons. For example, the demons may command the person to harm himself or others. These commands are to be distinguished from "command hallucinations" common in schizophrenics. In the case of schizophrenia, bizarre behaviors and disordered thoughts accompany the behavior. Very often, most of the behavior of demonized people appears normal. In fact, one has to listen very carefully to those who are demonized to detect the condition. Satan has many disguises and he sometimes appears even as an "angel of light" (2 Cor. 11:14). Demonized people may be well-dressed and articulate and yet be under some level of demonic control.

We mentioned earlier that the city seems to be a primary congregating point for demonic influence. Some common avenues of demonic activity in the city include the following:

- *Rock music* is an insidious entryway for the demonic. Lyrics sometimes have explicit references to Satan and demons. One well-known rock group is even called "Black Sabbath." It is reported that one member of this group began to hear voices telling him that workers in his house were trying to kill him. Unbeknownst to him, they were believers. When he accused them of trying to harm him, they offered to pray for him, and they did. He accepted the Lord and the Christians baptized him in the lake behind his house.

- *New Age Cult.* This is a new and very alarming movement with definite occultic practices. It is most dangerous because its adherents believe in the unity of all religions and that there are many ways to God. They believe that God is within each person and, like Satan, quote Scripture to support such an idea, "the Kingdom of God is within you."[17] This group believes in reincarnation and other antibiblical ideas but, most dangerously, it opens people to demonic influence through occultic practices such as "channeling," or the use of spiritual mediums.

- *Channeling* is another opening for Satan. Channeling is what Saul did when he consulted the Witch of Endor. The person who does the channeling charges a fee for consulting the reincarnated spirit.[18]

- *Gypsies and fortunetellers.* These are two of the most common means of demonic entrance. Even things as seemingly harmless as Tarot cards and Ouija boards have been known to cause serious problems.
- *Obeah.* Immigrants from the Caribbean practice *obeah*, which is an occult practice for "good" or "evil." The obeah man or woman might help a person get back a lover who has spurned the client. Or the obeah person might supply the answer to a problem. Often the client is given herbs or other potions. This occult practice can lead to demonization.

An obeah woman once rented a room in the house of a Christian family. Soon after moving in, she announced that she was leaving because the house was "too holy."

The demonic must flee from the presence of the Lord.

- *Brujeria.* Hispanic immigrants sometimes believe in *brujeria* or witchcraft, which clearly is Satanic. One sees the *brujo* (witch) to bring harm to someone else. In one case, a believer was having difficulty with a tenant. When he discussed this with a Hispanic co-worker, the person suggested that he consult a brujo who would get the person out of the house. The Christian refused, but this incident points out how easily Satan can gain access to the believer's life.

There are countless influences rampant in the city that can lead to demonization. These examples will but alert the reader to the possibilities for demonic invasion. The importance of understanding these avenues will become more apparent as we evaluate those who appear to be influenced or possessed by the demonic.

We noted earlier that it can be difficult to distinguish between an emotional problem and demon possession. Often the symptoms are almost identical, and yet we know that there are clear cases of demon possession. Sometimes the counselee will be able to tell the counselor that the problem is one of demon possession. Otherwise, one helpful criterion for distinguishing between emotional problems and demon possession may be the degree of chaos in a person's life. As people come more under the control of Satan, their lives become more psychospiritually chaotic. As they come under God's control, they demonstrate more control of themselves and they are less open to demonization.

Demonic activity lies in the area of personality where it is frequently impossible to clearly distinguish between soul and spirit. It may be impossible to make clear diagnostic distinctions in the area where soul and spirit appear to overlap or intersect. (See diagram below.) Although human diagnosis may be difficult, Hebrews 4:12 states that the Word of God can pierce "even to the dividing asunder of *soul* and *spirit*."

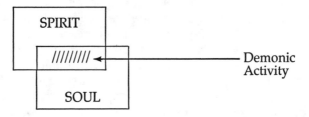

Some cases, however, are fairly easy to diagnose.

Sadie, a young black woman, approached a certain elder after a church service and requested counseling. However, she had a very strange, vacant stare and, at times, her body twitched uncomfortably. The elders suspected demon possession. So, instead of just one elder counseling her, several elders went into the pastor's study to counsel with her. During that time, Sadie admitted to having a problem with uncontrollable evil thoughts. Later, they discovered that tarot cards and occult literature paved the road she had taken. Fortunately for Sadie, one of the elders had had experience in casting out demons. He commanded the demon, in the name of Jesus, to state his name and come out of her. At this, Sadie made a low guttural sound and uttered some unintelligible gibberish. As the sound left her lips she convulsed in her chair, then went as limp as a rag doll. After about sixty seconds of silence, a look of serenity came over her face. She had been delivered after a long period of torment.

As with possession, evaluation is sometimes also fairly clear with regard to psychologically generated problems.

Jennifer, a white, middle-aged female in Sadie's church, was interviewed at her daughter's suggestion. The daughter, a believer, thought that her mother was possessed. After a short interview, the counseling elder discovered that the woman had a history of schizophrenia and had been hospitalized several times. Hers was not a case of demon possession, but rather a classic case of paranoid delusions.

Christian counselors who work in the field of deliverance typically postulate that (1) demonizing may appear without any mental disorder, (2) mental illness may occur without any demonic activity, and (3) mental disorder and demonizing may occur together.

Having said this, there seem to be certain characteristics that suggest the presence of the demonic. A Christian psychiatrist has rightly pointed out that demonic influence sometimes mimics multiple personality disorder.[19] This mental illness is one in which an individual may have two or more personalities. One may be "John," who is placid and nonassertive, while "Hank" may be hostile and combative. Two important differences exist between multiple personality disorder and the demonic.[20] First, in MPD the personalities are not aware of each other. In demonization not only may the two be aware of each other, but they may communicate with each other. Second, in demonization, the "other person" is evil. The personalities in MPD are not necessarily evil.

Another characteristic of demonization is the individual's reaction to the name of Jesus.[21] Just as the demons in Scripture were terrified at the presence of Jesus, so demons today react negatively and sometimes even violently to his name. This negative reaction to divine names and the Bible is supported by other Christian writers.[22]

A final characteristic of the demonic involves the biblical injunction to "test the spirits" (1 John 4:1). There are those in our day who doubt the ability to discern evil spirits. The Word of God, however, reassures us, "But you have an anointing from the Holy One, and all of you know the truth" (1 John 2:20). After careful assessment, if it appears likely that the problem is demonic, more direct evaluation and possible deliverance can begin.

Personal qualities and spiritual preparation are more important than any theory or technique when it comes to counseling the demon possessed. In Mark 9, the disciples were patently unsuccessful in casting out a demon. Jesus explained, "this kind does not go out except by prayer and fasting" (v. 29 NASB). Prior to dealing with demonic activities, the counselor needs to fast and pray and believe that the Holy Spirit will give him the ability to discern demonic activity. He should identify and confess any sin that the Holy Spirit reveals and ask for specific Scriptures and guidance for the session. Presumptuousness cannot play a part. Sincere dependence on the leading of the Holy Spirit must take precedence. There should be a team of people supporting the session with prayer and fasting as this is not normally a ministry for an individual to attempt alone. There should be one or two people directly involved in the actual deliverance and one or two others present to pray, quote Scripture, and sing spiritual songs. Others, whose presence is not necessarily needed, should also be asked to pray during the session.

Prior to a deliverance session, the counselee being evaluated should also renounce any known sin and Satanic strongholds, affirming his commitment to allow God to have total control over his being. After a time of prayer and praise, the deliverance can begin. In the name of Jesus, clear restrictions should be placed on any demonic spirits. They should be prohibited from harassing any of those present in the room or their families and they should be prohibited from any form of expression except the temporary use of the mind and mouth of the person being delivered, and then only on the direct command of the deliverer.

The believer has the right to address and command demons.[23] Passages such as Matthew 8:32, Mark 16:17, Luke 8:29, and Acts 16:18 support this position. In a deliverance session any evil spirits present are commanded to answer a series of questions affirming Jesus Christ as their Savior and Lord. If the spirit presence is unable to answer such questions affirmatively, it is clear that it is demonic presence. Dr. McGraw suggests questions such as "Do you confess Jesus Christ came in the flesh?" and "Who is Lord?" or "Is Jesus Christ *your* Lord?" be asked.

At this point, the demonic presence is commanded to give its name and rank, and the name of its leader. (Usually demons are linked in chains of authority under a lead demon.) This is done in a quiet but authoritative tone of voice. The command may have to be repeated. Demons are reluctant to identify themselves and their leaders because they do not want to leave the demonized person. The deliverer should command the demons to respond, asserting that they are under the authority and power of the blood of Jesus. Because demons are deceptive, it is often necessary to ask them if their answers can stand before the judgment bar of God, at which point they will answer reluctantly but truthfully.

After it has been determined if there are any grounds for each demon to remain, the demonized person is told to specifically renounce each demon by name, affirm that he wants nothing to do with them, and reclaim the territory they controlled, putting it under the lordship of Jesus Christ.

At this point, after prayer and praise together, the primary deliverer commands the demons by name to leave and go to the abyss, never to return. These commands must be repeated until all of the demons have left. A final re-evaluation is done by calling each lead demon to attention and asking if they or their subordinates are present. If there is no answer, the person is most likely delivered. Given the stubbornness of demons, however, the deliverer may wish to repeat the initial assessment process. Finally, the delivered person should be prayed for with the laying on of hands, and the Holy Spirit should be invited to fill the person with his presence. Satan will usually redouble his efforts to return through other demons in the days immediately following the deliverance, so the one delivered must carefully be followed-up and counseled and be given both spiritual and psychological support.

The issue of deliverance is complex and difficult. It is not something to be feared nor played at. Only those who are spiritually mature, who have sound biblical background, and who are filled with the Holy Spirit should tackle deliverance. There must be utter dependence on God at every step of the process. It is strongly advised that those entering into a deliverance ministry do so under the guidance of someone else who has extensive experience in this area.

NOTES

[1]L. Bennett, *Before the Mayflower: A History of Black America* (Chicago: Johnson Publishing Co., 1982).

[2]C. V. Willie, B. M. Kramer, and B. S. Brown, *Racism and Mental Health* (Pittsburgh: Univ. of Pittsburgh Press, 1973), 140.

[3]Ibid., 292.

[4]K. B. Clark and M. P. Clark, "The Development of Consciousness of the Self and the Emergence of Racial Identity in Pre-School Negro Children," *Journal of Social Psychology* 10 (1939): 591–99.

[5]Meeting of Latino educators and business leaders at Hostos Community College (December 1989).

[6]F. Butterfield, "Boston in Uproar Over Murder Case," *New York Times* (January 8, 1990).

[7]Among the helpful books available for children are:
A. Adoff, *Malcom X* (New York: Crowell, 1970); R. Bains, *Harriet Tubman: The Road to Freedom* (New Jersey: Troll Associates, 1982); C. E. Lincoln, *The Negro Pilgrimage in America* (New York: Bantam Books, 1967); J. Kunjufu, *Lessons from History: A Celebration in Blackness* (Chicago: African American Images, 1987); P. McKissick, *Jesse Jackson: A Biography* (New York: Scholastic, Inc., 1989); F. Sabin, *Jackie Robinson* (New Jersey: Troll Associates, 1985); L. Santrey, *Young Frederick Douglass* (New Jersey: Troll Associates, 1983); D. Walton, *What Color Are You?* (Chicago: Johnson Publishing, 1973).

[8]J. C. Coleman, *Abnormal Psychology and Modern Life* (Glenview, Ill.: 1976).

[9]W. H. Guier and P. M. Cobbs, *Black Rage* (New York: Basic Books, 1968).

[10]H. Hendin, *Black Suicide* (New York: Harper & Row, 1969).

[11]A. F. Pouissant, *Why Blacks Kill Blacks* (New York: Emerson Hall, 1972).

[12]Ibid.

[13]N. Boyd, "Family Therapy with Black Families," in E. F. Jones and S. S. Korchin, *Minority Mental Health* (New York: Praeyer, 1982).

[14]W. Ryan, *Blaming the Victim* (New York: Pantheon, 1971).

[15]H. O. Jones, *White Questions to a Black Christian* (Grand Rapids: Zondervan, 1975).

[16]We wish to express special acknowledgement to Dr. Gerald McGraw for permission to use his largely unpublished materials, upon which we rely heavily in this section. Dr. McGraw teaches at Toccoa Falls Bible College, Toccoa Falls, Ga.

[17]W. Martin, *The New Age Cult* (Minneapolis: Bethany House, 1989).

[18]R. K. Bufford, *Counseling and the Demonic* (Dallas: Word, 1988).

[19]M. S. Peck, *People of the Lie: The Hope for Healing Human Evil* (New York: Simon and Schuster, 1983).

[20]Bufford, *Counseling and the Demonic*, 116–32.

[21]Ibid.

[22]K. E. Koch, *Occult Bondage and Deliverance* (Grand Rapids: Kregel, 1970).

[23]G. McGraw, "Principles for Liberation of People Invaded by Demons," and "Procedure in a Deliverance Session," Unpublished manuscripts, Toccoa Falls Bible College, Toccoa Falls, Ga.

SECTION TWO

People of the City

Introduction

THE UNITED STATES of America is a land of immigrants. The so-called American Indians are quite correct in insisting that they be called Native Americans because they are the only ones who can be justifiably called "Americans." All the rest of us have come from distant lands, some willingly and others unwillingly. On one level America has welcomed her immigrants, as witnessed by the well-known inscription at the base of the Statue of Liberty: "Give me your tired, your poor, your huddled masses yearning to breathe free. . . ." Unfortunately, from America's earliest days, "people of color" have been accorded inferior status in relation to that of "whites." For example, the Chinese, who built the transcontinental railroad, were called the "Yellow Peril," and worse, the Chinese Exclusion Act of 1882 limited the number of Chinese people allowed entry into the United States. Hispanics, likewise, have had their share of ostracism, as evidenced by the "Zoot Suit Riots" of 1943 (see chapter 5). Finally, African Americans, the largest minority group of all, have been lynched, vilified, and segregated from the days of slavery to the present time. These minorities have, for economic and political reasons, gravitated to the cities. There they hoped to improve their lives, only to be hindered further by an inherently racist society.

Minority people suffer in different degrees, depending on their geographical location and the political and social conditions of the day, but they all have five criteria in common.

1. A minority person is distinguished by certain identifiable characteristics such as skin color, shape of eyes, language,

or a combination of these. These visible qualities make them easy targets.

2. Minorities are relatively powerless at the hands of the dominant group. Whites have been able to segregate minorities to certain parts of the city, certain schools, and (shamefully) certain churches. This segregation, by its very nature, has set up a system in which the visible minority is constantly reminded of their unequal status and their relative powerlessness to change it.

3. The status of minorities is castelike. Their visibility makes it easy for the majority to permanently relegate them to a lower socioeconomic status. While a certain amount of social mobility is enjoyed by minority people, it is nevertheless circumscribed by the dominant (white) group.

4. Minority groups are very conscious of their status in the eyes of the dominant group. A great deal of energy is expended in trying to show "them" (whites) that they are not inferior.

5. Minorities have sometimes accepted the view held by the dominant group and thus act accordingly. This is tragic.

The urban pastor must be ever vigilant against reinforcing this acceptance when it is has taken place. Obviously, however, not all have accepted their status as inferior. A kind of rage exists among minority peoples and it manifests itself in various forms. Some have reacted violently against the system in an effort to destroy it. Others have found a way to sublimate, that is, to find a more "acceptable" way to circumvent the racism that is so pervasive.

An urban pastor, then, should have knowledge of the counselee's culture as well as have very specific counseling skills. He must be sensitive to the plight of ethnic minorities and the social inequities they have endured if he is to be effective in counseling them. There is no doubt in our minds that the success of counseling is directly proportionate to the counselor's sensitivity to the social and cultural position of the counselee.

In this section the authors call on those who counsel inner city minority persons to first examine themselves. Counselors need to become aware of the extent to which they may have become tainted with institutionalized racism. To deny this problem is to risk harming those we hope to help.

In chapter 6, Siang-Yang Tan warns us to avoid stereotypes about Asians that are so prevalent among clinicians who are insensitive to and essentially ignorant of Asian culture. He emphasizes the need for a cultural match between counselor and counselee and culture-specific counseling if effective counseling is to take place. Finally, he suggests that common barriers to the effective counseling of Asians can be overcome with flexible counseling hours, affordable fees, and the use of an Asian co-counselor when the counselor is inexperienced in working with Asians.

In chapter 7, Edward Maynard warns that African-Americans are justifiably suspicious of anything that is a product of a hostile, racist system—including counseling. He notes, however, that there are a host of informal sources of counseling within the black community that have helped blacks deal with their problems. But, he continues, there are barriers even when both counselor and counselee are black, because the counselor may still be viewed as the tool of a racist society.

Luis Villareal stresses the role of communication in the counseling of Hispanics in chapter 8. The counselor may communicate negatively by words, gestures, and stereotypic attitudes that may have a deleterious effect on the counseling. While Hispanic counselees will often prefer a Hispanic counselor, they most of all want someone who understands them. Villareal emphasizes the counselor's need for self-examination with respect to his prejudices and predilections.

It is not our intention to make it appear that cross-cultural counseling is an impossible task. It is not. Culturally sensitive and psychologically-minded Christian men and women who are anointed by the Holy Spirit can very effectively alleviate the emotional suffering that is an integral part of inner-city living.

CHAPTER 6

Counseling Asians

SIANG YANG TAN

AMERICAN SOCIETY has become significantly more pluralistic
and culturally diverse in recent years. One of the fastest-growing
ethnic minority populations is Asian Americans. This chapter will
provide a description of the major characteristics of the Asian-
American population, as well as biblical perspectives and guidelines for effective cross-cultural counseling with Asians.[1]

CHARACTERISTICS OF THE ASIAN AMERICAN POPULATION

Over 700,000 Southeast-Asian refugees have settled in the
United States since the fall of Saigon in 1975. As part of the family
reunification resettlement this influx is ongoing, but has slowed
down considerably since 1984.[2] According to some estimates, at
least half of all Asian Americans are recent immigrants and
refugees,[3] with the total number at over three and a half million.[4]
Asian Americans came originally from East Asia, Southeast Asia,
the Indian subcontinent, and the Pacific Islands, but this group
now consists of more than twenty-nine distinct subgroups with
differences in language, religion, custom,[5] group identity, and
history. They may also share some common cultural values like
family orientation, interdependency, and particular Eastern religious or philosophical worldviews. The more specific term for
these people, Southeast Asian Americans, actually include people
of Vietnamese, Lao, Cambodian, Hmong, and Mien ancestry.
Earlier descriptions of Asian Americans as Japanese, Chinese,
Philippinos (or Pilipinos), Koreans, and Hawaiians, as in the 1970
census,[6] are therefore outdated and grossly inadequate.

Previous research conducted with stable Asian-American groups like the Chinese and Japanese may no longer be valid or generalizable. To conduct appropriate and valid clinical assessment of Asian Americans, the following factors must be explored and adequately considered: subcultural background, demographic variables, unique lifestyle, heterogeneity in socioeconomic status, and degree of acculturation to Western culture.[7] Generalizations about Asians and Asian Americans should, therefore, be made with great caution and necessary qualifications.[8] The term Asian American has become almost meaningless, unless it is used with further qualification and explanation. Sue and Sue[9] have aptly pointed out that " . . . clinicians should . . . be aware that on some characteristics, within-group differences may be greater than between-group differences . . . . Making generalizations about Asians or Asian Americans without taking into consideration subcultural differences can lead to faulty conclusions."

There is a widely held view that Asians and Asian Americans are relatively well-adjusted people with few psychological problems. This stereotype of Asian Americans as a model ethnic minority population is misleading and somewhat inaccurate.[10] For example, Indochinese refugees actually suffer from more psychological and physical complaints than the general population.[11]

With regard to rates of psychopathology or mental disorder among Asian Americans, there is a tendency to underestimate them. Research findings "support the view that Asian Americans seek treatment only when the disorders are relatively severe and that those with milder disturbances do not turn to the mental health system. If this is true, the treated-case method may significantly underestimate actual rates of psychopathology."[12] There is therefore a need for using large scale probability samples in epidemiological surveys[13] to arrive at more accurate estimates of the true prevalence rate of psychopathology among Asian Americans. The treated-case method is not as valid then because only individuals who seek treatment can be used in such a method.

With regard to personality assessment and deficiencies in personality adjustment, there is a tendency to overestimate such deficiencies among Asian Americans. A number of studies using relatively small or select samples (usually college students) have found that Asian Americans show greater feelings of isolation, loneliness, and anxiety, have lower self-concept scores, greater anxiety in social situations, and greater introversion, self-restraint, and passivity. However, there are serious methodological flaws and limitations with such studies. The untreated-case method used to determine the personality adjustment of Asian Americans tends to overestimate their deficiencies.[14]

A major area of concern in attempts to conduct valid and appropriate clinical assessment with Asian Americans is the use of interpreters during clinical interviews because of language difficulties or barriers. Interpreters have been found frequently to engage in at least three major forms of distortion during the clinical interview.[15] First, they omit, substitute, condense, or change the focus. Second, they normalize the patient's responses or complaints and therefore mislead the interviewer or clinician to underestimate the presence of psychopathology. And third, they deliberately attempt to minimize psychopathology, especially if the interpreter is a family member or close friend of the counselee's. Steps should be taken to ensure that if, and when, an interpreter is used in a clinical assessment interview, he is well-prepared so as to minimize distortions.

Accurate translation or interpretation is necessary not only in interview situations, but also in the use of personality inventories and other psychopathological rating scales.[16] If rating scales or assessment measures originally standardized with Western patient populations are to be used with Asian Americans, their reliability and validity should be established with Asian American subjects. Because cultural factors can influence the expression of symptoms of mental disorder or psychopathology, they should be taken into account when assessing counselee symptoms. For example, Asian Americans have a tendency to somaticize their psychological problems, especially if they involve depressive reactions.[17] For example, one study of depressed patients in Taiwan showed that 88 percent of them initially reported only somatic or physical symptoms, not depression.[18] Southeast-Asian refugees, in general, express psychiatric problems somatically with complaints of headache, insomnia, general aches and pains, heart palpitations, fatigue, and dizziness.[19] Special attention to somatic symptoms is therefore essential for a more accurate diagnosis of psychopathology (particularly depression).[20] To help in this regard, a few culture-specific rating scales of psychiatric symptomatology especially for Asian Americans have recently been developed. There is, for example, a Vietnamese rating scale for depression.[21]

Before I provide some biblical perspectives on cross-cultural counseling and some guidelines for effective counseling with

Asian Americans, it is also important to note several relevant cultural and historical perspectives in the Asian-American context.[22] Early research showed Asian Americans to be inhibited, law-abiding, nonassertive, reserved, and unlikely to express impulses. Such characteristics are consistent with Asian cultural values of restraining strong feelings, of unquestioning obedience to family authority, and of the primacy of family welfare over individuality. The historical record of prejudice and discrimination against Asian Americans as an ethnic minority population has significantly contributed to such findings as well. One example of blatant discrimination was the passage of the Chinese Exclusion Act in 1882, a racist immigration law that was not repealed until 1943. Much of current Chinese American stereotyped behavior may be attributed to historical white racism and prejudice.[23]

Recently, researchers have found that Asian Americans are actually as assertive as their Caucasian peers on behavioral measures, but less assertive (and more socially anxious) on self-report measures.[24] Again, the need for appropriate measurement of particular behavioral or personality variables in regard to research with Asian Americans (and other ethnic minorities) is crucial so that misleading stereotypes can be corrected, or at least qualified.

It is also essential to deal constructively with the issue of racism. A biblical perspective focuses on the sinfulness or fallenness of all human beings. There is a need for all ethnic groups, whether the majority or the minority, to develop greater respect for each other, and to repent of racism. This is particularly important if there is to be peace and justice in an American society that is increasingly pluralistic and culturally diverse. Racism in counseling exists and needs to be addressed.[25]

BIBLICAL PERSPECTIVES ON CROSS-CULTURAL COUNSELING AND MINISTRY

Several publications have recently examined biblical or Christian perspectives on cross-cultural counseling and ministry,[26] including a book on cross-cultural counseling written from a missiological perspective,[27] and another on counseling across cultures from a pastoral perspective.[28]

The need for the church and Christian mental health professionals to be more involved in services to ethnic minorities has been emphasized by Uomoto. Currently, Christian counselors reflect the profession's general tendency to prefer clients who are young, attractive, verbal, intelligent, successful—and white (i.e., YAWVIS clients).[29] Uomoto suggests several ways to promote a Christian, ethical human response to human needs,[30] with particular focus on prevention and the provision of community psychological interventions.[31]

The ministry of lay pastoral care and counseling conducted by Christian nonprofessionals or paraprofessionals is a significant component of outreach and prevention efforts.[32] Lay counseling may be particularly helpful in counseling ethnic minorities, including Asian Americans. I have, in fact, recommended the use of an informal but organized model of lay Christian counseling in Chinese and other ethnic-minority churches where there is a stigma against formal counseling.[33] This model assumes that lay Christian counseling should be an organized and well-supervised ministry that occurs in informal settings like homes, hospitals, and restaurants, rather than in formal church counseling centers. Some have recommended the use of early Chinese immigrants (residing more than six years in the United States) as lay helpers for more recent Chinese immigrants (residing six or less years in the United States) who are experiencing adjustment difficulties.[34] Intervention provided by such lay helpers may be more acceptable to Chinese individuals. An excellent example of an informal, organized model of a lay counseling ministry is the Stephen Series described in chapter 3.

More recently, I have emphasized the need from a biblical perspective to focus more on the ministry of the Holy Spirit (including appropriate spiritual gifts of exhortation, healing, wisdom, knowledge, discerning of spirits, and mercy), and spiritual power in lay-Christian caring ministries.[35] This perspective implies that Christian helpers—lay and professional—be yielded to the Holy Spirit, and exercise essential spiritual disciplines such as meditation, prayer, fasting, study, simplicity, solitude, submission, service, confession, guidance, worship, and celebration.[36] Christian helpers also need to be open to the use of what I have called "explicit integration" in counseling. Explicit integration is a biblically based approach that openly and systematically employs spiritual resources (such as prayer and the Scritpures) and deals with spiritual issues in a clinically competent and ethically responsible way.[37] Such a biblically based and spiritually oriented approach to people helping is particularly relevant to counseling with Asian Christians, who tend to be evangelical in their theological convictions. It has been my experience that the majority of Asian Christians, and especially Chinese Christians, who are courageous enough to seek counseling for their problems prefer to consult counselors who take a more explicit-integration approach.

Asians, in general, have worldviews that usually involve the supernatural. Asian Christians, in particular, believe in the reality of evil and the demonic. They may be more open to Christian counseling that includes the explicit and appropriate use of prayer (including prayer for inner healing and for deliverance where necessary), the Scriptures, and the power of the Holy Spirit.[38] Such "power counseling,"[39] however, should be used with clinical caution, ethical wisdom, and biblical balance, including a foundation of an adequate theology of suffering and grace.[40] Eastern religious practices of ancestor worship and worship of other gods and goddesses are prevalent and are adhered to in order to overcome misfortune or bad luck. Some Asian Christians may unconsciously or inadvertently hold onto such beliefs and practices, even though they are unbiblical and sometimes demonic. Because of this, ample biblical teaching as well as prayer may be necessary for deliverance and protection in counseling.

Furthermore, many Asians value material and educational achievements very highly. Problems with pride and materialism may be present, even among Asian Christians. Biblical values of simplicity and humility[41] will often need to be clearly taught and reinforced along with counseling. Finally, there is a tendency for male chauvinism and authoritarian styles of male leadership to predominate in many Asian families, including punitive or very strict parenting practices. More biblical, balanced styles of marital and parental interaction are often needed. These issues should be addressed where appropriate in Christian counseling, and done in a culturally sensitive, indirect way to allow some "saving of face" for the person involved.

My comments so far about Asians do not necessarily apply to all Asians nor all Asian Americans. They may be most relevant to those who are still traditional and less acculturated, especially those from East Asia and Southeast Asia, or those who have not long been in America. For those Asian Americans who are here to stay, a significant area of struggle for them is their ethnic identity as it relates to their acculturation into American society.[42] It is often difficult for them to integrate their Asian cultural backgrounds with American lifestyles and achieve an adaptive, bicultural ethnic identity. Their tendency is to become over westernized and to reject almost completely whatever Asian aspects of their ethnic identity remain. Effective counseling with Asian Americans will require work on these issues of ethnic identity confusion. Biblical perspectives on culture and biblical values must be incorporated, and counselees helped to respect the good in each culture while appropriately critiquing and rejecting what is bad and/or unbiblical.

Ridley's comments on cross-cultural counseling in a theological context are helpful here.[43] He delineated five theological implications related to cross-cultural issues that have been neglected in the Christian psychology literature. They are as follows:

1. The cultural transcendence of the Gospel (see John 4:4-42) means that the truth of Christianity should be preserved by avoiding cultural additions, subtractions, or corrections (cf. 1 Cor. 12:12-13; Gal. 3:26; Col. 3:10-11).
2. Christian counseling should be seen as a means of Christian liberation and not cultural oppression.
3. The dual targets of therapeutic change in a cross-cultural context should be the person and the social environment.
4. A holistic emphasis in counseling should avoid Western dualism and use biblical perspectives to evaluate behavior and beliefs, including value systems (particularly American middle class values).
5. Christian counselors should receive some training in cross-cultural counseling.

GUIDELINES FOR EFFECTIVE COUNSELING WITH ASIANS

I have elsewhere[44] described several guidelines for effective counseling and psychotherapy with Asian Americans, which I obtained from the recent growing secular literature on this topic.[45] I will now summarize these guidelines briefly.

First is the need to focus more on the cultural match between the counselor and counselee in terms of their attitudes, values, experiences, and behaviors, and translate this into more concrete behaviors in the counseling session.[46] The *ethnic* or *racial* match between the counselor and counselee may *not* be as crucial or as helpful as the *cultural* match. It is particularly important to consider individual differences, especially the degree of acculturation in people within the same ethnic minority group. S. Sue has therefore stated:

> Ethnic matches can result in cultural mismatches if therapists and clients from the same ethnic group show markedly different values (e.g., a highly acculturated Chinese American therapist who works with a Chinese immigrant holding traditional Chinese values). Conversely, ethnic mismatches do not necessarily imply cultural mismatches, because therapists and clients from different ethnic groups may share similar values, lifestyles, and experiences.[47]

Cultural match between the counselor and counselee should be more concretely defined in terms of variables that can be directly related to the counseling process. This would include an agreement between counselor and counselee on the conceptualization of the ethnic client's problems, the means for solving problems, and the goals for counseling, as S. Sue and Zane[48] have recommended. More recent research has shown, however, that ethnic or racial match between counselor and counselee appears to be the most important for Chinese American clients. This may be due to the fact that such an ethnic or racial match can also mean a language match (S. Sue, personal communication, March 21, 1990), which is crucial for effective communication and counseling.

Second, the need to link cultural knowledge and culture-specific counseling interventions to more basic processes has been noted in the literature.[49] Two basic processes in particular are *credibility*, referring to the client's perception or experience of the counselor as an effective and trustworthy helper, and *giving or gift giving*, referring to the counselee's perception that something was received from the counseling experience.[50]

The credibility of the counselor can be *ascribed* through the position, credentials, or role assigned to the counselor by others, or *achieved* through the counselor's own skills in the counseling situation. Gift giving does not mean that counseling has to be short-term or that quick solutions must be attempted. However, gift giving does imply that counselors should try to offer some concrete benefits early in counseling, even in the first session. Such immediate benefits or gifts may include " . . . anxiety reduction, depression relief, cognitive clarity, normalization, reassurance, hope and faith, skills acquisition, a coping perspective, and goal setting."[51] Recommendations for minimizing problems in credibility and maximizing gift giving[52] are particularly helpful for effective counseling with Asians and Asian Americans.

Third, a number of guidelines for counseling Asian Americans within a culturally sensitive systems approach have been delineated elsewhere.[53] The counselor must strive to break down barriers to continued counseling that are common in the Asian-American context. Clinic or private practice hours should be very flexible, for example, providing evening and weekend hours where possible. Sliding-scale fees in place of prohibitively high private-practice fees are a must. A co-therapist should be used if the primary counselor is not experienced in working with Asian-American clients. And, finally, the counselor should be prepared to help his Asian-American clients cope with legal or other social-service systems.

Guidelines for facilitating the initial counseling contact include the following:

- Determine counselee beliefs about mental and emotional problems.
- Provide an overview of the counseling or therapeutic plan, types of changes needed, and who needs to be involved. This will enhance trust in the counselor, since most Asian-American counselees expect the counselor to be an authority who will tell them what they must do to feel better.
- Use a brief therapy or counseling model since many Asian-American clients hope to have an answer to their problems and will look to more concrete methods of problem solving.
- Determine how open the family is to intervention and how one can earn the trust of ("join with") the family system.
- Anticipate reasons for which the family or counselee may not come back for a second session, and deal with such possibilities in the first session.

Similar guidelines for conducting family therapy with Asian Americans using a strategic-structural framework have also been provided.[54] They include the need for the counselor to:

- Establish and use authority.
- Take the directive stance and structure the initial session.
- Address family members appropriately by being sensitive to Asian family organization, including care to "protect the parent's face."
- Avoid direct confrontation too early in the counseling process.
- Engage in clear goal setting.

Effective strategies suggested by Kim include the following:

- Engage the family by initially defining the problem as the parents or family members perceive it (usually in terms of an identified patient in the family) so that parents do not lose face.
- Use reframing techniques to relabel in a positive way what people do, in order to encourage change.
- Assume flexible, multiple roles such as "expert" and "teacher".
- Use correct timing.

Other guidelines are now available in recent literature in the following specific areas:

- Sexual counseling for Asian immigrants.[55]
- Psychotherapy with Southeast Asian American clients.[56]
- A general family practitioner approach for Asian-American mental health services.[57]

Further work is needed in the more specific area of counseling with Asians who are *not* going to be American citizens or immigrants. These include Asian foreign students and Asian business or professional people who are in the United States for a limited period of time (several months to a few years). The adjustment issues they face are somewhat different from Asian Americans who are here to stay, since they will have to re-enter their own societies and cultures later.

There is also a need for more Asian Americans to be trained in the behavioral sciences and the mental-health professions. Psychology as a career option is highly underrepresented with approximately only one percent of all psychologists in the United States being Asian Americans.[58]

CONCLUSION

Counseling with Asians or Asian Americans is a crucial part of healing in the city, where the number of Asian immigrants continues to grow. This chapter has provided a description of the major characteristics of the Asian-American population, as well as biblical perspectives and guidelines drawn from the secular literature for effective cross-cultural counseling with Asians. Let me conclude with the following:

> There is an ongoing need to deal constructively with the issue of racism or discrimination against ethnic minority groups, including Asian Americans, in the United States. However, all

cultures and ethnic groups, whether majority or minority, have been tainted with sin and therefore need to be subject to the judgment of the Scriptures and to repent before God. The biblical injunctions to love God first and then to love our neighbor as ourselves (Matt. 22:37–39), and the biblical teaching that we are all one in Christ without human or cultural barriers (1 Cor. 12:12–13; Gal. 3:26–28; Col. 3:10–11) should challenge all ethnic groups . . . to develop greater understanding of and respect for each other, and therefore to overcome racism and prejudices against one another. Christian mental-health professionals, as well as the church, need to respond sincerely and sensitively to such a challenge. One way is to become more actively involved in the delivery of mental-health services to ethnic minority groups, including Asian Americans.[59]

NOTES

[1]Siang-Yang Tan, "Psychopathology and Culture: The Asian American Context," *Journal of Psychology and Christianity* 8 (2) (1989): 61–75.

[2]K. Nishio and M. Bilmes, "Psychotherapy with Southeast Asian American Clients," *Professional Psychology: Research and Practice* 18 (1987): 342–46.

[3]S. Sue and J. K. Morishima, *The Mental Health of Asian Americans: Contemporary Issues in Identifying and Treating Mental Problems* (San Francisco: Jossey-Bass, 1982).

[4]D. W. Sue and D. Sue, *Counseling the Culturally Different: Theory and Practice, Second Edition* (New York: Wiley, 1990), 189.

[5]R. B. Yoshioka, N. Tashima, M. Chew and K. Murase, *Mental Health Services for Pacific/Asian Americans* (San Francisco: Pacific Asian Mental Health Research Project, 1981).

[6]D. W. Sue, *Counseling the Culturally Different: Theory and Practice* (New York: Wiley, 1981), 113.

[7]D. Sue and S. Sue, "Cultural Factors in the Clinical Assessment of Asian Americans," *Journal of Consulting and Clinical Psychology* 55 (1987): 479–87.

[8]H. Kitano and N. Matsushima, "Counseling Asian Americans," in P. Pedersen, J. Draguns, W. Lonner and J. Trimble, eds., *Counseling Across Cultures* (Honolulu: Univ. of Hawaii Press, 1981), 163–80.

[9]D. Sue and S. Sue, "Cultural Factors in the Clinical Assessment of Asian Americans," 485.

[10]Ibid.

[11]J. Sutherland, R. Avant, W. Franz, C. Monzon and N. Stark, "Indo-Chinese Refugee Health Assessment and Treatment," *Journal of Family Practice* 6 (1983): 61–67;

J. Westermeyer, T. Vang and J. Neider, "A Comparison of Refugees Using and Not Using a Psychiatric Service: An Analysis of DSM-III Criteria and Self-Rating Scales in Cross-Cultural Context," *Journal of Operational Psychiatry* 14 (1983): 36–41.

[12]D. Sue and S. Sue, "Cultural Factors in the Clinical Assessment of Asian Americans," 480.

[13]W. Liu, *Research Priorities Development for Pacific/Asian Americans*, unpublished report (Chicago: Pacific/Asian American Mental Health Center, 1985).

[14]D. Sue and S. Sue, "Cultural Factors in the Clinical Assessment of Asian Americans."

[15]L. Marcos, "Effects of Interpreters on the Evaluation of Psychopathology in Non-English-Speaking Patients," *American Journal of Psychiatry* 136 (1979): 171–74.

[16]J. Westermeyer, "Cultural Factors in Clinical Assessment," *Journal of Consulting and Clinical Psychology* 55 (1987): 471–78.

[17]A. Marsella, D. Kinzie, and P. Gordon, "Ethnic Variations in the Expression of Depression," *Journal of Cross-Cultural Psychology* 4 (1973): 435–58.

[18]A. Kleinman, "Depression, Somatization, and the New Cross-Cultural Psychiatry," *Social Science and Medicine* 11 (1977): 3–10.

[19]J. Bokan and W. Campbell, "Indigenous Psychotherapy in the Treatment of a Laotian Refugee," *Hospital and Comminity Psychiatry* 35 (1984): 281–82.

S. Nguyen, "Mental Health Services for Refugees and Immigrants in Canada," in T. Owan, ed., *Southeast Asian Mental Health: Treatment, Prevention, Services, Training, and Research* (Washington, D.C.: U.S. Dept. of Health and Human Services, 1985): 261–82.

[20]H. Marsella, "Depressive Experience and Disorder Across Cultures," in H. Triandis and J. Draguns, eds., *Psychopathology: Handbook of Cross-Cultural Psychology* (Newton, Mass.: Allyn and Bacon, 1980), 237–89.

[21]J. Kinzie, S. Manson, D. Vinh, N. Tolan, G. Anh, and T. Ngog, "Development and Validation of a Vietnamese-Language Depression Rating Scale," *American Journal of Psychiatry* 139 (1982): 1276–81.

[22]Sue, *Counseling the Culturally Different.*

[23]B. Tong, "On the Confusion of Psychopathology with Culture: Iatrogenesis in the Treatment of Chinese Americans," in R. Morgan, ed., *The Iatrogenics Handbook: A Critical Look at Research and Practice in the Helping Professions* (Toronto: IPI Publishing, Ltd., 1983).

[24]D. Sue, S. Ino, and D. M. Sue, "Nonassertiveness of Asian-Americans: An Inaccurate Assumption?," *Journal of Counseling Psychology* 30 (1983): 581–88.

[25]C. Ridley, "Racism in Counseling As an Adversive Behavioral Process," in P. Pedersen, J. Draguns, W. Lonner and J. Trimble, eds., *Counseling Across Cultures* (Honolulu: Univ. of Hawaii Press, 1989).

[26]D. Augsburger, *Pastoral Counseling Across Cultures* (Philadelphia: Westminster, 1986).

D. Hesselgrave, *Counseling Cross-Culturally: An Introduction to Theory and Practice for Christians* (Grand Rapids: Baker, 1984).

D. Hesselgrave, "Christian Cross-Cultural Counseling: A Suggested Framework for Theory Development," *Missiology: An International Review* 13 (1985): 203–17.

C. Ridley, "Cross-Cultural Counseling in Theological Context," *Journal of Psychology and Theology* 14 (1986): 288–97.

Tan, "Psychopathology and Culture."

J. Uomoto, "Delivering Mental Health Services to Ethnic Minorities: Ethical Considerations," *Journal of Psychology and Theology* 14 (1986): 15–21.

[27]Hesselgrave, *Counseling Cross-Culturally.*

[28]Augsburger, *Pastoral Counseling Across Cultures.*

[29]E. Toupin, "Counseling Asians: Psychotherapy in the Context of Racism and Asian-American History," *American Journal of Orthopsychiatry* 50 (1980): 76–86.

[30]Uomoto, "Delivering Mental Health Services."

[31]R. Bufford and R. Buckler, "Counseling in the Church: A Proposed Strategy for Ministering to Mental Health Needs in the Church," *Journal of Psychology and Christianity* 6 (2) (1987): 21–29.

R. Bufford and T. Johnston, "The Church and Community Mental Health: Unrealized Potential," *Journal of Psychology and Theology* 10 (1982): 355–62.

S. Tan, "Prevention of Psychological Disorders," in D. G. Benner, ed., *Psychotherapy in Christian Perspective* (Grand Rapids: Baker, 1987), 81–87.

J. Uomoto, "Preventive Intervention: A Convergence of the Church and Community Psychology," *Journal of Psychology and Christianity* 1 (3) (1982): 12–22.

[32]J. Prater, "Training Christian Lay Counselors in Techniques of Prevention and Outreach," *Journal of Psychology and Christianity* 6 (2) (1987): 30–34.

Siang-Yang Tan, "Lay Counseling: The Local Church," *CAPS Bulletin* 7 (1) (1981): 15–20.

Siang-Yang Tan, ed., "Special Issue on Lay Christian Counseling," *Journal of Psychology and Christianity* 6 (2) (1987): 1–84.

Siang-Yang Tan, "Lay Christian Counseling: Present Status and Future Directions." Invited paper presented at the International Congress on Christian Counseling, Lay Counseling Track, Atlanta, Ga. (November 1988).

Siagn-Yang Tan, *Lay Counseling: Equipping Christians for a Helping Ministry* (Grand Rapids: Zondervan, 1990).

[33]Tan, *Lay Counseling.*

[34]S. Sue and N. Zane, "Academic Achievement and Socioemotional Adjustment Among Chinese University Students," *Journal of Counseling Psychology* 32 (1985): 570–79.

[35]Siang-Yang Tan, "Lay Christian Counseling: The Next Decade." *Journal of Psychology and Christianity* 9 (3) (1990): 59–65.

M. Gilbert and R. Brock, eds., *The Holy Spirit and Counseling: Theology and Theory* (Peabody, Mass.: Hendrickson, 1985).

M. Gilbert and R. Brock, eds., *The Holy Spirit and Counseling: Principles and Practice* (Peabody, Mass.: Hendrickson, 1988).

[36]R. Foster, *Celebration of Discipline* (New York: Harper & Row, 1978).

[37]Siang-Yang Tan, "Explicit Integration in Psychotherapy." Invited paper presented at the International Congress on Christian Counseling, Counseling and Spirituality Track, Atlanta, Ga. (November 1988). Also see Siang-Yang Tan. "Explicit Integration in Christian Counseling (An Interview)," *The Christian Journal of Psychology and Counseling* V (2) (1990): 7–13.

[38]J. Ozawa, "Power Counseling; Gifts of the Holy Spirit and Psychotherapy." Paper presented at the International Congress on Christian Counseling, Atlanta, Ga. (November 1988).

J. Ozawa, "Prayer and Deliverance in the Healing of Chronic Disorders: Hope for the Hopeless." Paper presented at the International Congress on Christian Counseling, Atlanta, Ga. (November 1988).

C. Kraft, *Christianity With Power* (Ann Arbor, Mich.: Vine Books, 1989).

[39]J. Ozawa, "Power Counseling: Gifts of the Holy Spirit and Psychotherapy."

[40]C. Brown, *That You May Believe: Miracles and Faith Then and Now* (Grand Rapids: Eerdmans, 1985).

J. Coggins and P. Hiebert, eds., *Wonders and the Word* (Winnipeg, MB: Kindred Press, 1989).

[41]R. Foster, *Freedom of Simplicity* (New York: Harper & Row, 1981).

[42]Sue, *Counseling the Culturally Different.*

[43]Ridley, "Cross-Cultural Counseling in the Theological Context."

[44]Tan, "Psychopathology and Culture."

[45]L. Comas-Diaz and E. Griffith, eds., *Clinical Guidelines in Cross-Cultural Mental Health* (New York: Wiley, 1988).

D. Ho, J. Spinks, and C. Yeung, eds., *Chinese Patterns of Behavior: A Sourcebook of Psychological and Psychiatric Studies* (New York: Praeger, 1989).

G. Hong, "A General Family Practitioner Approach for Asian-American Mental Health Services," *Professional Psychology: Research and Practice* 19 (1988): 600–605.

S. Kim, "Family Therapy for Asian Americans: A Strategic-Structural Framework," *Psychotherapy* 22 (1985): 342–48.

H. Kitano and N. Matsushima, "Counseling Asian Americans," in P. Pedersen, J. Draguns, W. Lonner, and J. Trimble, eds., *Counseling Across Cultures* (Honolulu: Univ. of Hawaii Press, 1981), 163–80.

F. Leong, "Counseling and Psychotherapy with Asian-Americans: Review of the Literature," *Journal of Counseling Psychology* 33 (1986): 196–206.

K. Nishio and M. Bilmes, "Psychotherapy with Southeast Asian American Clients," *Professional Psychology: Research and Practice* 18 (1987): 342–46.

P. Pedersen, J. Draguns, W. Lonner, and J. Trimble, eds., *Counseling Across Cultures* (Honolulu: Univ. of Hawaii Press, 1989).

M. Root, "Guidelines for Facilitating Therapy with Asian American Clients," *Psychotherapy* 22 (1985): 349–56.

S. Shon and D. Ja, "Asian Families," in M. McGoldrick, J. Pearce, and J. Giordano, eds., *Ethnicity and Family Therapy* (New York: Guilford, 1982), 208–28.

Sue and Sue, *Counseling the Culturally Different.*

D. W. Sue and S. Sue, "Asian Americans and Pacific Islanders," in P. Pedersen, ed., *Handbook of Cross-Cultural Counseling and Therapy* (Westport, Conn.: Greenwood, 1985), 141–46.

S. Sue, "Psychotherapeutic Services for Ethnic Minorities: Two Decades of Research Findings," *American Psychologist* 43 (1988): 301–8.

Sue and Morishima, *The Mental Health of Asian Americans.*

S. Sue and N. Zane, "The Role of Culture and Cultural Techniques in Psychotherapy: A Critique and Reformulation," *American Psychologist* 42 (1987): 37–45.

A. Tsui, "Psychotherapeutic Considerations in Sexual Counseling for Asian Immigrants," *Psychotherapy* 22 (1985): 357–62.

[46]Sue, "Psychotherapeutic Services for Ethnic Minorities."

[47]Ibid., 306.

[48]Sue and Zane, "The Role of Culture and Cultural Techniques in Psychotherapy."

[49]Ibid.

[50]Ibid.

[51]Ibid., 42.

[52]Ibid.

[53]Root, "Guidelines for Facilitating Therapy."

[54]Kim, "Family Therapy for Asian Americans."

[55]Tsui, "Psychotherapeutic Considerations in Sexual Counseling."

[56]Nishio and Bilmes, "Psychotherapy with Southeast Asian American Clients."

[57]Hong, "A General Family Practitioner Approach."

[58]J. Stapp, A. Tucker, and G. VandenBos, "Census of Psychological Pesonnel: 1983," *American Psychologist* 40 (1985): 1317–51.

[59]Tan, "Psychopathology and Culture," 72.

CHAPTER 7

Counseling Blacks

IN ORDER TO adequately counsel African Americans,[1] it is necessary to understand their historical roots. The success of the cotton crop in the southern United States and the sugar cane crop in Latin America and the Caribbean necessitated a large labor force. Native Americans (Indians) were originally forced into this work though unsuited for it, and were dying because of it. Plantation owners needed a better labor force so they turned to Africa as a source of almost unlimited slave labor. Africans were seized from West Africa—from Senegal in the north to Angola in the south—an area consisting of 3,500 miles. The Africa from which they were kidnapped was rich in history with a highly developed civilization. The notion that Africans were uncivilized savages was a fiction promulgated by European slave traders and plantation owners to justify the slave trade, and on top of that, the slaver often used the Bible to justify his actions. The Africans, told that they were the sons of Ham, the son Noah cursed, were therefore relegated to being "the lowest of slaves" (Gen. 9:25).

The journey from Africa to the West, called the Middle Passage, was one of incredible bestiality. Men were chained in the hold of ships where they were forced to lie in their own body waste for weeks at a time. Upon arrival in the West, if they had survived the trip, they were sold to plantation owners at auctions.

The plantation was a self-enclosed system. The owner answered to no one with respect to his treatment of the slaves, even if he took the slave's life.[2] It was common practice that the new slave's African name was taken away and he was assigned a name chosen by the slavemaster—the first step in his depersonalization. The work was arduous; slaves often worked as long as eighteen hours a day in temperatures that reached 105 degrees and both men and women were expected to pick the same amount of cotton—150 pounds per day!

After emancipation, the life of black people did not improve to any marked degree. They were segregated, mistreated publicly, refused employment, and generally degraded.[3] Many turned to sharecropping, which turned out to be another form of slavery. The black family lived on a plantation, worked the land, and were forced to sell the crop to the plantation owner at a price set by him, always far below the market value.

In addition to these indignities, the African American lived in terror of hate groups such as the Ku Klux Klan. The Klan dragged blacks from their homes, whipped and often murdered them. Lynchings were common practice. If a black man was accused of raping a white woman, or of even just looking at her, he could be taken to a public place, and without trial, hung from a tree, and then, often set afire.

In order to keep blacks "in their place," whites enacted Jim Crow laws, which prescribed absolute separation of the races. There were separate schools, separate public facilities of all kinds, and even separate churches. This system of segregation has left deep scars on the psyches of black people as two black clinicians have stated, "The psychological toll of second-class citizenship and a sense of powerlessness in American society is undeniable."[4] This feeling of powerlessness is evident in high-school dropout rates, in alcoholism, and in drug addiction currently found in the black community.

These historical realities form the social-psychological context of African Americans and suggest the need for a type of counseling that leads to empowerment. It is especially damaging to the African American when he accepts the appraisal of the dominant community about himself. This results in *internalization* of negative attitudes, which often leads to self-hatred and deep inner rage. The urban counselor must help the black counselee see that he is worthwhile and that the attitudes of some in the white community are false.

Empowerment counseling helps the counselee capitalize on his strengths. Each person who seeks counseling has some strengths—the act of seeking help in the first place is a sign of strength, and the counselor should point that out early in the counseling process. Research shows that a counselee who has a positive relationship with a counselor, and who is looked on as an equal, has the best chance for success.[5] The counselee who senses that he is not being looked down on can accept counseling that leads to empowerment.

Segregation, terrorism, and the failure of the cotton crop brought about wholesale changes in the lives of rural, Southern blacks. The migration of black people to the urban North in search of work took place in the early 1900s on a huge scale. However, it was in the urban centers that the African American was to experience a breakdown in the family, including a marked increase in juvenile delinquency and other social problems.[6] These problems will be dealt with in detail in the next section.

PSYCHOSOCIAL ISSUES

The unrelenting effects of racism have had a deleterious impact on the psyche of black people. As we noted in chapter 5, racism is very common—even appearing in dreams. It has been suggested that the psychology of black people has been studied from three points of view:
- The inferiority model.
- The deprivation/deficit model.
- The multicultural model.[7]

The chairman of the psychology department of Columbia University was one of the most vociferous proponents of the genetic inferiority model. He stated that "The weight of the evidence favors the proposition that racial differences in mental ability (and perhaps in personality and characters) are innate and genetic."[8] Arthur Jensen adopted this genetic position and in 1969 published an article in the *Harvard Educational Review*, stating that, based on intelligence tests, he had demonstrated the intellectual inferiority of blacks. He went on to state that environmental issues such as poverty, racism, and poor schooling were factors, but that the genetic factor was by far the most important.

Such misguided thinking has permeated our society. Many of our school officials either overtly or covertly subscribe to the theory of African-American inferiority and conduct education accordingly.

The cultural deprivation model states that years of privation have permanently marred blacks, and that their self-esteem has suffered irreparable damage. Championed by liberal whites who use it much the way Jensen and others did the inferiority model, the cultural deprivation school of thought has much the same effect—the condoning of racism.

The multicultural model, in a complete departure from the previous models, emphasizes that blacks have assets and liabilities just like any other cultural group. It recognizes the history of African Americans and notes the degree to which they have suffered certain privations, but does not accept at all that these privations are genetic or permanent. The work with Head Start, for example, has demonstrated that black children, if given opportunities early in life, can reach their potential. We will return to the issue of education later in the chapter.

THE FAMILY

The black family has been seriously maligned by insensitive sociologists for generations. The best known, Daniel Patrick Moynihan, wrote in 1965 that the African-American family was a "tangle of pathology" based on the relatively large number of female-headed families.[9] This negative appraisal of the family is not the first that Moynihan had voiced. It had been preceded by a host of uncomplimentary and blatantly racist comments about the black family.

Here, again, it is important to understand history. The reality is that slaveholders considered it legitimate to separate families, since they alleged that Africans did not have a family system. While some plantation owners attempted to keep families together, that was not the norm.[10] Indeed, no family tie was sacred during slavery—the African female was sexually abused whether she was married or not. In fact, many black men preferred not to be married to women on the same plantation so that they would not have to see them being sexually abused or whipped and be powerless to protect them. Over the centuries the maltreatment and denigration of black families has led to black family systems that are not typical of the dominant white family, but that are not necessarily pathological either. Indeed, given the realities of black family life, these atypical family structures should be seen as courageous attempts to deal with crushing social realities. The Christian counselor needs to affirm the strengths of the black family while preventively and therapeutically working for constructive change. Unfortunately, since Moynihan, many other writers have continued to see the black family as automatically "pathological."[11]

Research on the black family has followed five main themes:[12]
1. The poverty-acculturation theme.
2. The pathology theme.
3. The reactive apology theme.
4. The black nationalist theme.
5. The proactive-revisionist theme.

The *poverty-acculturation theme* suggests that the black family was successful to the extent that it followed the white middle-class model. The problem with this theme is that the African American does not fit into that model because of his historical context. The notion of the melting pot into which all races were to be assimilated as Americans regardless of ethnic identity was fine until the dark-skinned minorities wanted to get into the pot. Then that melting pot never became a reality and their exclusion from the American Dream has forced blacks to adopt a lifestyle that reflects the realities of their existence.

For example, many black families are extended families, typically involving many more members than the white middle-class model. Economic realities forced blacks into these family situations. Black income is only 56 percent of white income, so "doubling up" is a very common practice in black families where relatives are forced by economic necessity to live together. Besides the primary family, an extended family might include grandparents, aunts, uncles, and others.

The *pathology model* postulated by Moynihan emphasized the existence of a "black matriarchy," which led to family disorganization and other social ills. While we do not deny the vital need for a two-parent family, to say that a family is automatically pathological because it does not have a male present is suspect. The major problem for a single black mother raising children alone is poverty, which creates other problems such as inadequate housing, health care, child care, and, in some cases, dependence on welfare. Other significant problems include lack of time and energy, and the almost overwhelming dual role of mother and father. In addition, the absence of a father may leave children with a distorted view of a complete family system as God intended it. Although a common criticism, it should be noted that having a single mother as head of the house does not mean that there is no male role model. Many black families live in extended families that offer other male role models such as grandfathers and uncles.

The pathology theme seldom takes into account the reasons for female-headed black families. The black male often abdicates because he is unable to find employment—often as the result of direct or indirect racial discrimination—that will enable him to properly support his family. Until very recently, labor unions practiced blatant discrimination against black males. While the African-American female was often able to get work as a domestic, the male either had work that did not pay enough to support the family or had no work at all.

The *reactive-apology* model challenged the pathology model by stating that the black family was similar to the white family except for the effects of racism, poverty, and oppression. While this model sounds plausible, it ignores the events that have shaped the black family, such as its dislocation from Africa, its slavery, and its persistent denigration at the hands of a powerful white society. In other words, the African-American family is shaped not just by present circumstances, but by the antecedent forces that formed them.

The *black nationalist* model emphasized the strengths and competencies of the family. While this approach offered a positive look at black families, it tended to deny some of the realities. It does little good to adopt either the typical white liberal approach, which tends to state that what the black family needs is an increase in welfare benefits, or the black nationalist view that there are no problems at all. The truth is that the black family is simply different from the white family.

Finally, the *proactive-revisionist* model has reconceptualized the issues involved in regard to the black family. This model is more holistic and takes into account the social forces that have played on the family as well as the family's reactions to those forces. It then realistically evaluates social forces in the light of present realities. This school of thought considers the extent to which African values have been preserved in the family, along with other African survivals such as the value of the family as a kinship network.

IDENTITY ISSUES

Identity has been defined as "one component of an individual's overall self-concept. It involves the adoption of certain personal attitudes, feelings, characteristics and behaviors (personal identity), and identification with a larger group of people who share those characteristics. . . ."[13]

Early investigation of African-American identity centered

around the issues of low self-esteem and self-hatred.[14] The Clark study in which black girls chose white dolls as the prettiest is a case in point. Later, however, there was a total rejection of self-hatred among blacks.

Szasz has suggested that there is no such thing as mental illness, but that the individual we call mentally ill is responding to some life situation.[15] The African American has found himself in a world dominated by white images that are frequently presented as positive and black images that carry negative connotations. Due to prejudice, words in the English language connected with the word "black" are often negative—blacklist, blackball, blackhearted. Because of racial prejudice, they are emotionally loaded as judgments on the very personhood of African Americans. Those connected with the word "white," on the other hand, are often evaluated more positively. A so-called white lie, for example, is not as bad as a regular lie and a white knight is a good guy.

It is virtually impossible to grow up in a society that denigrates people because of skin color and be oblivious to it. On the other hand, to state that the individual is automatically crippled by such attitudes is equally dangerous because it suggests a permanent state of psychic paralysis. What most African Americans feel is what one writer called a sense of "twoness."

> One ever feels his twoness—an American, a Negro; two souls, two thoughts, two unreconciled strivings: two warring ideals in one dark body, whose dogged strength alone keeps it from being torn asunder.[16]

When speaking or thinking of identity, the issue is to develop a wholeness from the experiential duality. There must be a union of one's African being and one's American being. Initially one must deal with the denigration of one's culture by white society. Black, as we have stated, has more often than not been equated with what is negative. That which the white society has attempted to perpetuate on the African American is false and dangerous. To deny that these images have had a negative effect on black people is to deny reality. The job of the counselor is to help the black counselee come to terms with herself; as a black person who has value and absolute self-worth in her own right. We shall return to this issue when we deal specifically with counseling issues.

COUNSELING ISSUES

Given the historical experiences of African Americans, it should come as no surprise that many are suspicious of the counseling process. While blacks have sought counseling from any number of persons in the community such as barbers, bartenders, hairdressers, and the like, they have looked on formal counseling as something alien and have erected barriers to keep from going. This has been especially true of black men, who have been taught to be strong and to take care of their own problems. Other blacks, having been to white clinicians who have been insensitive, have confirmed for themselves the stereotype that counseling or psychotherapy is not for black people. The lack of money has caused many blacks to see counseling as a luxury— especially when the rent is due and the children need clothing.

> The decision to seek psychotherapy flies in the face of culturally revered coping styles in the black community. Emphasis is placed on the active—managing difficult situations without showing stress.[17]

What often happens is that the person will try to resolve the situation in dysfunctional ways, including alcohol abuse, overeating, or domestic violence. These methods are all preferable to seeing a "shrink."

> A thirty-two-year-old black woman went for counseling because she was experiencing difficulty in her marriage. In order to facilitate the counseling, the counselor requested that her husband come to the next session. He came, but he made it clear that he did not believe in counseling and that no one was going to tell him how to conduct his affairs. The counselor tried to reassure him that the purpose of counseling was to reestablish a more satisfying relationship. However, he refused to accept this and walked out in the middle of the session.

Other barriers to counseling for African Americans also exist. One is reluctance to openly discuss personal matters with a stranger.[18] Black people having been betrayed in many ways fear that it may happen again—especially when their counselor happens to be white. For example, a study comparing black children's I.Q. test scores after having first been tested by white psychologists and then by black psychologists found dramatic differences. The children scored as much as fifteen points higher when tested by a black psychologist.[19] Another is mistrust of white people, in general. This is especially true of those raised in the

South.[20] Richard Wright in his autobiography, *Black Boy*, recounts an incident involving two white men and two black men. The white men, wanting to see the two blacks fight, told one black man that the other had insulted him and, as if this were not enough, then told each black man that the other had a knife.[21] The whole episode was a complete fabrication designed to get them to fight. When incidents like these are multiplied, it is no wonder that mistrust has developed.

However, when both counselor and counselee are black, there can still be barriers. The counselee may view the counselor as belonging to a higher class by virtue of his educational background or social status. What is really at stake here, in the case of either a white or black counselor, is the issue of trust. Trust must be built in either case, but trust is often more difficult to establish when the counselor is white.

In a case of cross-cultural counseling, the issue of race should be raised at the first session. An African-American psychologist offers the following advice:

> Although this does not always interfere with the treatment process, at least at the overt level, the willingness of a white clinician to raise the issue of race with a black family often gives the message that "anything can be discussed here," [thus] clearing the air and removing a possible obstacle to the development of trust.[22]

There are enough impediments in counseling so resolving the racial issue is important to a productive relationship. The counselor, however, must also be aware that the counselee may use the racial issue to subvert the counseling process. A warning must be given here: people do not always come to counseling to change their behavior; sometimes they want their dysfunctional behavior sanctioned. At some point in the process, this type of counselee will offer any number of reasons why the therapy is not working. However, the real issue is that he is not prepared to deal with the fundamental issues that are causing difficulty. When all is said and done, this type of resistance to counseling is by no means limited to blacks. It is a universal phenomenon.

> Gerald, a thirty-four-year-old black male, because he felt insecure and sorry for himself and was in a destructive marriage began counseling with a black counselor. Gerald was a successful executive with a major corporation but felt that he had never accomplished very much. His wife, in treatment with another therapist, and not wanting to come in for marital therapy

reinforced this appraisal. She made it a point never to compliment him on any achievement, however great it may have been. Along the way, he reported that his father had been an autocratic, domineering man whose word was law. Then, as the counseling moved in the direction of Gerald's poor self-image and his relationship to his father, he terminated treatment.

Here the issue was not race but the counselee's fear of dealing with a threatening issue. In all fairness, it should be pointed out that the issue of race may not be the major concern of the counselee. In fact, for most black counselees, the issue of race may not be central, but it is certainly in the picture somewhere.

A black West Indian couple made an appointment for counseling in regard to the wife's depression, which was putting a strain on their marriage. They had been referred by someone who did not tell them the race of the therapist. As soon as they entered the treatment room the husband blurted out, "I'm so glad you're black!" The issue of race never came up again, but the fact that the therapist was black obviously influenced the treatment.

In dealing with African Americans, the way in which the counselor presents himself is crucial. A black family therapist uses the concept of "vibes" as a central issue in black culture.[23] Vibes refers to the way in which a person comes across to others. Blacks are particularly attuned to verbal and nonverbal cues. The tone of voice, choice of words, and body language in all its dimensions are key to the development of a good working relationship.

A forty-six-year-old black woman quit therapy after the first visit because the therapist "tossed her check into a drawer as if it was nothing." Because the counselor knew of her modest means, he had charged her less than his usual fee. However, the smaller fee combined with the counselor's action made the counselee deduce that he valued neither her small payment nor her personhood.

In this case, the flight from treatment may have been for many other reasons. The fact remains that the counselee seized on the issue of the check to rationalize leaving counseling, and I mention it here merely to point out that black people are sometimes sensitive to every movement. This does not mean that the counselor must put on an act for the counselee, because this too will be picked up. It does mean that the best policy is to be authentic. The black counselee, for the most part, will respond to that kind of authenticity.

FAMILY COUNSELING

Family counseling with African-American families must take into account three major factors:
1. Kinship bonds and role flexibility.
2. Extended kinship networks.
3. Ecological realities.[24]

The historical realities of black family life mean that the typical white, middle-class norms of family structure do not always apply to black families. There are in the black family, for example, strong kinship bonds between structurally distant relatives such as cousins, uncles, and aunts. In addition, there are others involved with the family who have no blood ties but who may be closer to the family than blood kin.

The structure of some black families also affects traditional roles. Often, for example, the female is employed, but the male is not. In this situation, the father takes over the care of the household, acting as a mother normally would. However, it is not only males who get pressed into the "mother" role. Very often grandparents act as primary caregivers, or "mother," while the real mother is employed. Somehow the traditional roles must be flexible for the black family, especially when the mother's employment takes her away from her children for long periods of time, as in the case of "sleep-in" domestic workers.

It is important to clearly understand this kinship network when doing family counseling. It is naïve always to expect the typical nuclear family constellation. Family therapists suggest the use of the "genogram" to diagram family relationships.[25] The genogram is a graphic representation of the multi-generational system that summarizes family relationships and emotional patterns. It is a psychosocial family tree.

The Jones Family

The Jones family consisted of Mrs. Hyacinthe Jones (age 38), her two children Joseph (age 16) and Susan (age 12), Mrs. Jones' mother, and the sister of Mrs. Jones' mother, Sadie Bynoe, whom the children call "Auntie." The Jones children have different fathers, neither of whom ever married Mrs. Jones. Joseph's father sees him only sporadically. Susan's father is very much involved with her and frequently takes her for weekends.

Joseph, the identified patient, was referred by his high school

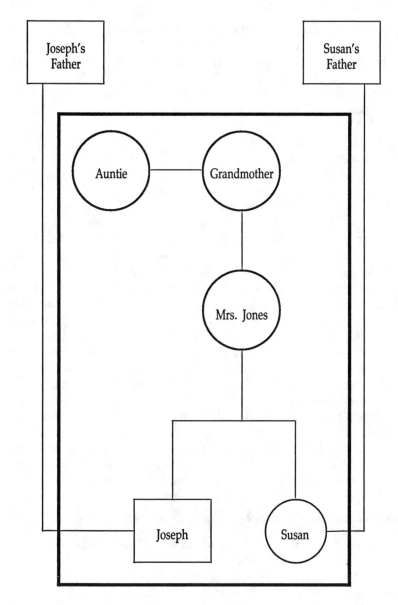

Genogram of Jones Family
(Heavy line encloses those involved in counseling)

guidance counselor. He has frequently been truant and is hostile and belligerent to teachers and fellow students. Mrs. Jones states that she can "do nothing with him." Mrs. Jones has had to work full time as a nurse's aide and often does private duty nursing on weekends in order to make ends meet, because she receives no support from Joseph's father. The genogram in this case would look like this:

Those family members involved in the counseling are bounded by the line around their names. Susan's father refused to participate because he felt that his child was not involved. During the course of treatment it became apparent that Joseph had long been angry at his mother for "chasing his father away." The therapist helped Mrs. Jones explain that Mr. Sneed, Joseph's father, had been an alcoholic who was largely unavailable to the family and that when he did visit, he was verbally and physically abusive. Because of therapy, Mrs. Jones was able to show Joseph an order of protection she had secured because of Mr. Sneed's physical assaults on her; Joseph was able also to express his anger toward Susan, who unwittingly flaunted her relationship with her father; and Mrs. Jones was helped to see that she needed to spend more time with Joseph and provide positive male role models for him. Consequently, she got him involved in a program for teens at the local Baptist church. Both Grandmother Jones and Auntie were counseled to be supportive without undermining Mrs. Jones's authority with her children, which they both had been doing.

The *ecological* model is crucial in working with black inner-city families because it takes into account the many social and economic issues that complicate the family's internal struggles. The Jones family, for example, had to deal with the school authorities, whose only solution to Joseph's problem was to suspend him from school rather than seek the help he obviously needed. It was through the intervention of the pastor at Auntie's church that the guidance counselor was contacted.

When treating black families, many orthodox methods must be discarded and adjustments made to accommodate the unusual situations these families face. Appointments may have to be scheduled at unusual times and the counselor may have to visit the home if the situation warrants. In a word, the counselor must be flexible in order to serve a group of people whose needs are atypical.

SUMMARY

African Americans, making up 11.5 percent of the U.S. population and numbering 30 million, form a unique group. They were violently torn from their motherland, kept in bondage for 300 years, and shamefully mistreated from the time of emancipation until the present. During World War II, German prisoners of war were able to eat in canteens that refused service to black servicemen who had been conscripted to fight for democracy! These historical realities have in part formed the African-American personality and have affected the black family. The counselor who works with black people must be attuned to these facts and be able to use the tools available to him to heal the wounds that inevitably result.

NOTES

[1]The term "African American" is a more accurate sociohistorical appellation than "Black." In this book we will use them interchangeably while believing that "African American" is preferred.

[2]J. H. Franklin, *From Slavery to Freedom: A History of Negro Americans* (New York: Alfred A. Knopf, 1980), 134.

[3]A. Pinkney, *Black Americans* (Englewood Cliffs, N.J.: Prentice-Hall, Inc., 1975), 20–21.

[4]A. Thomas and S. Sillen, *Racism and Psychiatry* (Secaucus, N.J.: Citadel Press, 1972).

[5]A. H. Jenkins, *The Psychology of the Afro-American: A Humanistic Approach* (New York: Pergamon Press, 1982), 173–74.

[6]Franklin, *From Slavery to Freedom*, 311.

[7]J. L. White and T. A. Parham, *The Psychology of Blacks: An African-American Perspective* (Englewood Cliffs, N.J.: Prentice-Hall, 1990), 6.

[8]Thomas and Sillen, *Racism and Psychiatry*, 30.

[9]D. P. Moynihan, *The Negro Family: The Case for National Action* (Washington, D.C.: U.S. Dept. of Labor, Office of Planning and Research, March 1965).

[10]J. W. Blassingame, *The Slave Community: Plantation Life in the Antebellum South* (New York: Oxford Univ. Press, 1979), 150–51.

[11]White and Parham, *The Psychology of Blacks*, 26–27.

[12]Ibid.

[13]Ibid., 42.

[14]Ibid., 42–43.

[15]T. S. Szasz, "The Myth of Mental Illness," *American Psychologist* (1960): 113–18.

[16]W. E. B. DuBois, *The Souls of Black Folk: Essays and Sketches* (Chicago: A. C. McClurg & Co., 1928), 3.

[17]A. S. Marsella and P. B. Pedersen, *Cross-Cultural Counseling and Psychotherapy* (New York: Pergamon Press, 1981), 179.

[18]N. Boyd-Franklin, *Black Families in Therapy: A Multisystems Approach* (New York: Avilford Press, 1989), 102.

[19]R. L. Jones, *Black Psychology* (New York: Harper & Row, 1972), 71.

[20]Ibid., 70.

[21]R. Wright, *Black Boy* (Harper and Brothers, 1937), 207.

[22]Boyd-Franklin, *Black Families in Therapy*, 102.

[23]Ibid., 96.

[24]P. Moore Hines and N. Boyd-Franklin, "Black Families" in M. McGoldrick, J. K. Pearce, and J. Giodano, eds., *Ethnicity and Family Therapy* (New York: Guilford Press, 1982), 86–95.

[25]Ibid., 91.

CHAPTER 8

Counseling Hispanics

LUIS VILLAREAL

COUNSELING HISPANICS is an underrepresented topic in counseling-related journals and books.[1] Generally, research on counseling and psychotherapy for Hispanics shows that many Hispanic counselees have criticized "traditional counseling approaches" as being culturally inappropriate, demeaning, irrelevant, and oppressive.[2] An analogy given by Dr. Jose Angel Cardenas regarding education for Hispanics illustrates the dilemma of giving "ineffectual counseling" to Hispanics. Dr. Cardenas compares the American educational system to a shoe store. He tells the story of Hispanic children "going to the educational shoe store, asking for a size seven, and the salesperson replied that the requested shoes only come in size six."[3] To make the educational "shoes" fit the feet of the Hispanic consumer, the salesperson "cuts off the consumer's toes to make the shoes fit."[4] The salesman's assumption that one size and one style fits all is widely held, even in the field of counseling. The upshot is that Hispanics underutilize and often avoid the whole range of mental-health services offered them.[5]

While underrepresented in psychotherapy received, Hispanics are overrepresented among the poor and lower class.[6] The majority of psychotherapists describe their model of the "good and desirable patient" as one who is "young, attractive, verbal, intelligent, and successful."[7] For the most part, Hispanics (like other low income and minority individuals seeking counseling) do not fulfill the YAVIS stereotype. Most Hispanics seeking therapy have objectives that are "very concrete, sometimes limited, and simple"—much different than those of the typical Anglo-American therapist.[8] If counselees do not clearly communicate these issues and concerns to their counselors, therapists often will make inappropriate inferences and assessments regarding the counselee's needs.[9]

WORLDVIEW

When crossing cultures, it is important to understand that every individual has a worldview unique to his or her culture. Counseling someone from a different culture demands our stepping back and taking an objective inventory of ourselves. Personal perspectives can prevent accurate psychosocial assessment and appropriate intervention patterns that are necessary for effective counseling. An individual raised in a white middle-class community typically views opportunities in careers, housing, and medical care much differently than does a Hispanic family head-of-house who may work in a factory or follow the harvesting of agricultural crops.

Worldviews are composed of attitudes, values, and opinions. They "affect how we think, make decisions, behave, and define events."[10] The detailed components that make up a worldview make it difficult to understand the lifestyle and values of someone outside it. Varying worldviews may act as roadblocks to effective communication across different cultures.

Differing worldviews are shaped by history as well as personal life experiences, and in working with Hispanics, it is important to understand their history. Guerrero[11], for example, cites a history of "physical, psychological, and spiritual colonization" that continues to shape and influence the Hispanic even today. Their low level of trust toward those from the dominant culture, including professional helpers, results from that history, which is filled with evidence of the racial oppression, discrimination, and dominance that shape the worldviews of both the white therapist and the Hispanic client.

One quickly comes to realize that counseling across cultures is filled with potential conflict. Client worldviews, when combined with unexamined and insensitive worldviews in the counselors, may promote division and misunderstanding. The unfiltered worldviews held by many insensitive counselors subtly demand that Hispanics assimilate or accommodate to the style of the dominant society. The only option may be for the Hispanic counselee to avoid or drop out of therapy.

In effective counseling across cultures, the counselor must closely examine both his personal worldview and that of his Hispanic counselee. The counselor must ask self-revealing questions that will help him prepare for the counseling task at hand. These might include: "What stereotypes do I have of Hispanics?" "What has been my history with individuals like my present Hispanic client?" "What value have I given to such people in the past?" "What experiences have shaped such a value or evaluation?" "What am I intending to communicate?" "What am I responding to (person, clothing, skin color, words, facial expressions, silence, body language, style of language)?" "What is my Hispanic client receiving from me?" The therapist should also try to understand the client's worldview by "walking a mile in his shoes." The following questions may be helpful in understanding the Hispanic counselee's point of view: "What history does my Hispanic client have with individuals like myself?" "What is he communicating?" "What is he intending to communicate?" "What is he responding to in me as he sits before me in my office (person, clothing, skin color, vocabulary, expressions, body language, hospitality/reception, office location, seating arrangements, etc.)?" "What words is he communicating?" "What do such words mean to me?" "What meaning do the words have to him?" "Are the meanings different?" "What stereotypes does he have of me?" "What am I receiving from my Hispanic counselee?"

It should be noted that Hispanics tend to prefer Hispanic counselors because they are seen as more credible sources of help. Common skin color and ethnic familiarity encourage trust—a preference that holds consistent across all levels of acculturation.[12] Given this preference, the non-Hispanic counselor faces a difficult task, though not an impossible one. The Hispanic is seeking someone who can understand him and who does not negatively judge his culture or his identity.

CROSSING TO ANOTHER CULTURE

Ineffective communication, coupled with counselor insensitivity, will most likely result in misunderstanding and a negative evaluation of the counselee. For example, if the counselee fails to show up for a scheduled counseling appointment, the counselor may label her as being poorly motivated or unwilling to invest in treatment. In reality, however, the therapist's intended communication may never have reached its target, or the counselee may have been wounded by the counseling interaction. Hispanics drop out of counseling in greater numbers than do individuals from other ethnic groups and they also stay in counseling for shorter periods of time. Much of the reason for this is related to misguided therapy.[13]

Ethnicity and Treatment Fate

Ethnic Group	Treatment Rejection
Hispanics	57%
Blacks	36%
Asians	7%
Whites	0%

Treatment rejection was defined as the rejection of treatment after the intake interview and results were similar to early termination.

V. Gong, "Patient-Therapist Mismatch on Locus of Control and Its Effects on Treatment Rejection by Lower Socioeconomic Minority Patients," Unpublished Doctoral Dissertation, City University of New York, 1984 (60).

The question can then be raised, "Should the therapist be expected to adapt to the cultural expectations of the Hispanic client, or should the Hispanic client be expected to adapt to the cultural expectations of the therapist?"[14] What leads to the best results? The answer is that it is less desirable for the clients to "conform to the therapist's expectations (conformity prescriptions) than for treatment to be reformulated to fit the client's expectation, which some have called reformity prescription."[15] Unfortunately, the former occurs most frequently because counselors are characteristically inflexible and bound to their worldview.

WHEN HISPANICS DO REQUEST HELP

For most Hispanics, the family is the most important social unit.[16] Hispanics view the family as a reliable reservoir of emotional and spiritual strength.[17] After the nuclear family, Hispanics, first, go to extended-family members for assistance with emotional difficulties and, then, to close friends or neighbors. Hispanics who are in need characteristically move toward their kin network for help, in contrast to Anglo-Americans who move away from their kin networks.[18]

While one might traditionally diagnose this dependence on the family as detrimental, pathological enmeshment, this is often not the case with Hispanics. Their traditional agrarian existence focused on the importance of the family and community, not the individual, which in turn promoted a healthy interdependence and the carrying of one another's burdens. When one suffered, all suffered. Thus, everyone in the nuclear and extended families was concerned. Communal concern and care is a well-known cultural theme of the Hispanic and is clearly supported by Scripture.

Underlying the request for care is the issue of trust. Hispanics value highly the recommendations of family and friends as to which professionals they should turn to for help with emotional difficulties. The client wants personal care[19] and if a family member or close friend was helped by someone, then this recommendation is particularly significant. A professional counselor's education and expertise are of secondary importance.

It is obvious, then, that the professional counselor may be the last resource for a prospective Hispanic client. When Hispanics do request psychotherapy, they want it now, immediately. It is not unusual for a Hispanic family to equate the role of the family therapist with that of a pastor or a priest, and to expect immediate help, such as spiritual absolution through confession or interceding prayer. They want immediate help and they prefer help that is directive and concrete. An indirect style of counseling is less appealing. It is typically interpreted as "distant" and "uncaring," leaves the impression that the therapist does not want to be involved or does not genuinely care.

Since the Hispanic family is strongly hierarchical and therefore quite authoritarian in structure, there is a deeply ingrained respect verging on obedience for the counselor, who is seen as the expert. This respect often promotes a guarded or passive reception of the assistance given, however, due to the newness of the relationship. Initially, counselees use indirect statements to convey resistance or disagreement.[20] Some therapists would label this guardedness and nonchallenging presentation-of-self as pathological and extremely passive. One must be careful, however, to view it in its cultural context. It is most likely merely a sign of respect toward the counselor's role and not an inability to disagree or to assert oneself.

To insure an accurate assessment and the elicitation of the counselee's true feelings, the counselor should solicit feedback from the Hispanic client in a subtle manner, instead of presenting a direct demand for complete disclosure. Therapy must be attentive and affective in tone. "Does this make any sense?"

"Which piece of what I have said makes more sense than others?"
"Which parts of what I said don't seem very clear?" A subtle
approach avoids alienating and embarrassing the client while at
the same time respecting and preserving privacy.

The Hispanic family seems to respond best to short-term
counseling (four to ten weeks) that is focused on the present and
is "problem-oriented."[21] To many Hispanics, long treatment
suggests a poor prognosis for improvement and personal motivation and investment in the problem-solving process are likely to be
discouraging. While open-ended treatment drags on until the
counselee finally decides that improvement has eluded her,
treatment for a short length of time often increases the chances of
success. In fact, change seems to come more readily in the first
four to ten weeks of treatment than later in the treatment process.[22] Actual and desired change seems to vastly decrease after this
brief period, but the positive change may be credited to an
expectation of change on the part of the client and the therapist. A
brief therapy schedule forces counselees to be motivated toward
change, anticipate it, look for it, and seek to achieve it.

In the past, the use of folk medicine among Hispanics to meet
mental health needs was a common practice. During the last
twenty years, however, such practices have declined. The role of
curanderos ("those who can 'cure' and claim to have some skill in
the healing arts"[23]) in East Los Angeles, for example, has been
declining.[24] In related research of 400 Hispanics, fewer than 1
percent of the respondents sought curanderos for emotional and
psychiatric disturbances. With the increased numbers of medical
professionals and the improved economic position of more
Hispanics, the overall use of the curandero has decreased. Even
so, curanderos, those who manipulate not only the supernatural
world but also the physical world for the healing of sick clients,[25]
still practice. In the poorer, more rural areas, curanderos have
always been more popular because of the unavailability or the
exorbitant cost of professional medical care.

Curanderos who use their services for mental health purposes
commonly do not divide the natural from the supernatural as
Anglos do. Emotional problems are often seen by Hispanics as
emanating from God or other spiritual forces, and are seen as the
result of an imbalance between those forces. As a result, the
people always seek a harmonious relationship between the natural
and the supernatural because a lack of harmony can produce an
undesired illness or bad luck.[26] Curanderos are usually sought out

for this purpose. For example, Hispanics believe that one can be hexed (*embrujado*) or given the evil eye (*mal ojo*). If such an equilibrium is not found, someone—a curandero—must be mediator between the sufferer and the evil spirit causing the disruption. Surprisingly, the curandero's role as mediator is even viewed by some as scripturally sanctioned (at least according to their interpretation of 1 Corinthians 2:7–11 and James 5:14). According to their interpretation, the role and ability of the healer is seen as a gift or *don* given by God, just as he gives other spiritual gifts. The healer's faith in God as well as faith displayed by the person seeking to be healed are considered mandatory for the desired healing to take place.

HOLISTIC TREATMENT CONSIDERATIONS

As stated earlier, Hispanics are overrepresented among the poor. Due to the contextual needs that may arise, the counselor must be holistic in his counseling approach. Concrete needs like food or housing may interfere with successful psychological or spiritual counseling. According to Scripture, it seems clear that man is not a bodyless soul or soulless body.[27] Instead, God created man a body-soul-in-community, and therefore "if we seek to serve our client as God made him, we must inevitably be concerned for his total welfare, the good of his soul, his body, and his community."[28] This is especially true with Hispanics because of their predominantly lower socioeconomic status.

The counselor's role may become that of an advocate or mediator on behalf of the counselee. The interrelated issues of discrimination, oppression, and racism as they affect the counselee's ability to function may have to be addressed by the counselor through advocacy and mediation on his behalf. It is not uncommon, for example, for a child's low educational functioning to be related to stress at home. Without proper networking by the therapist, the school or other agencies may initiate changes that will give the school relief but in the end will significantly disrupt and retard the future educational and psychosocial development of the child. Thus, it is the responsibility of the counselor to address such contextual issues even if they fall outside of the traditional counseling framework. It is critical for the counselor to avoid "victim-blaming." Many of life's variables are outside the counselee's personal control. These need to be confronted, but in the meantime, they negatively impact the counselee's emotional state.

COUNSELING IS A MOVE TOWARD FRIENDSHIP

The traditional role of most trained counselors is one of emotional distance from the client. If a client solicits any personal information from the counselor, the counselor has been trained to subtly redirect the questions back to the client. It is often taught that responding to such questions would only cause the counselor to lose his objectivity. His ability to effectively confront and assist the counselee would be thereby diminished. It is also feared that the loss of objectivity could result in the therapist's enmeshment in the family system's dysfunction, thus diminishing his therapeutic value.

Such a position of professional distance can easily be interpreted by the Hispanic counselee as being unfriendly. If, indeed, this perception is made, it will work against the healing process. As stated earlier, Hispanics want personal care. When Hispanics request treatment, they are entrusting their lives to one deemed trustworthy. Though psychotherapy may begin in a formal and reserved fashion, Hispanics slowly move toward establishing a close relationship and even friendship with the counselor. The premise here is that one shares the private, personal details of one's life only with people one can trust, which for the Hispanic is a friend. The personal sharing of one's life (*personalismo*), and the focus on relationships instead of tasks are important cultural characteristics of the Hispanic. The foundational thinking here is that distant and impersonal helpers are easy to find. Helpers who are friends, however, are of great value, and can accompany one all through life, which is perceived as an endurance run, and close friends are essential to persevere in the ordeal ahead.[29]

Over the course of therapy, then, the counselee may come to view the counselor in an almost "kinship" fashion.[30] In contrast to Hispanics, Anglo-Americans are often very casual and friendly at the time of initial introduction. When social intimacy finally does develop for the Anglo-American, however, "they will customarily continue to maintain a certain distance,"[31] and fail to attain the enduring closeness that characterizes Hispanic culture.

It is not uncommon for Hispanic counselees to give small gifts or food to their counselor in order to display appreciation for help received. Such gifts are also an acknowledgement and affirmation of the valued relationship. Sometimes a gift may be the only means of payment possible for poorer families, or it may be an intermediate step for delayed payment. The gesture, however, is one of appreciation from the client to the counselor. To reject their gifts is to reject them[32] and to generate mistrust. Typically, the traditional view of counseling would interpret such behavior as manipulative or as a way to avoid difficult issues relating to the counselee's dysfunction. That is not the case. Among Hispanics, friends readily express love, care, and appreciation for each other and the giving of gifts is one such expression.

THE ACCULTURATION AND ASSIMILATION CONTINUUM

To understand Hispanics is not to understand every Hispanic. There are those who are almost completely Anglo or acculturated on one end of a Hispanic cultural continuum, and those who are completely Hispanic or unacculturated at the extreme and opposite end. One who is acculturated has given up his "old ways" and has become completely Anglicized by adopting the new ways of the Anglo culture.[33]

The client's amount of cultural assimilation must also be considered in order to accurately assess his position along the continuum. Assimilation is similar to acculturation in that it refers to the extent "an individual becomes a part of a given culture."[34] In other words, How well is the Hispanic accepted by the dominant Anglo culture? Does he retain his language and ethnic identity? Acculturation and assimilation can be assessed by examining diet, preferred language, clothing style, traditions claimed, circle of friends and acquaintances, and dominant activities. One can be acculturated and yet not be assimilated, or vise versa.

The fully acculturated and assimilated client may best be assisted by an approach used with middle-class Anglos. Hispanics on the opposite end of the continuum would be best suited to an approach that is more culturally relevant. Persons termed bicultural (somewhere in the middle) require an approach that takes into account the influence and strength of both cultures in the life of the client. In determining the appropriate approach to treatment, the therapist must understand that regardless of where on the continuum the client falls, there will be specific psychological stresses for that client because the adoption or consideration of new cultural values or a new culturally driven identity always introduces new stresses.

However, in all of this, one must not disregard the role played by factors like oppression and discrimination. The imposition of unjust and harmful burdens and the experience of debilitating and differential treatment because of one's culture or ethnicity obviously affect one's ability to function.

INTERVENTION WITH THE HISPANIC MALE: IS IT POSSIBLE?

Much has been written about the topic of *machismo*, which refers to the Hispanic male's sense of manliness and virility. The case is made that Hispanic boys are raised to be aggressive, tough, stoic, courageous, yet distant and self-controlled in the expression of feelings and pain. The Hispanic male in his role as father is seen as the ultimate disciplinarian and final authority. He is seen as dominant, the protector of his woman and children, while acting as primary provider.[35] Often this description of the male discourages his participation in therapy because it promotes the denial of illness, feelings, pain, or difficulties in the family. To gu ird the family's privacy, the Hispanic male is characteristically silent. It is said that when feelings surge to the surface, Hispanic men attempt to divert them.[36] These stereotypes often lead to the misconception that the Hispanic male is an improbable therapy participant who has no personal desire to get involved with outsiders.

In spite of the possible misinterpretation of the Hispanic male as being strictly macho, it must be clearly stated that the stereotypical machismo of the Hispanic male still exists. At the same time that the male is claiming the role of the protector and defender of his family he will demand absolute autonomy as he engages in adolescent-type activities like excessive drinking, time away from his family with his peers, and extramarital sexual conquests.[37] Such autonomy automatically rejects any attempts by wife or family to get him to account for his time or his money.

However, when push comes to shove and outsiders seek contact with the male head of the family they are likely to be intercepted by the wife, girlfriend, or live-in female friend who shields him from such inquiries. While the woman may not like her role, her inability to assert herself against his demands for absolute autonomy wins out. This is substantiated in many ways.

The female may answer his telephone calls, letting him choose which calls he will return. (This carries the lowest risk for him.) The woman may also carry messages to others on behalf of her male partner, whether to creditors, landlords, or school officials. She, in effect, becomes the representative of the macho male. Ironically, the wife or female partner thus becomes the macho male's protector from those outside the family circle.

The woman may complain privately about such an arrangement, but in those relationships where machismo is the norm, she has come to accept her role as being her destiny. She often consoles herself by thinking that when the time comes, she will encourage something different for her children.

The relationship of the macho male to his wife can also be seen as an ambiguous husband-son role.[38] He is very demanding, yet very much dependent on his wife for the practical matters of everyday living. Minuchin describes the macho male as a person who believes that his duty ends with his role as provider. He strongly feels that he has consequently "earned his freedom" from the family[39] and such freedom logically follows from the responsibility. The dilemma, however, comes in the male's struggle to become an integral part of the family at the same time his emphasis on independence has pushed him to its emotional fringes. The man who dominates his wife usually causes her to become alienated from him, with the children usually replacing him as the significant other in her life.

Close examination of Hispanic families shows that this description of the male can sometimes be inaccurate. While the husband may appear domineering, he often relies heavily on his wife for major decisions and the handling of the finances. With more Hispanic women obtaining employment outside the home, there has been a shift toward a more egalitarian power structure.[40] An increase in earning power does often translate into a shift in the governing and decision-making power. Though Hispanic males and females may initially espouse patriarchal attributes, research shows that decision making was a shared skill instead of a male-dominated skill only. It seems that where the male was the overbearing and domineering one, it was usually in a dysfunctional family system.[41] In spite of the shifting norms within the Hispanic marital subsystem, the strong stereotypes of machismo still prevail, however.

Further examination of the Hispanic male often reveals a positive side to the stereotypical view of machismo. The male's aloofness can be a reaction to the way the dominant society regards him. The macho male is portrayed as one lacking feelings for others. He is described as being dominated by his personal hedonistic pleasure at his family's expense. For the Hispanic to open his life to a professional counselor who holds such a view would be to agree with the stereotypes.

There is a proverb, popular in the Southwest that says, "*Pretencioso, flojo y vano, Mexicano.*" Translated, it means, "Pretentious, lazy, and vain is the Mexican." After years of hearing this said, the Hispanic male will likely resist anyone who seeks to help him. This, and other sayings like it, probably influences the male to be stoic and strong, and allows him to perpetuate the negative portrayal that others impose on him.

Machismo must be understood systemically, however. The first thing that we must understand is the Hispanic male's need to be strong, to *sobrevivir*, to survive. To survive means that the Hispanic male must develop an ability to conceal any and all weaknesses, or else his family will suffer. Stereotypes, misinterpretations, and mistreatment he has experienced convince him that those outside the family will never help. The proverb, "*Con los anos vienen los desenganos,*" which translated means, "As the years pass I see things more as they are," strengthens the resolve to be strong. If he can be strong, his family will be strong, and they will survive. To his way of thinking, cooperation with outside forces would prove futile at best and dangerous at worst.

The second thing we must understand is that his quietness, or what seems to be noninvolvement, should not always be interpreted as unwillingness to improve himself or his family. Instead, a close look at the Hispanic male will usually show a deep sense of loyalty and responsibility toward his family. These qualities can become a bridge rather than a barrier to engaging Hispanic males in therapy.

Given these principles, and in order to effectively intervene in therapy, the counselor must decide to recruit the Hispanic male. Recruitment means to get the Hispanic male to address the difficulties in his family. As in any recruitment attempt the recruiter must play the role of a salesman. The salesman (counselor) seeks to sell a product he believes the client needs. He must convince the potential customer (Hispanic male) of the need for the product. (In the actual field of sales, convincing the client may involve manipulating the truth. In counseling, it does not.) In the recruitment process, the counselor must inform the Hispanic male that his help is badly needed and that his input is an important factor in his family's ability to function well. (If God has appointed the husband and father to the primary leadership role in the family, the counselor must assist in the healthy execution of that role.) The counselor may say something like, "I need your help with a difficulty that I have been presented with regarding your family. Your view of the family is extremely important. Can we possibly meet briefly about this?" This approach affirms the Hispanic's leadership, wisdom, and importance. In essence, the therapist is emphasizing the positive side of machismo and the centrality of the father in the family.[42]

THE HISPANIC FEMALE

The Hispanic female has traditionally been described as one whose lot in life is dominated by *la sufrida*, or "destiny of suffering." The dominant theme for the Hispanic female, many say, is that she must suffer for the sake and love of the family. It is a role that is deeply entrenched by tradition and her own observations of her mother. Female children are "taught that their destiny includes three areas: superlative femininity, the home, and maternity."[43] The Hispanic female is admired and protected, and her feminity is reinforced only in the years before marriage. Once married, she assumes a maternal, subservient role shaped by the theme of self-sacrifice or *la sufrida*. Because her needs are the last to be fulfilled, she struggles to be assertive. The female will display much public passivity but much private aggressiveness toward her children and although obedient in public to the direction of her macho partner, she will privately express anger about his irresponsibility and lack of communication.

The dominant (Anglo) view may accept the view that Hispanic women are trained to be fatalistic, passive, nonassertive, and ultimately masochistic and dysfunctional. Hispanics, however, provide an alternative view. Altruism and the sacrifice of one's time and energy for the family is highly regarded and considered a godly virtue. After all, to give one's life for another is even scriptural—Jesus did it. Self-denial and suffering, then, are promoted in different religious rituals of the Catholic faith.[44]

Whereas men may acquire power by demanding respect (*respeto*), mothers generally derive their power from love.[45] Although the father may be respected, he may not be loved like the mother. The mother comes first and is held in the highest esteem. This is the reward that balances out la sufrida for the female.

This so-called *marianismo*, or covert centrality of the mother is positive as long as there is respect for both mother and father and both are affirmed in their roles and functions. A systemic problem arises, however, when the "self-sacrificing mother" is given high esteem by family members at the expense of respect, love, and good relations with the father. This produces an unhealthy imbalance in the family with the father's leadership diminished and the marital structure taking on the appearance of having an overadequate mother, an underadequate father, and a devalued family.

In this kind of unhealthy arrangement, the children's love may become the emotional focus for each parent, taking the place of the emotional investment in the marital relationship. Minuchin calls this a "blurring of the boundaries" between the marital subsystem and the subsystem of the children.[46] The ultimate tragedy, however, comes at the time the children leave the home. The parents may ultimately find themselves estranged from each other and considering and then seeking divorce. Some, however, stay married for the "sake of the children" and because "God and the Church" speak against divorce. For all practical purposes, however, the pair are already emotionally, physically, and spiritually divorced.

Therapeutically, there is a danger in looking at the Hispanic female with pity and sympathy. Pity produces a diminished view of her psychosocial functioning. Likewise, one must not be quick to incriminate the Hispanic male for "subjugating her." Advocating a more egalitarian life for the wife may be culturally inappropriate as well. Any assessment procedures must address the possible maneuvering of each marital partner, and the ways in which these maneuvers have affected the family's structure. Inelegantly asked, "What is the payoff of this kind of marital arrangement?" As Jay Haley has claimed, "To describe a marriage or union as one where there is a dominating husband and a dependent wife does not include the idea that the wife might be provoking her husband to be dominating so that actually she is the dominating force of what sort of relationship they have."[47] "Helpless maneuvers may actually be the powerful agents in managing whatever happens in the relationship."[48] The acceptable Hispanic family norm of functioning called *marianismo* or *hembrismo*, is often the foundation of these maneuverings.

Hispanics accord the family much importance. Therefore, treatment must be oriented toward the family system instead of exclusively focusing on any one individual. The female may initiate the treatment and may describe her man in stereotypical fashion, but if the therapist agrees to meet with the female client alone, he may alienate her husband who, in turn, may refuse treatment. When it is impossible to see the male and female together during the initial session, it is recommended that any meeting with the woman alone should be followed by a subsequent meeting with her husband alone. This demonstrates respect for his leadership role in the family, and gives the man the important opportunity to give his side of the story before the counselor proceeds to examine the larger family arrangement. This adjustment helps the couple feel that they are on equal footing as they begin counseling. It also removes the stigma that one of them is to blame.

HISPANIC CHILDREN

Children are highly regarded in the Hispanic culture. Some would even go so far as to say that children take on more importance than the marriage relationship itself. In his article, "Mexican American Families," Falicov states that "it is the existence of children that validates and cements the marriage."[49]

Children are taught several very important principles that shape who they are. First, Hispanic children are taught to have respect (*respeto*), which means a dependence on and duty to those in authority. Second, Hispanic children are taught to be cooperative rather than competitive, which stands in stark contrast to the competitiveness and achievement orientation of Anglo-American children.[50] However, cooperation should not be interpreted as a tendency toward passivity, but rather as a desire that all involved be taken into account, and that everyone's needs be considered. Third, Hispanic children are taught to be loyal. The children are taught that the family itself is the most important resource in life. The family is a place of refuge and strength for the child and as a result there is deep pride regarding one's membership in his family. In spite of these early lessons, when Hispanics swing into the mainstream of American society, such cultural distinctions gradually change.

On the other end of the loyalty-to family spectrum, Hispanic children are taught that they may not be able to trust the world outside of the family. The family is the resource of love and support. In a study of young Hispanic children ages seven to thirteen, it was concluded that "in the child's eye view the central feature is the home, and the people at home."[51] Hispanic children are given their self-confidence, worth, security, and identity through membership in the family.[52] This push for the centrality of the family can be seen as a positive survival and self-preservation response to the discrimination and oppression that it often receives from society at large.

HOW TO BEGIN TREATMENT

It is culturally correct to begin treatment with the father or both parents (parental subsystem) by asking them to describe their reasons for coming to treatment. To begin with the children would be to show disrespect for the hierarchy of the family, and would most likely doom the therapy. Beginning with the parental subsystem gives importance to parents and supports the boundaries separating them from the subsystem of the children. If the wife or a child in a traditional Hispanic family takes the lead in the initial, problem-definition stage of treatment, the therapist should use that data to ask questions about the overall functioning of the family.

As a way to understand and best assess the family, the therapist may want to join the family, a process that Minuchin describes as "emphasizing the aspects of his personality and experience that are syntonic with the family's."[53] This helps the therapist to feel the difficulty or dysfunction of the family and is in keeping with the Hispanic's cultural view of relationships—those with whom one is close will share something of their private lives and personalities. A couple of words of caution are necessary though. The therapist must be sure to retain his freedom to therapeutically interject those measures he deems necessary, and to avoid the pitfall of becoming enmeshed in the family's dysfunction. The therapist must accommodate to the family system only to the extent that he is able to assess the stress and pain of the family.

In gathering information about the identified problem(s), the therapist will develop a working hypothesis of the problem. At the end of each therapy session, it is helpful for the therapist to give the family a small homework assignment related to the identified problem. This is consistent with the family's expectation—the therapist must be direct and issue concrete assistance. The assignment should be something simple that can easily be attained or completed. When the homework is returned, assess its completeness, but do not blame the family if they fail to carry out the assignment. Unlike Anglo-Americans, Hispanics are sometimes uncomfortable with the idea of scheduling certain times to express affection or resolve problems.[54] Hispanics more readily value "serendipity, chance and spontaneity in interpersonal relationships."[55] Homework should be given with this cultural value in mind. You will find, though, that many families will complete their homework in spite of this cultural trait.

The therapist must not hesitate to evaluate the content of his homework or instructions to the family. The family may complete the assignment poorly or not at all because the counselor's instructions were faulty or poorly communicated. The homework chosen by the therapist must always be translated into the client's own language, and here I do not mean either English or Spanish. The homework must account for the client's worldview or his way of conceptualizing reality. When clients fail to carry out the work the therapist has assigned there is a natural inclination to blame the victim, which in this case is the client. Failure, however, always involves the input of two parties, which in this case includes the therapist.

THE CHURCH, PRAYER, AND THE HISPANIC CLIENT

The church is highly important in the life of the Hispanic, especially when emotional problems arise. It is not uncommon for Hispanics to seek help at their church. At the church, Hispanics try many different paths in their search for help. They will make promises to God in the form of personal deprivations (resembling the practice of fasting) as a way to persuade him to answer their prayers for relief through supernatural intervention. (Hispanic Catholics are no different from Protestants and cultic groups in this regard.) Many Hispanic Catholics in the Southwest will offer medals, amulets, candles, prayer offerings, and votive offerings as a way of "paying" for relief from God.[56] Others will pay for church novenas or masses. Some Hispanics may believe that their emotional discomfort is a punishment from God for their sinful living. They petition, therefore, for God's forgiveness and mercy.

It does not take a very large leap to realize that prayer, the reading of Scripture, or the recitation of Scripture by the therapist can play a very significant role in therapy. Whereas offerings, medals, amulets, promises, and different forms of deprivation have the purpose of keeping evil away from the client, prayer and the use of Scripture in therapy have the clear purpose of drawing the Lord near to the client. The emphasis has to be on the "drawing near" of something positive, as opposed to an emphasis on keeping away the negative. Just as a child and a parent can comfort each other and know each other best through an intimate friendship, so the client, through prayer and Scripture, is drawn to God, his maker, whose specialty is loving, helping, and protecting humanity. He is the Great Physician and Counselor.

Hispanics readily welcome prayer and the use of Scripture in therapy sessions. They have a deep respect for the work and ministry of God in the Trinity. The reading of Scripture is viewed as a personal, tailor-made intervention of comfort or admonition for the client. Given to the client in typewritten form, Scripture that articulates a promise from God is, in fact, useful.

It should be carefully and nonmanipulatively stressed in therapy that Jesus Christ desires a relationship with the client. Christ's desire is to push evil away, and to draw closer to humanity. Jesus wants to be a close friend and a Savior to the client. Although close relationships are highly esteemed by Hispanics, a close friendship with God is somewhat foreign to the culture. Still, friendship with God is something that a Hispanic welcomes rather than shuns and this openness to the moving of God's Spirit makes the Hispanic receptive to spiritual counseling input. A poor Hispanic has very little to trust in materially, but James 2:5 holds true, "the poor are rich in faith" because God himself becomes trust.

NOTES

[1]Derald W. Sue, *Counseling the Culturally Different* (New York: John Wiley & Sons, 1981), xi.

F. Acosta, J. Yamamoto, L. A. Evans, and S. A. Wilcox, *Effective Psychotherapy for Low-Income and Minority Patients* (New York: Plenum Press, 1982), 1.

Carmen Fernandez, "Cultural Implications in the Mental Health Delivery Systems for Spanish-Speaking Population," in E. R. Myers, ed., *Race and Culture in Mental Health Service Delivery Systems* (Washington, D.C.: University Press of America, 1981), 98.

A. G. Wilkeson, "Mexican Americans," in Gaw Albert, ed., *Cross-Cultural Psychiatry* (Boston: John Wrigth PSG Inc., 1982), 98.

Carmen Carrillo, "Changing Norms of Hispanic Families: Implications for Treatment," in E. Jones and S. Korchin, eds., *Minority Mental Health* (New York: Praeger, 1982), 252.

[2]Wilkeson, 88.

Sue, 1981, xi.

Albert Vasquez, "Chicago, Chicano, and Mexicanos: A Community Perspective," in G. Gibson, ed., *Our Kingdom Stands On Brittle Glass* (Silver Spring: National Association of Social Workers, 1983), 82.

[3]A. G. Guerrero, *A Chicano Theology* (New York: Orbis Books, 1987), 50.

[4]Ibid.

[5]R. A. Ruiz and M. J. Casas, "Culturally Relevant and Behaviorist Counseling for Chicano College Students," in P. B. Pedersen, J. Draguns, W. J. Lonner, and J. E. Trimble, eds., *Counseling Across Cultures* (Honolulu: Hawaii Univ. Press, 1976), 181.

[6]Carillo, 250.

[7]W. Schofield, *Psychotherapy, the Picture of Friendship* (Englewood Cliffs: Prentice Hall, 1964).

Acosta, Yamamoto, Evans, and Wilcox, 5.

[8]Ibid.

[9]Sue, 28.

[10]Sue, 73.

[11]Guerrero, 25.

[12]F. Ponce and D. R. Atkinson, "Mexican-American Acculturation, Counselor Ethnicity, Counseling, and Perceived Credibility," *Journal of Counseling* 36 (2) (1989): 203–8.

Vasquez, 82.

[13]Acosta, Yamamoto, Evans, and Wilcox, 3.

F. Baekeland and L. Lundwall, "Dropping Out of Treatment: A Critical Review," *Psychological Bulletin* 82 (1975): 738–83.

[14]P. B. Pedersen, "The Cultural Inclusiveness of Counseling," in P. B. Pedersen, J. Draguns, W. J. Lonner, and J. E. Trimble, eds., *Counseling Across Cultures* (Honolulu: Hawaii Univ. Press, 1976), 36.

[15]B. Gomes-Schwartz, S. W. Hadley, and H. H. Strupp, "Individual Psychotherapy and Behavior Therapy," *Annual Review of Psychotherapy* 29 (1978): 435–72.

A. Goldstein, "Expectancy Efforts in Cross-Cultural Counseling," in A. J. Marsella and D. Pedersen, eds., *Cross-Cultural Therapy* (New York: Pergamon, 1981).

[16]N. Murillo, "The Mexican-American Family," in M. J. Haug and N. N. Wagner, eds., *Chicanos: Social and Psychological Perspectives* (St. Louis: C. V. Mosby Co., 1971).

[17]J. I. Escobar and E. T. Randolf, "The Hispanic and Social Networks," in R. M. Becerra, M. Karno, and J. I. Escobar, eds., *Mental Health and Hispanic Americans: Clinical Perspectives* (New York: Grune and Stratton, 1982), 47.

Bernal and Flores-Ortiz, "Latino Families in Therapy," *Journal of Marital and Family Therapy* 8 (1982): 357–65.

M. K. Ho, *Family Therapy with Ethnic Minorities* (Newbury Park: Sage Publications, 1987), 124.

[18]C. H. Mindel, "Extended Families Among Urban Mexicans," *Hispanic Journal of Behavioral Sciences* 2 (1) (1980): 21–34.

[19]Bach-y-Rita, "The Mexican American: Religious and Cultural Influences," in R. M. Becerra, M. Karno, and J. I. Escobar, eds., *Mental Health and Hispanic Americans: Clinical Perspectives* (New York: Grune and Stratton, 1982), 38–39.

[20]C. J. Falicov, "Mexican American Families," in M. McGoldrick, J. K. Pearce, J. Giordano, eds., *Ethnicity and Family Therapy* (New York: Guilford Press, 1982), 149.

Escobar and Randolf, 151.

[21]Falicov, 147–48.

[22]P. Watzlawick, J. H. Weakland, and R. Fisch, *Change* (New York: W. W. Norton and Co., 1974), 113.

[23]R. T. Trotter and J. A. Chavira, *Curanderismo* (Athens: Univ. of Georgia Press, 1981), 1.

[24]R. B. Edgerton, M. Karno and Fernandez, "Curanderismo in the Metropolis: The Diminishing Role of Folk Psychiatry Among Los Angeles Mexican Americans," *American Journal of Psychotherapy* 24 (1) (1970): 124–34.

[25]Ibid., 9.

[26]Ibid., 14.

W. Madsen, *The Mexican Americans of South Texas* (New York: Holt, Rinehart and Winston, 1964), 68.

[27]J. Scott, *Christian Mission in the Modern World* (Downers Grove: InterVarsity Press, 1975), 29–30.

[28]Ibid.

[29]Pedro Ruiz, "The Hispanic Patient: Sociocultural Perspectives," in R. Becerra, M. Karno, and J. I. Escobar, eds., *Mental Health and Hispanic Americans: Clinical Perspectives* (New York: Grune and Stratton, 1982), 22.

[30]Falicov, 148.

[31]Ibid.

[32]Ruiz, "The Hispanic Patient," 23.

[33]Ruiz and Casas, 194.

[34]Ibid., 195

[35]Falicov, 139.

[36]Bach-y-Rita, 37.

[37]S. Minuchin, *Families of the Slums* (New York: Basic Books, 1967), 239.

[38]Ibid.

[39]Ibid.

[40]G. Hawkes and M. Taylor, "Power Structure in Mexican and Mexican-American Farm Labor Families," *Journal of Marriage and the Family* 31 (1975): 807–11.

S. Mirande, *The Chicano Experience* (Notre Dame: Univ. Press, 1985), 156–57.

[41]G. Canino, "The Hispanic Woman: Sociocultural Influences on Diagnosis and Treatment," in R. M. Becerra, M. Karno, J. I. Escobar, eds., *Mental Health and Hispanic Americans: Clinical Perspectives* (New York: Grune and Stratton, 1982), 124.

[42]Falicov, 140.

[43]Wilkeson, 89–90.

[44]Bach-y-Rita, 33.

[45]Ruiz, 22.

[46]S. Minuchin, *Families in Family Therapy* (Cambridge: Harvard Univ. Press, 1974), 53–56.

[47]Jay Haley, "Marriage Therapy," in G. D. Erickson and T. B. Hogan, eds., *Family Therapy: An Introduction to Therapy and Techniques* (Monterey: Brooks Cole, 1972), 180–210.

[48]Ibid.

[49]Falicov, 140.

[50]G. Canino, 129.

[51]M. Goodman and A. Beman, "Child's-Eye-Views of Life in an Urban Barrio," in N. N. Wagner and M. J. Haug, eds., *Chicanos: Social and Psychological Perspective* (St. Louis: C. V. Mosby, 1971), 111.

[52]Keung Jo, 124.

[53]Minuchin, *Families in Family Therapy*, 91.

[54]Falicov, 153.

[55]Ibid.

[56]Ibid., 146.

SECTION THREE

Pressing Problems

Introduction

WE NOW TURN our attention to the critical problems that the urban pastor or counselor will inevitably face. The issues examined in this section are not unique to the city, but they are unquestionably exacerbated by the urban setting. The sheer concentration of these problems in cities makes them infinitely more intractable. In suburban or rural areas, the same types of problems are more amenable to intervention because resources are not strained to the breaking point as they are in the inner cities. Administrators in large cities frantically look for assistance from the federal government because the problems they face are not municipal but national. People migrate to the cities looking for a better life, only to have their hopes dashed by a multitude of forces that militate against their aspirations. Frequently the urban migrant turns to dysfunctional ways of anesthetizing his pain, but the original problem is compounded when these methods fail.

As we noted in section two, ethnic minorities are drawn to the city. They struggle, as do whites, with the same issues, but they do so with the added overlay of racism. What might be considered merely an obstacle by a white urbanite becomes an impenetrable barrier to a minority person when racism is injected. When a society denies its people of color even the most basic rights, they must find alternative means to achieve their objectives. Unfortunately, these means are then labeled "deviant" by the larger society. Because it affects both the perpetrator and the victim, this so-called deviant behavior contributes to the distress of living in the city.

The city, as we have stressed, is the home of the immigrant—

those from within the country and those who have come to our shores from other lands. One issue that all migrants must deal with is rootlessness. They have left behind the supports that nurtured them all their lives: community, church, and family. The city is heartless and the migrant finds himself alone and anonymous before its cold, compassionless face. Despite the poverty and problems at home, there he at least knew who he was and where he stood in the community. In the city he has no status, so he must try to create one, sometimes in ways that society does not condone.

The scene we have sketched is not a pretty one, but life in the city is often not pretty. The urban landscape is painted in drab tones, but the urban church has the potential to present another palette with brighter and more pleasing colors. In the words of Jesus, we are to "heal the brokenhearted."

With this in mind, this section presents some of the major issues you will confront as you minister to the pain of those within and outside of your church family. We sent a questionnaire to a sample of urban pastors and asked them to rank the problems they saw as causing the most distress. The problems highlighted herein are ones urban pastors consider the most pressing.

It may come as a surprise to some that drugs have not been included. Interestingly enough, our pastor-respondents did not rank this very high on their lists. Drugs are so pervasive in the urban center that they lie at the heart of many problems in the city. They are certainly related to AIDS; many intravenous drug users are infected with the virus. Drugs and victimization go hand in glove because so much crime is drug-related. Often marital conflict is a result of drug abuse by one of the partners. Therefore, even though the drug problem permeates city life, we feel that those involved with drugs are best treated by specialists for their chemical addiction.

We now turn to the treatment of the problems themselves. In each chapter we emphasize short-term treatment. Counselors in inner-city churches and outreach ministries do not have the time nor the training necessary to allow them to offer long-term therapy. We suggest that the counselor be aware of the problems that are beyond his scope and refer such problems to those equipped to handle them. The counselor should confine himself to the treatment of selected problems and, in addition, a timetable should be established at the outset so that both counselor and counselee keep in mind that the counseling is time-limited.

Closely connected to the setting of goals and the establishment of a timetable is the assessment of the counselee's motivation for change. It is important for counselors to realize that not everyone who asks for help may be ready to change. For example, there will be those who want you to confirm the way they have been living. They do not need to change. It is the rest of the world that needs to change.

If the counselee is sufficiently motivated toward real change, however, the counselor then needs to examine herself to determine if the problem is one she can handle. This is not a question of expertise but of attitude. To be effective, she must be able to put herself in the person's position. She must ask, "Can I be understanding without being judgmental, no matter what the nature of the problem?" It is possible to adopt this stance even though the dilemma confronting the counselee is one which is, from the counselor's standpoint, quite sordid. To be judgmental is to lose the counselee. There will be time to deal with unscriptural conduct, but this will come after a counseling alliance has been formed.

The counselor will now need to assess the problem the counselee presents. She will have to sift through a number of problems to determine which of them is the core issue in the person's life. Very seldom will matters be so crystal-clear that the counselor can immediately determine where to start.

There are five principles we believe are crucial at the assessment phase. First, once it has been clearly established, deal with the crisis at hand, and act to stabilize the individual as much as possible. A woman who has just been assaulted by a chronically abusive husband needs to be taken to a place where she and her children can be safe before any counseling can take place. Second, pray for discernment. We do not mean that prayer is in any sense secondary, but once the issue is clarified, pray that the Holy Spirit will give you the insight you need to counsel effectively. Rely on God's Word: "If any of you lacks wisdom, he should ask God, who gives generously to all without finding fault, and it will be given to him" (James 1:5). Third, focus on the greatest source of discomfort. The question you might ask is, "Where does it hurt most?" Fourth, ask the person which aspect of the problem she wants to deal with first. Only she knows what troubles her most about the issue at hand. Finally, analyze the problem using the Multi-Modal Profile or BASIC ID, as revised to include the spiritual dimension (see chapter 2).

Initially this method may look confusing, but it will help you to determine which aspect of the problem is causing the most pain. If her answer is not clear to you, do not hesitate to ask, and then listen carefully. When does she get angry? When does she start to choke up or cry? When does she drop her head or avert her eyes? Use every clue at your disposal to do your analysis of the case. If all that we have said thus far sounds like a tall order, it is, but with time, experience, and the Holy Spirit's anointing, you will be ministering effectively to hurting souls.

Each chapter in this section is structured in a similar manner. First, there is a brief overview giving the general parameters of the problem, how it originates, and how it affects people in similar circumstances. Then we present a case study to illustrate the problem. In some instances, we give more than one case study, but one case focuses on the BASIC ID method of analysis. The one exception to this format is in chapter 18 on victimization, where we present several cases before we do a composite analysis.

Next, we present a number of goals for the counseling, which come out of the analysis. We show how the counselor attempted to reach those goals using counseling interventions. We also include supportive environmental interventions such as self-help groups, halfway houses, and sponsors.

Chapter 9 begins this section with an examination of non-chemical addictive behaviors. It is possible for people to become addicted to things other than alcohol and drugs. Romance, relationships, eating, sex, and gambling can be as addictive as chemical substances. The essential characteristics of addictions are outlined, as are the types of problems they create and the ways in which persons so afflicted can be counseled.

In chapter 10 we present the problems of adult children of alcoholics, commonly known as ACOAs. The chapter discusses the effects an alcoholic parent has on an individual, both when he was a child and now as an adult. This includes the fact that ACOAs are at risk of becoming alcoholics themselves. Some salient physiological and psychological issues follow members of this group and the problem of codependency is stressed.

AIDS is the subject of chapter 11. This problem has devastated the urban center. The way it is contracted is outlined, as are common characteristics of PWA (People With AIDS). Some of the physical and emotional issues facing PWAs are outlined, and counseling interventions that can be used to minister to this desperate group are provided.

Marital conflict, which is much more prevalent than separation or divorce, is treated in chapter 12. The major causes of marital conflict are presented along with the ways in which the couple can be counseled about them. The use of the genogram, a graphic representation of the families of origin of both spouses, is introduced as a useful technique in treating troubled marriages.

Chapter 13 deals with domestic abuse and its painful physical and psychological consequences. Abuse may be active or passive. The senior citizen who is abused by his uncaring adult children, and the fetus who has been aborted are part of this hapless population. In this chapter we focus on spouse abuse. Crisis intervention is a critical aspect of this counseling and we spend some time presenting this counseling technique. We also develop the reasons as to the need to counsel both the wife and the husband, who is typically the abuser.

Divorce is an ever-present reality in our country, but even more so in the urban center. In chapter 14 we present some counseling techniques that are useful in ministering to those recovering from divorce. We use the term "divorce" to mean any kind of permanent separation, because formal divorce proceedings are not often carried out in the inner city. This often leaves the woman without the financial or emotional support of her former husband.

Single parenting is endemic to the urban center. Socioeconomic conditions almost dictate the marital separation and desertion that often takes place, leaving the woman (most often) alone to care for her children. Chapter 15 addresses the needs of the children and the necessity of the single parent to take care of herself so that she can be an effective parent.

Chapter 16 addresses crisis pregnancies. Pregnancy by its very nature creates a certain amount of anxiety even when it is desired and planned. When it is unwanted and unplanned, when the mother is unmarried or married with more children than she can care for, a crisis exists. The pastor or church worker who undertakes to counsel such people must be prepared for the fact that despite counsel, some will elect abortion. We suggest some strategies to help you deal with this very grave problem.

The painful problem of sexual abuse is taken up in chapter 17. While obviously painful for the victim, these cases are also stressful for the counselor, especially when young children have been victimized. The critical emotional issues are presented with some counseling interventions that can be helpful to the victim.

Included is a list of steps that should be taken when a child reports abuse, as well as some precautions that should be taught to small children to prevent its occurrence.

Chapter 18 examines the urban dweller's nightmare—victimization. Here we present several cases and offer a composite analysis, since victimized people have similar reactions. We outline the major issues involved in counseling victims: feelings of vulnerability and helplessness, alternating between denial and acceptance, and the desire for revenge.

Finally, chapter 19 concludes this section with a discussion of stress. This is not an exclusively urban issue, but it is exacerbated by the conditions of urban life, especially those of the inner city. The counselee is taught to recognize the indices of stress and to take some practical steps to alleviate the symptoms before they worsen. Emphasis is placed on physiological, cognitive, behavioral, and social intervention.

CHAPTER 9

Addictive Behaviors

UNTIL RECENTLY, addiction was viewed exclusively in terms of chemical dependency. Addicts were those who were hooked on drugs or alcohol; they were substance abusers. To view cigarette smoking as addictive seemed far-fetched, in spite of the U.S. Surgeon General's assertions. After all, addicts are a selfish, disgusting, criminal minority, and cigarette smokers are ordinary people! We are now learning that there are millions of ordinary people who are addicts. We are discovering that people can be addicted to romance, relationships, eating, sex, soap operas, power, gambling, religiosity, activity, and stealing, for example, as well as to alcohol, cocaine, heroin, and tobacco.

Addictions begin as attempts to avoid pain and to experience well-being. The degree to which we elevate the desire to live life with the least pain and greatest pleasure possible is the degree to which we are susceptible. Indeed, our society's shift to a pleasure ethic may be feeding the plethora of addictive behaviors ensnaring people. People who do not know how to have healthy relationships; those who have difficulty trusting;[1] and those who place a low value on achievement, desire instant gratification, and have habitual feelings of elevated stress[2] seem most susceptible to life-controlling problems.

Addictive behaviors are persistent attempts to produce a desired mood change through an emotional attachment to an object, event, person, or experience. Initially, the behaviors produce temporary relief from stress and emotional pain, and give transient feelings of euphoria—what is commonly referred to as a "rush." These initial behaviors are repeated and a powerful

167

psychological and biochemical reinforcement is derived from the association between particular actions and the desired mood elevation and an attachment forms.

Over time, the repeated association between pain relief/euphoria and the particular behavior pattern becomes psychologically entrenched. What began as an apparently ingenious choice that seemed to put the person in control of his emotional state progressively results in the loss of choice and the appearance of out-of-control thoughts, feelings, and behaviors—adiction. If it is not indulged, the addiction eventually begins to threaten severe emotional pain thus creating, in the form of inner shame and guilt, a new layer of pain on top of the initial pain it was intended to overcome. Shame "creates a loss of *self* -respect, *self* -esteem, *self* -confidence, *self* -discipline, *self* -determination, *self* -control, *self* - importance, and *self* -love."[3] The apparent solution turns on the addict and intensifies the original pain.

Once an addictive pattern and, some suggest, personality, is formed, the specific object of addiction may be fairly easily switched.[4] A person may go from alcohol to cocaine, from relationships to running, from soap operas to eating. The bottom line becomes whether or not the object-relationship will repeatedly and predictably bring about the desired mood change.

There are five essential characteristics of true addiction: (1) tolerance (always wanting or needing more of the addictive behavior or object of attachment to be satisfied), (2) withdrawal symptoms when the addictive behavior is curtailed, (3) self-deception, which includes denial that one has a crippling problem, (4) lack of will power (inability to stop the addictive behavior), and (5) distortion of attention (the addictive relationship demands one's focus and emotional energy, thus becoming a god).[5]

The ultimate problem with addictive behaviors is the emotional, biological, and relational destruction that they produce. Failure to address unmet psychospiritual needs within the God-given boundaries of contingent freedom gives the temporary illusion that one has total freedom to meet personal needs in whatever way one wants in the pursuit of a pain-free paradise. When the god of mood-alteration is served, however, the result is bondage.

> Addiction exists wherever persons are internally compelled to give energy to things that are not their true desires. To define it

directly, addiction is a state of compulsion, obsession, or preoccupation that enslaves a person's will and desire. Addiction sidetracks and eclipses the energy of our deepest, truest desire for love and goodness. We succumb because the energy of our desire becomes attached, nailed, to specific behaviors, objects, or people.[6]

CREATIVE COMPULSIONS

Once we are freed of the conception that addictions always involve some form of chemical dependency, we are able to discover commonalities in the pattern and dynamics of the compulsions, as well as in intervention approaches appropriate for several types of addictive behaviors. The range and creativity of nonchemical addictions reflect the complexity of the human psyche, and the desperate attempts to which many will go to avoid or remove psychospiritual pain. The following are a few examples of creative compulsions people have become trapped in.

CASE STUDIES

Tom

As a young boy, Tom had a lot of free time on his hands. To keep himself occupied, he spent a lot of his time at home looking around in the attic, the basement, the closets, and dresser drawers. By the time he was about eleven, he had discovered his father's pornographic magazines. Shortly thereafter, he began to masturbate three or four times a day.

During his teen years, he hung out with the wrong crowd. Vandalizing, stealing, and fencing became a common practice for him, but he told his parents that he was selling items for a friend. (His father apparently also brought home hot merchandise and sold it.) Tom felt he was putting one over on his parents.

As a young Catholic, he would confess these sins but then compulsively repeat them. When Tom came for counseling, by this time a born-again believer, his wife had moved out and he was an anxiety-filled, depressed man. On two occasions he had been caught stealing to buy pornographic material (one a break-in and the other from pocketbooks), and had gone to prostitutes on several occasions. His transgressions had hit the local papers, and he had been disciplined by his local evangelical church.

Sandra

Sandra's parents are divorced. All but one of her mother's five siblings have been divorced as well. Everyone thinks her mother's remaining sibling is gay. Several family members on her mother's side are alcoholics. Her father, a violent alcoholic and heavy gambler, has lived an irresponsible, carefree lifestyle. One of her great-aunts is reputed to be a spell-casting witch. Emotional dysfunction and interpersonal conflict dominate this multigenerational family system.

Sandra struggles with addictive buying binges and has run up several thousand dollars worth of unpaid bills. Initially, her buying binges became a way of nurturing herself, a way of overcoming feelings of deprivation and loneliness caused by her father's neglect. Even now the temptation to go on a buying binge is greatest when her husband is working long hours and she is at home feeling abandoned and angry.

Harry

Harry, molested by a babysitter when he was about five years old, began a downward slide into addictive behavior. At age eleven, he lifted girls' dresses. As a high-schooler, he was into heavy petting (no intercourse) with many girls. The year after he graduated from high school, he dated over eighty girls. Since his marriage over thirty years ago, he has engaged in petting with two of his wife's sisters, sexually abused one of his daughters, and, after becoming a Christian, had sexual interactions of varying kinds with over a dozen girls, married women, foster daughters, and a step-granddaughter.

Jane

Jane struggles with addictive eating and relational dysfunctions. She has tremendous animosity toward her father because he lets himself be dominated by his highly controlling wife (Jane's mother), as well as because of his compulsiveness, rigidity, and isolation. During therapy she realized that she had been sexually abused by him. Apparently there is also some deep family secret about her grandfather, who was a minister. Jane's mother communicated her hatred of men and sex to Jane. Jane's husband left her for another woman, plunging Jane into depression and a terrifying fear of loneliness. After going through a severe eating binge, she began an affair with a minister. During much of her life she has alternated between eating and relationship addictions, triggered by her twin fears of being lonely and of being controlled, and fed by her tremendous ambivalence toward men and toward sexuality.

Sabrina

Sabrina and her friend arrange their workdays and lunch hours around a favorite television soap opera, rushing to her nearby home to view the program every weekday. The excitement of the romance and the adventure of the convoluted relationships contrast greatly with the boredom of Sabrina's twenty-five-year marriage and draw her like a magnet. Ever since she was a teenager she has read romance novels and fantasized about men, following a pattern she saw in her mother. If she is forced to miss her soap opera, Sabrina becomes depressed, irritable, and unsociable. This noontime television ritual has been followed for over ten years.

David

David dresses impeccably and speaks articulately. A Christian since the age of ten, he came in for counseling because he was trapped in the dual web of workaholism and sexual addiction. A visit to a prostitute two weeks earlier had precipitated his entrance into therapy. Feeling greatly distressed and inextricably trapped, and with his stomach in knots, he wondered if he was developing an ulcer. He had difficulty sleeping, even though he was tired after consistently working twelve- to fourteen-hour days, six days a week.

David has always worked hard, and during counseling, realized that he has a deep inner sense of having to prove himself. He also has a need to let others know of his accomplishments, especially extended family members.

David was introduced to pornographic material as a little boy by uncles who seemed to talk more about sex than about anything else. It was clear that they viewed sexual activity as the sign of manhood. David's mother frequently commented that all of the men on her side of the family were womanizers. (Her father had had twelve children by three or four different women. Her brothers each had three or four children by three or four different women as well.) As David grew up, he was surrounded by older people. David's parents, separated during most of his childhood, had gotten back together during his teen years though David was aware that during the separation his mother had had men friends and his father had had women friends.

As a junior high-schooler, David was given pornography by other boys and his sexual fascination grew. As a high school student, he watched pornographic videos at his friend's house, and began going with that friend to strip joints. A key incident occurred after high school when he engaged in oral sex with a stripper brought in for a friend's bachelor party. He then became increasingly obsessed with pornographic literature and videos, strip shows, and occasionally, prostitution.

These addictive behaviors continued even after his marriage, though he expressed great appreciation for his wife's love and talked of her in loving tones. She, however, was not aware of his problem. David described his state of mind when engaged in these behaviors as a "numbness, a compulsion, an almost uncontrollable urge." He began to discover that his workaholism and sexual addiction were interrelated. His boss put him down often, making him feel like a child and his workaholism, even though relieving his sexual obsession, also created stress that demanded some form of relaxation. That usually came in the form of sexual "acting out" after a period of long hours and demanding work activity.

During counseling, David began to realize that television viewing frequently triggered temptation for him. In the early phases of counseling, David frequently remarked about the intense pain and inner void he felt. He commented several times about a deep sadness that he felt whenever he thought back to about age five. He felt that he simply could not overcome the strong urges of his addiction, yet he wanted to be free.

ANALYSIS: DAVID

Construction of a family genogram showed a pattern of widespread relational instability, sexual focus and acting out, occultic involvement, and emotional dysfunction throughout the multigenerational family system.

A multimodal analysis of David's case would include the following:

BEHAVIOR:	1.	Compulsive viewing of pornographic literature at work.
	2.	Compulsive purchasing and rental of pornographic videos.
	3.	Compulsive attending of strip shows.
	4.	Periodic sexual liaisons with prostitutes.
	5.	Working six days a week, twelve to fourteen hours per day.
	6.	Feelings of inadequacy.
AFFECT:	1.	Feelings of distress.
	2.	Feelings of inadequacy and powerlessness.
	3.	Feelings of shame and guilt.
	4.	Feelings of loneliness and emptiness.
	5.	Feelings of sadness.
SENSATION:	1.	Tension prior to addictive behavior.
	2.	Lethargy and tiredness.
	3.	"Rush" and intense focus when engaging in addictive behaviors.
IMAGERY:	1.	Uncles talking about sex and looking at pornographic material.
	2.	Sadness and depression at age five.
	3.	Little boy.
	4.	"Nobody loves me" (during parents' breakup).
	5.	Parents' involvement with others during their separation.
	6.	"All the men in this family are womanizers" (mother's voice).
COGNITION:	1.	If I act older, I'll be loved.
	2.	To be a man is to be sexual; to be nonsexual is to be a puny little kid.
	3.	To be accepted, I must be sexual.
	4.	I deserve recognition for working so hard and achieving more than anyone else in my family.
	5.	I have to prove myself.
	6.	I don't deserve my wife.
	7.	I deserve to relax, a reward for working so hard.

INTERPERSONAL RELATIONSHIPS:	1.	Controlled by mother's emotional reactions; does not want to hurt her; feels the need to be there and support her.
	2.	Positive relationship with wife.
	3.	A "loner"; no close friends; generally distant and emotionally uninvolved with others; task-oriented.
DRUGS/ BIOLOGY:	1.	Shingles (about six months into therapy).
SPIRITUAL:	1.	Describes self as believer in Christ.
	2.	Did not connect spiritual commitment with addiction.

GOALS

The primary goals for helping those struggling with the compelling urges of addictions are to help them to:
1. Recognize and own the addiction.
2. Identify their unmet psychospiritual needs.
3. Understand the addictive cycle.
4. Grasp long-range consequences.
5. Face pain courageously and deny the "false self."
6. Develop a strategy.
7. Strengthen the "true self."
8. Develop accountability.
9. Embrace and exercise their ability to choose.
10. Resolve shame and guilt.

Recognize and Own the Addiction

Depending upon the depth of despair and degree of disintegration that a person has experienced, admitting to addiction will be met with varying degrees of resistance. Most people with nonchemical addictions, especially those in nonsexual areas, will see themselves as just having a "problem." The person may go so far as to admit that he is compulsive or has an addictive pattern. However, it is not until the addictive behavior(s) have reached the degree of intensity where the person has lost control and appears to have no choice, or where the person has engaged in a pattern of swapping addictions, that he will more readily receive the painful truth that he is an addict. This does not mean that he is hopeless. It does mean that he will find himself compulsively attached to a variety of objects, experiences, and even people. Without such attachment he will experience a significant degree of pain and emptiness. It also means that his current focus of addiction will have the power to draw him back into a highly intense attachment, even when he has apparently conquered it. He will always need to be careful in relation to his addiction; the dragon in his soul will spring back to life with very little nurturing.

As David began to realize that he did not have the power to "just say no" and to let go of his intense focus on either work performance or sexual acting out, he began to accept the fact that he was, indeed, an addict.

Identify Unmet Psychospiritual Needs

Addictions are attempts to remove or numb the emotional pain that comes from unmet psychospiritual needs.[7] Because we are all products of the Fall, we are born with existential deficits that threaten us with feelings of disorder, distress, and disintegration. The degree of pain experienced during socialization in the form of rejection, isolation, inadequacy, victimization, anxiety, worthlessness, and in the lack of life purpose can be intensified through faulty parenting or other negative experiences. This pain leads to a search to satisfy unmet needs, thus unleashing the potential for addictive behaviors. Addictive patterns begin as the child is exposed to others who handle their pain addictively, or as she experiments and discovers that a certain behavior seems to relieve emotional pain and give a surge of pleasure.

In David's case, these addictive patterns were established before he was five years old as he observed his uncles and listened to his mother's comments. His addictive potential grew with exposure to sexual material during the critical years of adolescence. The identification of his underlying deficits in regard to identity, competence, significance, and especially, loneliness were necessary before therapy could be effective. Once the deficits were identified, David began wrestling with other, healthier ways of dealing with them instead of dealing with them through workaholism and sexual addiction.

Understand the Addictive Cycle

As a person moves further into an addiction, feelings of being out of control grow. An awareness of the addictive cycle, however, helps the counselee begin to introduce a sense of order into the midst of obsession and chaos. Awareness brings increased opportunities to alter the addictive pattern.

The addictive cycle is essentially the same regardless of the specific addiction. It begins with feelings of distress, discomfort, and emotional pain. Often some current experience is linked to the person's specific array of existential deficits and the pain is magnified. When a particular behavior pattern provides quick relief from this distress, an addictive connection is formed. Then, when pain is triggered, there is a strong urge to repeat the behavior that previously relieved pain and provided comfort. If the urge is acted upon, relief is again felt. However, as time goes on and the person begins to lose control over stress-relieving behavior, acting out leads to further pain in the form of guilt, shame, or the deepening of psychospiritual needs created by the particular "fix." Thus, a cycle or stereotypic ritual is established, but it must be interrupted at the initial stages of distress so that healthier coping behaviors can be introduced.

David began to see the connection between his deficits of competence and significance, his need to prove himself through his workaholism, the build-up of stress, the need to relax, and the onset of his sexual addiction. He was then able to take constructive steps to prevent and interrupt the cycle.

Grasp Long-Range Consequences

Addiction is characterized by immediacy. The intensity of the addictive pattern focuses the addict's entire being on the immediate emotional and physical experience. As the addiction becomes entrenched, the addict begins to live for the addictive moment—for the "high" or "rush" that allows him to momentarily escape the emptiness and emotional pain that otherwise plagues him. The desire to avoid pain, which promotes quick-relief solutions, makes it difficult for the addict to consider long-range consequences. There is often a subtle, underlying belief that one will be unable to handle pain—that one will be destroyed by it and thus must immediately get rid of it. That thinking, together with deceptive temptations of Satan that emphasize consequences as being minimal or nonexistent, traps countless people in addictive attachments.

Counseling must help the counselee actively imagine the

consequences of his addictive pattern if it continues (as it most likely will) and intensifies over time. He needs to mentally picture and talk about the "down" side of his feelings *following* the addictive behavior. He needs to evaluate how effective the addiction is in meeting his underlying needs. At the same time he should be helped to explore other ways of meeting his psychospiritual needs that would provide longer-term satisfaction. The counselee will need to understand, however, that he will initially have to fight off very strong urges to use the quick-relief option before he gets to the point of enjoying long-term satisfaction. This is where a recovery group or a mentoring relationship with someone further along the road to recovery is important for most. The example of others, together with candid and honest relationships, helps the addict gain strength to resist temptation.

David was periodically encouraged to discuss the immediate and long-range consequences of his addictive pattern. As he thought through, imagined, and verbalized the spiritual, emotional, marital, and financial consequences of his behavior, he realized that he had allowed himself to think that a single addictive act did not really matter. He then saw the tremendous destructiveness of his choices. He determined with new strength to choose the upward path, and seemed strengthened by keeping the consequences consciously before him.

Face Pain and Deny the "False Self"

A critical element in overcoming addictive patterns is courage. Courage is doing what one knows to be right in spite of the pain that may result. In order to overcome addictive behaviors, one must experience the pain of saying no to the "false self" that promotes addictive urges. One must discover the lies that the false self promotes, "You'll die if you don't do it," "You'll go crazy if you don't have it," "You'll fall apart if you don't do it." These emotionally crippling, catastrophic messages simply are not true. To be freed, the addict must deny his (false) self, pick up his cross (the excruciating pain of false-self denial), and follow Jesus. The pain of saying "no" may indeed be intense, but it will give way to self-respect, self-control, integrity, and eventually, to well-being.

It should be obvious that there is a tremendous need for emotional support during this phase of withdrawal. Twelve-Step groups are very helpful to many. The addict must understand that the temporary pain (which may last anywhere from a few weeks to a few months, depending upon the addiction and the person) is the necessary pain of psychospiritual surgery. It is a healing pain that will not destroy. If, on the other hand, the "cancerous" growth of the addiction is allowed to continue, it will eventually bring about the permanent pain of disintegration.

When David began counseling, he was filled with pain. The thought of denying his false-self urges seemed overwhelming and impossible. As he began to understand that he was able to make choices, and that the pain of saying no to the addictive demands of his false self would not kill him, he began to courageously resist temptation. Although his initial steps were faltering, he began to believe that he could say yes to his true self and not fall apart. As he began to experience successes, he experienced an inner sense of being strengthened, which in turn made him feel better. Over time he began to enjoy the feelings of once again being in control of his life instead of being at the mercy of the false-self demands. He found it easier and easier to deny the false self.

Develop a Strategy

Conquering addictive behaviors is akin to winning a war. Wars are usually not won by brute strength alone, but must be combined with careful strategy. Strategy includes a thorough examination of the enemy's resources, typical tactics, and points of vulnerability. It also requires an honest and comprehensive self-examination to determine a workable plan for seizing and keeping control of one's objectives. Understanding one's own addictive cycle is vitally important so that triggering stimuli, stress intensifiers, and stereotypic rituals can be identified and strategically altered to prevent or short-circuit acting out.

The recognition of triggering stimuli and stereotypic rituals is a vital part of defeating addiction. Typically the triggering stimuli (which may be fantasy, a visual stimulant, an internal biological state, or an action), because of repeated and highly reinforced association with the addictive ritual, unleashes a stereotypical (rigid, unchanging) sequence of thought, emotion, and action, or ritual. The triggering stimuli may not immediately precede the addictive behavior. Sometimes, for instance, fantasy begets more fantasy for a period of weeks or months before the *immediate* triggering stimulus (in David's case, a girlie magazine lying around at work) incites the behaviors that are linked to the stereotypic ritual.

A significant triggering stimulus for many is a build-up of stress and tension. The addictive behavior, then, becomes a way of trying to relax or relieve stress. David's workaholic pattern contributed directly to intensified stress. His internal messages about manhood and his need to prove himself promoted a pattern of overwork that was further exploited by a boss who demanded high levels of output.

David began to see the link among (1) his normal workaholism (punctuated by periodic high demand times), (2) his attempt to reduce stress by watching television, (3) his sexual fantasies fed by television, (4) his attempt to get "innocent" relief by reading pornographic magazines at work, and (5) his rental of pornographic videos, attendance at strip shows, and visits to prostitutes during the unstructured, boring times at work that followed high-stress periods. He was then able to strategize and interrupt the cycle. He learned to counter the false messages from his childhood regarding manhood, sexuality, performance, and personal adequacy. He reduced his work hours and began a regular exercise program. He structured his free time, especially on weekends, and spent much more time during weekends and evenings with his wife. He strictly monitored his television viewing, especially in times of high stress, and controlled his fantasizing.

Strengthen the "True Self"

The "true self" that still reflects the image of God, though in damaged form, must be strengthened if the deceptions and condemnation of the false self are to be overcome. David's true self was strengthened through interaction with the counselor, through memorization and meditation on Scripture passages relevant to his struggles, and through reading (see Resources p. 323ff.). This combination helped David understand the roots of his addiction, the faulty filters and rotten rules that he had internalized (see the cognitive dimension of the multimodal analysis), the self-defeating patterns he had chosen to use in coping with the pain of his unmet psychospiritual needs, and the elements necessary for him to consistently walk on the upward path (in opposition to the downward path of addiction).

Develop Accountability

Isolation is one of the primary characteristics of people who have become addicted. Although the addict may maintain an appearance of relationships, more careful examination shows that those relationships tend to be dependent, manipulative, controlling, parasitic, or sexual. Addiction accentuates egocentricity in all of its forms. Addicts use other people because genuine intimacy is either minimal or nonexistent in their lives. This is because genuine intimacy requires that they focus on someone besides themselves, that they care, that they sustain commitment despite misunderstanding and conflict, and that they develop trustworthiness. Accountability, then, is critical because it corrects the subtle deception of the false self and the truth-avoiding ego defenses that maintain the addiction.

In addition to seeing a counselor, it is highly recommended that the counselee participate in an appropriate recovery group. In most major urban areas there are Twelve-Step programs available for a wide variety of addictions (see Resources p. 331ff.). The National Association for Christian Recovery is a new nationwide organization developed to assist in the development of Christ-centered support groups through consultation, training, and a quarterly newsletter, *Steps*. It provides a link between the addict and resources, support groups, workshops, and conferences on recovery throughout the United States. Turning Point, another nationwide Christian organization is designed to help the church reach out to people with life-controlling problems through support groups within the local church.

Exercise Ability to Choose

Addictions appear to rob people of the ability to make choices. The power of the addictive urge makes one feel that one must act out the addiction in order to survive. In reality, though addiction makes it more difficult to choose, even the advanced addict still has choice. This is one of the most enduring and God-like qualities of humanity. As long as there is life, there is choice. As long as there is choice, there is hope. Many who become addicted have a relatively passive view of life with an external locus of control. That is, they do not see their choices and actions as being linked in any consistent way with good or bad consequences. As a result, they tend to develop a sense of personal powerlessness that fosters the belief that they cannot control life in general, or their addiction in particular. The common feeling of being "out of control" is a reflection of their belief that they cannot truly be "in control." Effective counseling must help the counselee to see that he can choose to change, that the past does not have to be the future as well. Often, assertiveness training teaches the addict that he can make a difference in how he feels, and even in what happens to him, if he exercises good choice.

The other dimension has to do with overcoming a pattern of irresponsibility often associated with the sense of powerlessness. One frequently sees addicts immaturely dependent—a dependence that requires others to "take care of" or nurture them. The counselee must be helped to see the disadvantages of such dependency and the advantages of responsible, mature adulthood, including the reduction and resolution of shame and guilt.

Resolve Shame and Guilt

Shame and guilt seem to be two automatic consequences of choices and behaviors that contradict God's intended design for human functioning. When Adam and Eve sinned, they made coverings for their nakedness and tried to hide from the presence of God. Their responses signaled the automatic internal consequences of shattering shame and overwhelming guilt. The results of going against the God-given limits of their humanity included the release of terrifying, anxiety-generating thoughts and feelings of condemnation. Because addictions also involve attempts to relieve pain or find well-being in ways that violate the rules for healthy human functioning, a similar flood of anxiety, triggered by thoughts and feelings of guilt and shame, follows the temporary rush or euphoria of the addiction.

Sometimes the pain that the addictive behavior is designed to relieve is the pain of shame. Those who have received parental messages that they are "not good enough," "bad," "different or weird," "a burden," or "defective" become shame-based. Filled with toxic shame, they seek ways to find relief from constant feelings of condemnation.

Resolution of shame and guilt involves recognition and confession of sin, acceptance of forgiveness, and a change in self-perception from "bad" (or worse) to "loved and accepted."

Thorough examination of Scriptures having to do with acceptance of those who have acted shamefully in one way or another is important. The attitudes and interaction of the counselor are critical as well. Negative, condemnatory nonverbal and verbal feedback from the counselor only drives the shame deeper. The Scriptural knowledge of healing grace and the experience of it in interaction with the counselor will gradually result in a changed perception of self. As the addict begins to "get hold of" the reality that he is not only forgiven, but accepted, and that God's grace means that he has permission to feel positive about himself, he will be freed from the addiction-promoting shackles of unresolved shame, guilt, and self-hatred.

Addictions *can* be overcome. Although they are difficult to control, appropriate counseling and participation in support groups can help many say no to addictive patterns and find healthy and holy ways to deal with the pain of unmet psychospiritual needs.

NOTES

[1]Craig Nakken, *The Addictive Personality: Roots, Rituals, Recovery* (Center City, Minn.: Hazelden Books, 1988), 26.

[2]Stanton Peele, *The Meaning of Addiction: Cumpulsive Experience and Its Interpretation* (Lexington, Mass.: D.C. Heath & Co., 1985), 16.

[3]Nakken, *The Addictive Personality*, 28.

[4]Ibid., 25.

[5]Gerald R. May, *Addiction and Grace* (San Francisco: Harper & Row, 1988), 25–30.

[6]Ibid., 14.

[7]Craig W. Ellison, *Finding Shalom: Counseling and the Stress of Life* (Dallas: Word Books, forthcoming).

CHAPTER 10

Adult Children
of Alcoholics

IT IS ESTIMATED that 28 million Americans have at least one alcoholic parent. Approximately one-third of all American families report alcohol abuse by a family member.[1] If adult children of alcoholics are distributed equally throughout the population, there are over five million evangelical Christians who have grown up in alcoholic homes.[2]

The psychological, interpersonal, and spiritual impact of being raised in such an environment is often devastating.[3] Children of alcoholics are three to four times more likely than the general population to become alcoholics. They are also at high risk for birth defects, stress-related medical problems, and attention-deficit disorder. Boys with an alcoholic grandfather are three times more likely to become alcoholics than are other boys. Girls from alcoholic homes are very likely to marry men with alcohol problems. Children of alcoholics often have difficulty trusting other people, or forming and maintaining intimate relationships. They tend to deny their feelings, and exhibit an extreme need for control and the approval of others. Repressed anger, guilt, and shame characterize their emotions.

Many ACOAs also doubt their perceptions of reality and are confused about what is normal. They think in black-and-white, all-or-none terms, struggle with a deep-seated fear of abandonment, suffer from a sense of shame that comes from feeling fundamentally flawed as persons, and have a crisis orientation toward life. ACOAs typically are codependents as well. Codependents are caretakers or enablers who focus their lives around another person to such a degree that they not only promote irresponsibility in the other person, but they also do not take appropriate emotional care of themselves.

CASE STUDY: LOUISE

Louise is a petite woman in her early forties, married to her second husband, George, a man five years older than she. She has four children ranging in age from eighteen to twenty-six. The oldest son and daughter are from her first marriage.

Louise's childhood was very unhappy. She was the fifth of nine children, and both her parents were heavy drinkers. A filthy, abusive mouth, and constant screaming and cursing characterized Louise's mother. Her mother made Louise the primary object of her wrath, in part because Louise reminded her of her husband, whom she called a "filthy Swede." Seemingly angry all the time, Louise's mother would react by throwing whatever she could get her hands on at the children. Once she threw boiling water at Louise's face, and on another occasion she threw a knife at another daughter. Verbal and physical abuse, however, were only two of the many dysfunctions in Louise's family. Her mother also read palms and tea leaves, made use of the ouija board, and would think nothing of walking around half-naked in front of people. No matter what Louise did to try and win her mother's approval (for example, by constantly trying to keep the house clean), she never received a positive word in return. Nevertheless, she felt that her role was to be the family servant. As if an abusive mother were not enough, Louise's older brother would creep around in the middle of the night and try to sexually molest his sisters.

At age fifteen Louise was pregnant by a drug addict. She married him and had a second child during their three-year marriage. The marriage was anything but tranquil—her husband put a loaded gun to her head three times, tried to push her out of the apartment window, and tried to smother her with a pillow while she was sleeping. Every day she wanted to die. During the ninth month of her second pregnancy, Louise's husband would force her to stay awake all night, night after night. After her son's birth, Louise acted on her death wish and, after swallowing a whole bottle of pills, was near death for a week. Her son cried constantly and could not be comforted during his first several months. Eventually Louise's husband kicked her out and she lived in her brother's filthy basement apartment for two years (he had just gotten out of jail at the time). At age twenty she met George, who "fooled her" by pretending to like her children. Although she never felt anything for him, she married him as a way to escape her miserable existence.

When Louise came in for counseling, she was extremely angry and tense. She indicated that she wanted to obey the Lord (she is a born-again believer), but could not believe that he meant for her to continue to live in misery with George. George exhibited a total lack of love, caring, and companionship constantly and expected Louise to take care of his needs while never acknowledging any of hers. He had promised to stop smoking pot but never did. George was also frequently verbally abusive (yelling, cursing, dirty words), usually showed no affection toward Louise, and had been occasionally physically abusive toward her and the children. Finally, the week before she came in, Louise had lost her temper. She told her husband that she felt like she was married to a dead man, and that if another man told her what she needed to hear, she might very well leave. This brought about only a temporary increase of attention and affirmation. As she entered counseling, Louise felt only intense hatred toward her husband.

Adding to her stress was the continuing uncertainty over her oldest son's behavior. He had recently returned home to live after having been released from prison where he had served time for several armed robberies (mostly against women) and drug charges. Even though he verbally abused his mother and disregarded her household rules, Louise found it hard to insist on any boundaries for his behavior. She blamed the problems in his life on her own failings including her first marriage to his drug-addicted father. Then, on top of everything else, he appeared to be taking drugs in violation of his parole.

Louise's husband and son were not the only ones who caused stress in her life. Louise's oldest daughter had become involved with a physically abusive man and was seeking Louise's help and emotional support. In addition, her physically disabled, wheelchair bound father, who lived about an hour away expected Louise to regularly run errands for him. Louise felt that she could not deny his requests (demands?), even though other family members lived closer. She said he needed her and was helpless. She could not say "no" because she felt that her purpose in life was to take care of people.

Louise's inability to say "no" stemmed from her fear that loved ones would leave her. She did not know how she could survive on her own. She always felt as if she did not know how to be a person for herself, or even if she had a self.

The final complicating factor in Louise's life as she entered counseling was that she was unable to work (an important form of escape and release for her) because of disabling neck and back problems. She was physically exhausted, in part because of those difficulties, which eventually required surgery, but everyone expected her to keep serving them.

ANALYSIS

Construction of a family genogram,[4] with questions aimed at discovering any dysfunctional family-of-origin patterns, quickly revealed that both of Louise's parents were heavy drinkers. This is highly significant because of the emotional, cognitive, and relational distortions commonly suffered by children of alcoholics (COAs).[5]

A multimodal analysis of this case follows. (It should be noted that several items are included in the analysis that were revealed in counseling but not detailed in the brief overview of Louise's problems.)

BEHAVIOR:
1. Alternating suppression of thoughts and feelings and outbursts of anger.
2. Caring for other's needs regardless of how she feels physically and emotionally (codependent; nonassertive).

AFFECT:
1. Feelings of anger.
2. Feelings of helplessness.
3. Feelings of hatred.
4. Feelings of stress.
5. Fear of abandonment.
6. Feelings of being used/leaned on.
7. Feelings of loneliness.
8. Feelings of depression.
9. Feelings of rejection.

SENSATION:
1. Tension and pain in back and neck.
2. Physical exhaustion.

IMAGERY:
1. Mother screaming, cursing, throwing boiling water.
2. Mother calling her a "no good Swede."
3. Mother and father drinking heavily.
4. Finding mother in bed with boyfriend.

	5.	Mother at bar.
	6.	Father disregarding her caring efforts.
	7.	Swallowing bottle of pills.
	8.	"Squirrel" dream.

COGNITION:

1. I'm an oddball.
2. I exist to serve others and take care of their needs.
3. I am nothing.
4. What I think or say has no value to others.
5. I'm under the control of everyone else in my family.
6. My needs don't matter.
7. I have nobody to protect me and take care of me.
8. I'm not garbage–don't treat me this way (preceding angry outburst).
9. I've been a dumping ground.
10. No one is there to comfort or care for me.

INTERPERSONAL
RELATIONSHIPS:

1. Alienated from mother.
2. Exploited by complaining father.
3. Verbally abused and unaffirmed by husband; hates him and wants to leave.
4. Conflict with oldest son.

DRUGS/

BIOLOGY:

1. Three herniated discs and bone spur in back.
2. Tension focused in neck and back.
3. Abscessed teeth.

SPIRITUAL:

1. Identifies self as born-again, charismatic Christian.
2. Feels that her faith is the only thing keeping her together.
3. Bothered by discrepancy between anger and hatred for husband and need to show Christ's love to him.

GOALS

The primary goals for helping those crippled by the impact of alcoholism during their childhood are:
1. To correct false controlling beliefs.
2. To develop healthy relational patterns.

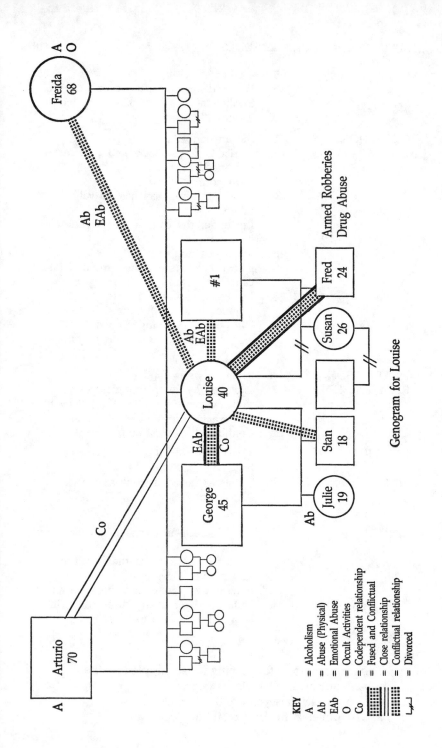

Genogram for Louise

KEY

A   = Alcoholism
Ab = Abuse (Physical)
EAb = Emotional Abuse
O   = Occult Activities
Co = Codependent relationship
▓▓▓ = Fused and Conflictual
     = Close relationship
     = Conflictual relationship
     = Divorced

Armed Robberies
Drug Abuse

3. To identify and express emotions appropriately.
4. To teach realistic expectations.
5. To help them face their fears and risk.
6. To forgive and let go of the past.

One of the most notable characteristics of alcoholic families is the way in which they organize themselves around denial. The alcoholic and his entire family frequently conspire to keep the alcohol abuse a secret from themselves as well as from those outside the immediate family. Anger, violence, withdrawal, broken promises, hangovers, and unpredictability are excused or rationalized. Consequently some ACOAs cannot admit to or even recognize an alcohol problem. The extreme loyalty encouraged in these families also makes it difficult for many to face the truth. As a result, the Children of Alcoholics Screening Test (C.A.S.T.)[6] or the Children of Alcoholics Quiz[7] may be helpful in therapeutically confronting the denial and helping the counselee deal with the basic truth. It is important for the counselor to be aware that children of alcoholics are also frequently victims of physical abuse and incest. As part of the family secret or as a way to avoid facing the horrible pain of the truth, these painful experiences may be deeply repressed.

When Louise entered therapy, she was primarily aware of her anger and her physical and emotional pain. She had not yet connected the alcoholism of her parents with her continuing misery in life, and did not understand that her anger and pain were the products of multiple distortions in the way she thought, felt, and related to her alcoholic family of origin. She could tolerate neither her mother nor her husband, was unable to think of anything good about her marriage, and remained in it only because she did not want to leave out of vindictiveness, and she was unable to work because of her bad back.

Release of Pent-Up Emotion

The initial process of counseling was aimed at allowing her to express all of the bottled-up feelings of anger, hatred, and rejection she had been carrying within her. Involved in this was giving her "permission" to express her feelings and suggesting that her physical tension and back problems were probably related to the tremendous emotional stress that had built up over the years. She was able to express her feelings of "nothingness," her resentment over the ongoing profanity and verbal abuse she received from her husband and son, and her sense of being abandoned by her husband and parents at several major crisis points (such as at the arrest and imprisonment of her son).

Correct Controlling Beliefs

Once Louise had been able to fully discuss her history (including the flagrant and frightening abuses suffered in her first marriage) and her current family experiences, counseling was aimed at helping her correct false beliefs that controlled her. The most damaging were, "I am nothing," "What I say has no value," "I exist to serve others," "I have no right to expect anything from others," and "My needs don't matter." (Other major misbeliefs among ACOAs include "I don't deserve to exist," "I must be perfect," "I must not upset others," "I have to be in control.") These beliefs had led her to become highly nonassertive and to accept as legitimate whatever demands were made of her. The "wounds" inflicted on her body, soul, and spirit had been blocked out of her awareness for years, but they had accumulated until her health broke down and her ego defenses no longer worked to shield her from emotional pain.

Correction of false controlling beliefs involves *identifying* the primary controlling beliefs; *encouraging* counselees to consider God's view of their worth and purpose in life through study and discussion of selected Scriptures; *contradicting* the controlling beliefs through counseling interaction that affirms the counselee, shows respect, encourages expression of feelings, and validates their worth; and *helping* the counselee to identify, memorize, and affirm healthy controlling beliefs until they replace "sick" ones.

The ACOA Bill of Rights (Figure 10-1) is a helpful tool to use in encouraging correct thinking. The counselor can go over each of the points in detail and encourage the counselee to memorize them and put them into practice. A daily journal is helpful for the ACOA to record her correct choices as she learns healthy patterns of thinking.

Figure 10-1
ACOA BILL OF RIGHTS

1. I have the right to make other choices besides the choice merely to run away.

2. I have the right to say "no" when I feel unready or unsafe.
3. I have the right not to be molested by fear.
4. I have the right to feel all feelings.
5. I have the right to believe I'm probably not guilty.
6. I have the right to make mistakes.
7. I have the right not to smile when I cry or feel hurt.
8. I have the right to terminate conversations with those who put me down or humiliate me.
9. I have the right to be healthier than those around me.
10. I have the right to change and grow.
11. I have the right to be relaxed, playful, and frivolous.
12. I have the right to set limits and to be selfish.
13. I have the right to get angry, even at someone I love, without fearing that I, the other person, or the relationship will dissolve.
14. I have the right to do stupid things without believing that I am a stupid person.
15. I have the right not to be ashamed of what I don't know or can't do.

Develop Healthy Relational Patterns

Intervention with ACOAs frequently requires the teaching of assertiveness skills because of their common patterns of codependency and nonassertiveness. *Nonassertiveness* is characterized by tendencies to avoid emotionally intense (negative) confrontation, people-pleasing and trying not to "make waves," stuffing (denying and repressing) one's real thoughts and feelings, and self-blame. Also included are behaviors that allow control by others, attitudes of fatalism and feelings of victimization, and hierarchical relationships in which the ACOA normally plays a "child" in relation to another adult who acts as a controlling, criticizing, and correcting "parent."

Assertiveness properly understood is *not* a selfish, aggressive push for personal rights; it is *not* a demand to get whatever one wants; it is *not* an insensitive coercion over other people. The core meaning of assertiveness is found in Ephesians 4:15, which urges believers to "speak the truth in love." The three key words in this exhortation are *speak*, *truth*, and *love*. Correct assertiveness is speaking and acting in ways that respect the dignity and worth of selves and others. When a problem arises, these types of people are problem-focused and partner-oriented. They say things like "Let's talk about this and make a decision together," "We have a problem, let's work on it." Assertive people do not hide behind agreeability or anger—they are direct and honest.

Assertiveness is speaking the truth—that is, telling what one really thinks and feels, openly but appropriately. Assertive people are not gossips or deceptive in their dealings, telling one person one thing and another something else. As a result, assertive people are seen as trustworthy; there is a sense of security rather than chaos.

Assertiveness is speaking the truth in love. Truth without love can be unnecessarily hurtful in the way it is spoken or in insensitive timing. Assertive people exercise self-control. They are not controlled by others, nor is it their aim to control others. They carefully and prayerfully measure when and how to speak so that there is a *con*structive (building up) effect and not a *de*structive one. They are able to say yes or no depending on their principles and priorities and as the situation warrants.

On one hand, assertive people make themselves vulnerable. They do not hide behind silence, half-truths, or lash out; thus they cannot slip by with innuendos and other self-protective tactics. In addition, they tend to irritate aggressive people because they cannot be intimidated or dominated like nonassertives. On the other hand, assertiveness allows one to experience a full range of mostly positive feelings. Assertive people have less anxiety, greater self-worth, and better physical health. They are more likely to be understood rather than misunderstood and they are able to form and maintain healthy, intimate relationships.[8]

Assertiveness involves developing an identity of one's own. This is often a big change for ACOAs who have been dominated, intimidated, and controlled by powerful persons who have sought to submerge the ACOA in their own identities or make them function as extensions of themselves.

Louise needed to learn to be assertive. Her first task was to read selected materials and then she was taught to distinguish among nonassertive, assertive, and aggressive interactions. Her first practical assignment was to make one assertive response each day and record it in a notebook. Later, the assignments were refined to focus on assertiveness with her husband and son. The number of assertive choices per day was also gradually increased. During counseling sessions Louise was asked to reflect on how she felt while making assertive responses and how she felt afterward. Her feelings were then linked to her faulty filters (controlling beliefs). Gradually, she learned to identify when she *should* have been assertive and began choosing to make those responses. As she practiced assertiveness and was able to breach the inner rules that kept her bound in unhealthy interaction patterns, she began to feel better about herself, and did not feel as angry.

Assertiveness counseling also involved role-playing difficult situations Louise anticipated in her family interactions, so that she could rehearse an assertive response. The counselor role-played the "difficult" party and gave her instructive guidance throughout the role playing.

Another troubling relational issue for many ACOAs is that of boundaries. ACOAs frequently have to be helped to separate themselves emotionally from their spouses, children, and parents, so that they are not enmeshed and acting as though the other person is an extension of themselves for which they are responsible. Failure to establish personal boundaries that allow for both individuality and intimacy usually leads either to constant attempts to control a spouse or children, or leads to extreme people-pleasing behaviors. The chaos, unpredictability, and enmeshment of their childhood experiences produce behaviors that are intended to avoid anxiety and feelings of life being out of control. Unfortunately, these efforts at control require huge expenditures of energy and typically drive those who are emotionally closest away from the ACOA.

Identify and Express Emotions

Because of all the feelings she had repressed, Louise had shut down emotionally except for intense anger, which had not even been identified until the months immediately preceding therapy. As is typical in alcoholic families, Louise had learned that it was bad to have (negative) emotions, that she was not supposed to upset the family's emotional apple cart, and that she was selfish if she had any feelings that did not conform to family reality as defined by her alcoholic parents or abusive husbands. Louise found it very difficult to talk about her feelings. The huge backlog of emotional pain threatened to overwhelm her if she even tried to talk about the past.

Gradually and gently, with several starts and stops on Louise's part, the counselor was able to get Louise to use a Feeling Words List[9] of over 350 words. She was gently encouraged to identify one or two feelings she experienced each day and then to record these feelings in her journal, briefly describing what they felt like and noting any past experience of that emotion. Initially she found that reflection on past experience was so overwhelming that she stopped after the first word "abandoned" (much helpful information came from her sharing, however). Subsequently, she was again able to focus on her feelings through this exercise, although not consistently.

Fear is a major force in the lives of adult children of alcoholics. One of the most prominent, though not usually expressed on the surface, is that of abandonment. This fear feeds codependent patterns of enmeshment and control. Other fears that also are typically hidden are the fear of being found out, the fear of ridicule and rejection, the fear of trusting, the fear of disapproval, the fear of confrontation, the fear of insanity, and the fear of impending doom.[10]

Shame is another significant issue for many ACOAs and overcoming it is very hard. Shame is induced in several ways. The episodes of abnormal and embarrassing behavior by one's alcoholic parent(s) frequently drive a deep sense of shame into the ACOA. Alcoholic parents themselves frequently use shame and blame to control ("If you weren't such a problem, I wouldn't have to drink"). They may even let a relatively healthy child who does not go along with the "family secret" know that he or she is weird and different. Typically, the lack of affirmation and attention experienced by children in alcoholic homes conveys a message, "not good enough."

Shame develops out of a sense of deficiency about one's being. Healing the wounds of shame involves becoming aware of it, recognizing distorted defenses, and accepting it as part of the human condition, and at the same time challenging the false messages behind the particular sources,[11] often a slow process. Twelve-step recovery programs may be helpful with their emphasis on coming out of hiding, finding God's power, finding a new family affiliation, breaking the "no talk" secrecy rules, learning to feel feelings, grieving lost developmental experiences, reprogramming, and cultivating intimacy with God.[12]

Teach Realistic Expectations

Unrealistic expectations frequently held by ACOAs include, "We will be as one and do everything together," "You will instinctively anticipate my every need and desire," "We will trust each other totally and immediately," or its opposite, "Trusting and being vulnerable in a relationship always brings pain." [13] Other unrealistic attitudes include the belief that normal people do not have to struggle to get what they want, normal people are perfect, and recovery from the effects of alcoholism should be rapid.

Louise had to come to grips with the reality that her parents, husband, and son could not realistically be expected to protect and care for her because of their entrenched perceptions of her role, their aggressiveness, and their self-centeredness. She could, however, insist on being treated with respect and could draw that respect out of them by being self-respecting and acting assertively.

Help Face Fears and Risk

One of the most difficult tasks for the counselor of ACOAs is to encourage constructive risk-taking. Change and growth always require risk-taking because the counselee is being asked to try something unfamiliar, unpredictable, and thus potentially painful. The emotional pain that ACOAs feel is usually associated with the unpredictability of their alcoholic parents' erratic behavior. It requires considerable courage for them to try something new, in spite of the misery of their current experience.

It is at this point that the counselor needs to gently lead the counselee into a deeper understanding of God's care for him or her. This may be difficult if the counselee sees God as unresponsive to her distress or blames him for her plight. Setting the situation in the context of the ongoing battle between God and Satan frequently helps counselees gain faith and trust in God, as well as the determination to fight the enemy of their souls.[14]

Counselees must be helped to see that positive change will require facing possible pain and working through it; avoiding it through unhealthy defenses and faulty patterns of behavior will not work. They must be encouraged to believe that therapeutic pain (the pain that comes from choosing healthy patterns and refusing to continue habitual ways of finding false security) will not destroy them. Establishing small experimental steps, such as being the first to be assertive in situations where there is not much to lose, is important. As those steps are successfully taken, a series of graduated risks should be introduced until the counselee is able to face his or her worst fears. Participation in self-help groups often provides the extra encouragement needed, as the ACOA hears of others taking risks successfully.[15]

Forgive and Let Go

Perhaps the most difficult step of recovery for ACOAs who come from extremely abusive alcoholic families is to forgive and let go of past pain and injustice. When we are treated unjustly and our personhood is violated physically or emotionally, we naturally yearn for and even demand justice. To forgive is not natural; judgment and reparation are.

As nonassertive ACOAs absorb the hurtful actions and words of those who are important to them, resentment and bitterness grow inside. Because the ACOA often fails to address and resolve the injustices (they usually cannot as children facing powerful and even violent parents), the wrongs accumulate and begin to define who the person is emotionally. Letting go becomes difficult, then, because it feels like there would be nothing left of one's self if all the hurts around which the person has constructed an identity are released.

Christian counseling first involves helping the person consider and internalize the psychospiritual meaning of Christ's sacrificial act of forgiveness on the cross. Christ became sin; that is, he took the place of the offending alcoholic parent and became the object of God's righteous judgment. But Christ also forgave sin ("Father, forgive them, for they do not know what they are doing," Luke 23:34). He has *already* suffered the just punishment of Holy God for *all* mankind. Our bitter attempts to punish others are totally unnecessary! He has given us both the example and the power to forgive through his resurrection. Thus, as the ACOA follows Jesus and lets go, he experiences a sense of self-sacrifice also. He gives up a wounded self that has become very familiar.

This brings us to the second task, which is to help the person to find a new identity that is not based on hurt and resentment, but is rooted in the mercy and forgiving love of Christ. This involves guiding him in the study of the Scriptures and discussing over time what it means to be a child of God. Finally, the counselor helps the wounded one to see that holding onto the hurts of the past with an unforgiving spirit is actually an act of codependence, of defining one's self through enmeshment with the faulty, dysfunctional behaviors of the offending parent.

NOTES

[1]Jane Miller, "Alcohol Abuse in America: Problems and Solutions," *Alcoholism Magazine* (February 1983): 8–9.

[2]Sandra D. Wilson, *Counseling Adult Children of Alcoholics* (Dallas: Word, 1989), xii. This is an outstanding resource written from an evangelical pespective.

[3]Ibid., 3–60.

[4]Emily Marlin, *Genograms: The New Tool for Exploring the Personality, Career, and Love Patterns You Inherit* (Chicago: Contemporary Books, 1989), and Monica McGoldrick and Randy Gerson, *Genograms in Family Assessment* (New York: W. W. Norton & Co., 1985) are two excellent guides for genogram analysis and construction.

[5]Emily Marlin, *Hope: New Choices and Recovery Strategies for Adult Children of Alcoholics* (New York: Harper & Row, 1987).

[6]John Jones, *The Children of Alcoholics Screening Test* (Chicago: Camelot Unlimited, 1983). The CAST and its test manual are available from Camelot Unlimited, 5 N. Wabash, Suite 1409, Chicago, IL, 60602.

[7]The COA Quiz taken from *Alcoholism & Addiction* magazine is reported with scoring key in Marlin, *Hope,* 254–55.

[8]Two good resources for understanding assertiveness are Robert E. Alberti and Michael L. Emmons, *Your Perfect Right* (San Luis Obispo, Calif.: Impact Publishers, 1986), and Charles E. Cerling, Jr., *Assertiveness and the Christian* (Chicago: Tyndale, 1980).

[9]Steven J. Danish, Anthony R. D'Augelli, and Allen L. Hauer, *Helping Skills: A Basic Training Program,* 2d ed. (New York: Human Sciences Press, 1980), 40–42. Contains a list of over 350 feeling words.

[10]Marlin, *Hope,* 17–31.

[11]Ronald Potter-Effron and Patricia Potter-Effron, *Letting Go of Shame* (San Francisco: Harper & Row, 1989).

[12]John Bradshaw, *Healing the Shame that Binds You* (Deerfield Beach, Fla.: Health Communications, 1988), 135.

[13]Wilson, *Counseling Adult Children of Alcoholics,* 177–78.

[14]Craig W. Ellison, "The War of the Ages," unpublished manuscript. Available from the author at Alliance Theological Seminary, Nyack, New York, 10960.

[15]Marlin, *Hope,* 88–103, and Wilson, *Counseling Adult Chilren of Alcoholics,* 281.

CHAPTER 11

AIDS

"A SENSE OF CRISIS is hard to sustain. It thrives on earthquakes and tornadoes, plane crashes and terrorist bombings. But forces that kill people one at a time have a way of fading into the psychic landscape."[1] In less than ten years we have witnessed the thunderous onrush of one of the most monstrous diseases to have visited humankind in recent history. And according to experts, it has just begun. We have no way of knowing the extent of the repercussions ahead. The number of "people with AIDS" (PWA) is expected to reach six million by the year 2000.[2]

Urban centers have been hit hard. San Francisco, because of its large male homosexual population, has one of the largest HIV (human immune-deficiency virus) positive populations[3] anywhere. Other major urban areas with large numbers of intravenous drug users have large numbers of PWAs also.[4]

AIDS is contracted when body fluids are exchanged. The persons most at risk are male homosexuals, intravenous drug users, and prostitutes. Drug users contract AIDS when they come in contact with infected blood through the use of shared hypodermic needles. Homosexual males pass it to each other through anal intercourse, which involves the tearing of anal tissue and the introduction of infected semen into the bloodstream. Prostitutes, infected by bisexual males or by contaminated needles, are often doubly at risk. The virus may remain dormant in the body for years before it begins its rampage through the system.

In addition to the adults at risk is the rising number of babies being born with AIDS that has been passed on to them by their AIDS-infected mothers, most of whom are drug users. Many of these women are African Americans.[5] Another group at risk are the hemophiliacs. In urban centers, in order to support their habits, drug addicts sell their blood to blood banks. The tainted blood products have been used to treat some hemophiliacs. Thus, some hemophiliacs have contracted AIDS through the use of Factor VIII, a blood plasma product needed to help their blood to clot.[6]

Along with medical and psychological problems, many PWAs experience severe prejudice. A young hemophiliac boy in Florida, for example, was banned from school when it was found that he was infected with AIDS. And as if that were not enough, neighbors set fire to the family's house. When AIDS was believed to have originated in Haiti, Haitians were ostracized. The cause of all this, of course, is ignorance about the transmission of the disease. It cannot be passed through casual contact, such as shaking hands, or even by kissing. Contamination occurs through the exchange of body fluids such as blood or semen.

CASE STUDIES

John

John contacted an urban pastor he had heard on a local radio program. He had led a homosexual life for many years and had just been informed that he had AIDS. The prognosis was bleak. Even though he had had many sexual partners, he was a solitary person. His major concern was that he did not want to die alone. During the course of the disease, he exhausted every medical option available to him, even traveling to Mexico for an experimental treatment. While being counseled by the pastor, John accepted Christ as his personal Savior. Later he died.

Pedro

Pedro was both an IV drug user and a homosexual. As a teenager, he had come to the U.S. mainland from Puerto Rico. Almost immediately, he fell into a homosexual lifestyle and was introduced to drugs by one of his lovers eventually becoming addicted. At that point, he began to engage in sex with a multitude of men to earn money for drugs. HIV positive but symptom-free, he, too, has accepted Christ and meets with a group of PWAs that is sponsored by an urban evangelical church.

These cases are typical of the PWAs that the Christian counselor will meet. They are frequently depressed and overwhelmed by their situation. Often they have been abandoned by friends and family. One PWA had to live in the streets until he found a public shelter for PWAs because his mother would not allow him in her house. She feared that he might pass AIDS on to the family by eating from the same plates and drinking from their glasses.

Gladys

Gladys is a pert, bright, and pleasant black woman. She is thirty-three years old and the mother of a three-year-old son. At age twenty-three, she owned a dry-cleaning establishment that employed eight people. She is a Phi Beta Kappa college graduate in the top ten percent of her class. She grew up in a comfortable, middle-income home as an only child, and describes both parents as being alcoholics. Her mother, a registered nurse, has just stopped drinking in the last year. Prior to that, she had consumed half a bottle of gin a day for as long as Gladys could remember. Her father, recently retired as a captain in the fire department, has drunk a fifth of scotch per day all of Gladys's life.

Gladys loathed her parent's drinking and vowed never to touch alcohol. To this day she does not drink. About six years ago, though, she was invited to a party where guests were using cocaine. Influenced by a boyfriend to try "just a little," she at first resisted, but eventually she gave in because she was afraid of losing him. The feeling of exhilaration she experienced hooked her from that day on. She lived for "coke," and began to take money from her business to buy it. Soon she could not pay for supplies and equipment. Consequently, the quality of her employees' work deteriorated, and finally she was forced to close the business. She lost her car to the bank and used up all of her other assets to buy cocaine. Desperately, she began to forge her parents' signatures on checks and cash them. However, their account was soon overdrawn and they then realized her plight. They tried to get her into treatment but she refused to go. The pleasure of "getting high" was too compelling.

When her parents would no longer support her habit, she left home to work as a call girl in a brothel. The money she made was not enough to supply her habit, so she became a streetwalker. By this time she was mainlining (injecting drugs) and became infected with the AIDS virus through the use of shared needles. While working as a prostitute, she became pregnant and her son was born addicted and had to be detoxified before she could take him home. Gladys's parents have custody of him because the courts threatened to have him placed in foster care. She complains that her father "smothers" him the way he smothered her. She also complains that, growing up, she did not have a life of her own—at least no social life. Her father demanded that she go to a nearby college and drove there each Friday night so she could spend the weekend at home, driving her back on Sunday night. All weekend he "programmed" her every move, but her mother was rather remote and "stayed in her cups."

Gladys is now in her fourth rehabilitation program. Typically, she becomes detoxified, but just as she is about to get her life back together, she returns to drugs. While in her last program, she realized that "the Higher Power" spoken about in Narcotics Anonymous was not enough. She was introduced to the Lord Jesus by a Christian worker at the rehabilitation center and accepted him as Lord and Savior. Since that time, she has had one "slip" with drugs but came back to the Christian AIDS group and confessed it openly, receiving the group's support.

ANALYSIS: GLADYS

BEHAVIOR:	1.	Hyperactivity; unable to stay with a task or thought; pressured speech.
	2.	Preoccupied with her condition; every physical change, however slight, is feared.
	3.	Morbid fear of returning to drug use; afraid to be alone, believes that being with another believer will prevent her from "slipping."
AFFECT:	1.	Feelings of depression.
	2.	Feelings of fear.
	3.	Feelings of anger (especially at father).
	4.	Feelings of helplessness.
	5.	Feelings of rejection.
SENSATION:	1.	Skin seems to tingle.
IMAGERY:	1.	Father dictating her every move.
	2.	Parents sitting in house drinking.

	3.	Dry-cleaning establishment in other people's hands.
	4.	Working the streets looking for "Johns."
	5.	Constant search for cocaine.

COGNITION:
1. I am a mess.
2. As soon as I begin to get it together, I mess up.
3. I am a slut.
4. My father still controls my life; he wants me to die so that he can have my son all to himself. He wants me to disappear.
5. I'm going to "fall" (go back to drugs).
6. How many more drug programs will it take for me to get straight?

INTERPERSONAL
RELATIONSHIPS:
1. Love/hate relationship with father.
2. Feels that mother is not there for her and, therefore, does not seek her help.
3. Difficult to ask for help from group.

DRUGS/
BIOLOGY:
1. Craving for cocaine.
2. Constant sniffing as a result of damage to nasal passages from snorting cocaine.
3. Trying to stop smoking cigarettes.

SPIRITUAL:
1. "Baby" Christian who has not yet learned to use the enabling power of the Holy Spirit to combat the craving for drugs.
2. Still unwilling to submit herself completely to the will of God the Father because she sees him as her smothering father.
3. Does not have a church to fellowship in and feels spiritually isolated.

GOALS

The primary goals for people with AIDS are to:
1. Help them deal with the fear of dying.
2. Help their families deal with the reality of the PWA's condition.
3. Help them resolve feelings of shame.
4. Develop positive relationships with others.
5. Help them handle rejection from family and friends.

Process

Gladys requested counseling when she realized that she "sabotages" herself. As noted, she has been in three treatment programs and is now in her fourth, from which she was almost discharged for using drugs while in treatment. She admits that she cannot accept success, and must always do something to spoil it. Objectively she recognizes that she is bright, but her self-image is poor. We have listed individual goals for Gladys's treatment, but the overarching goal is the enhancement of self-esteem as it is for those PWAs who are male homosexuals.

This brief profile of Gladys is typical of many PWAs who have contracted the disease through IV-drug use. They live with a great deal of psychic pain and use drugs as a psychological anesthetic. In Gladys's case, her mother told her that she was not wanted, and, thus, she has never felt valued. Gladys's mother also tells her grandson, as well as Gladys, that she does not like children around her.

Albeit, Gladys is, in addition to being highly intelligent and introspective, painfully aware of the psychological dynamics that have led up to her present situation. The danger is that she may intellectualize her pain rather than allowing herself to experience it, which would lead to relief. There are moments when she does experience real joy, but only for a moment before it dies.

Help Them Deal with the Fear of Dying

Gladys has an ambivalent attitude toward death. On one hand, she expresses a desire to live, but on the other, death seems like it would be a welcome relief from suffering. Because Gladys has a real, living link with the Lord and an increasing knowledge of the Word, the counselor has been able to use these powerful forces in counseling her. She now sees that God has an important function for her and her life has meaning—something that she could not have imagined before her conversion. She is beginning to understand that the quality of her life is more important than the length of it. Involved in counseling other PWAs, she is forcefully reminded of the value of her own life. The counselor also is encouraging Gladys to return to graduate school. Ultimately, however, what really undergirds Gladys's faith is God's Word, "If we live, we live to the Lord; and if we die, we die to the Lord.

So, whether we live or die, we belong to the Lord" (Rom. 14:8).
Again and again she needs to be reminded of this, but each time it
comforts and sustains her. Counseling also helped her understand
the very real influence Satan trys to have on her life—that he
(Satan) will constantly try to undermine her faith and that she
must have on the "full armor of God" (Eph. 6:13).

Counselor's must be prepared to see almost total regression in
PWAs from one session to the next. It may appear that all the
achievements from the previous session have been wiped out. It is
not quite that way, however. Rather, this is a typical step in the
PWA's coming to grips with the awesome reality of death. The
Christian counselor always has in mind the salvation of his
counselee, but never is this more important than with a PWA
whose death is imminent. PWAs not only fear death, but, rather,
the dying process itself.[7] Almost all PWAs have seen their friends
die horrible deaths and must be helped to deal with the possibility
that that may be how they will die. The counselor needs to allow
the counselee to talk about his or her fears.[8] There are five typical
stages through which dying people pass:

1. Denial and isolation.
2. Anger.
3. Bargaining.
4. Depression.
5. Acceptance.[9]

The counselor need not force the dying person through these
stages, but should be sensitive to them and prepared to minister
to the needs of each stage.

Help Families Deal with the Reality of the PWA's Condition

The families and friends of the PWA experience a wide range
of emotions with fear, anger, and a feeling of helplessness
prevalent. The counselor must be ready to help the family deal
with these emotions, and must not deny the family the free
expression of these emotions.

The fear of losing a loved one is very real, as is fear about the
dying process itself. As noted, it is not just death but dying that is
the issue. Having witnessed an emaciated PWA near death they
thus fear the experience for their loved one. In the final stages of
AIDS, the counselor needs to help the family think of their family

member as he or she was, and help them empathize with their loved one. The PWA needs them now more than ever.

Anger is a very real emotion that must be addressed. Families of HIV infected IV-drug users and homosexuals often feel that the person could have avoided contracting this disease because it is true that AIDS is a direct result of high risk acts. The anger, however, is often unconscious, and sometimes must be brought to the surface by the counselor so that it can be dealt with. The counselor must give them permission, as it were, to express their anger.

Helplessness is also an emotion that attends the family of dying patients. It is at this point that they need to be put in touch with the One in whose hands both life and death are held. God is the One who gives life, and he has the right to take it. The counselor assists the family in bowing to Divine Providence and leading them to understand that his way, however painful, is best.

Help Them Resolve Feelings of Shame

The counselor must acknowledge that feelings of shame are a consequence of having AIDS. It is important to allow the PWA to express his feelings freely, "I feel so stupid. I knew what shooting drugs could do. I saw my friends die but I didn't think it would happen to me." Sin came into the world long ago, and we all live with the consequences of our behavior. It is important that the PWA accept this truth. Here again there is the need to emphasize the forgiveness of God. "Therefore there is now *no condemnation* for those who are in Christ Jesus" (Rom. 8:1 italics mine). The PWA must see that, after God forgives, he no longer condemns and therefore he need not condemn himself any longer. "Neither do I condemn you. . . . Go now and leave your life of sin" (John 8:11). Gladys had a great deal of trouble accepting the forgiveness of God. The thinking, *"I* am bad" must be separated from, "my *behavior* is bad." Gladys had to see that God loved her, though *not* her behavior.

Develop Positive Relationships with Others

Gertrude, a PWA, was experiencing difficulties adjusting to a relationship with a young man who was very much in love with her. In a session she blurted out, "I don't know how to be a sober girlfriend." This epitomizes a major issue for PWAs—those who have been IV-drug users, as well as male homosexuals who have come to faith in Christ and no longer wish to lead a gay lifestyle. Both groups have to learn to establish relationships with straight and sober people. The drug and gay communities have their own subcultures with norms and values peculiar to those cultures. Those who no longer want to continue those lifestyles must be resocialized into the mainstream culture.

We spoke earlier of developing a cadre of lay counselors to deal with a host of issues confronting the urban pastor. Here is a place to use them. The lay counselor can be the one person who will be a bridge between the established culture and the PWA, but this person must be chosen with extreme care. He must be accepting of a very different lifestyle; the PWA has experienced enough condemnation. The goal here is not so much "talk" counseling but the establishment of a genuine relationship with a straight, sober person. This may simply involve regular conversation, which allows the PWA to talk about his feelings without interruption. It may be as simple as playing a game of checkers or chess, looking at a TV program together or just walking and talking—essentially, just being a friend to the PWA. He needs time to find out how to relate again.

Gladys's counselor was able to begin that type of relationship with her because he knew the neighborhood in which she grew up. They began by talking about places in the community, and thus began to build the bridge. Most of Gladys's relationship with men (the counselor was male) had been that of a prostitute to a customer. Therefore, a relationship with a male who did not want anything from her was something new. She did not know how to receive (in this case counseling) without also giving, which in her experience involved sex. This was a tricky problem for the counselor because he wanted to affirm her personhood, including her femininity. After a time, though, Gladys was able to accept affirmation that did not involve sex.

An AIDS support group is also vital to the establishment of positive relationships. In addition to the lay counseling that Gladys received, she belonged to a support group made up of PWAs and "straight" people, which was an excellent way to have non-PWA contacts. The members had been well-chosen by the pastor and the PWAs were greatly strengthened by the group.

Help Them Handle Rejection from Their Family and Friends

Fred's mother would not allow him back into her house after he was diagnosed as being HIV positive. She had many objections to his living there. She told him that she could not sterilize his dishes and glasses; she was afraid that if he sneezed, he would infect everyone in the house; and she was especially concerned about her three-year-old granddaughter, who lived with her. The most she would do for him was hand him a few dollars at the door, being careful not to touch him. As each of his old buddies from the neighborhood found out, they too shunned him, making their chance meetings on the street very brief. Fred, at times, considered suicide because he felt there was no point in living any more.

Introduced to the AIDS support group, Fred at last felt accepted. The group encouraged him to look for work (he is a skilled carpenter), which he did. This helped him feel even more accepted. He was counseled, though, not to tell others about his illness because that would only lead to further rejection. As others in the group shared their experiences with rejection, Fred realized that he was not alone in his plight. The PWA must be reminded repeatedly that the rejection is ignorance on the part of the rejecter and is *not* necessarily a reflection on him. He must see it as the rejecter's problem and not his own. This, by the way, has been a great help to minorities who have experienced discrimination. Do not allow the racist's problem to become yours: Fred seemed very much heartened by this advice.

The group's acceptance gave Fred a place in which to feel belonged. It enabled him to better handle the rejection of the outside world. Fred's support group does a great deal of touching and hugging. One AIDS counselor put it well, "Touching is healing."[10]

NOTES

[1]G. Crowley, M. Hagen, and Ruth Marshall, "AIDS, the Next Ten Years," *Newsweek* (June 25, 1990), 20.

[2]Ibid., 20.

[3]C. Kain, *No Longer Immune: A Counselor's Guide to AIDS.* (Alexandria, Va.: American Association for Counseling and Development, 1989), 32.

[4]Crowley, op. cit., 27.

[5]B. Lambert, "AIDS in Black Women Seen as Leading Killer," *New York Times* (July 11, 1990).

[6]Kain, op. cit., 15.

[7]W. Hoffman and S. Grenz, *AIDS: Ministry in the Midst of an Epidemic* (Grand Rapids: Baker, 1990), 219–22.
[8]Ibid., 221.
[9]Ibid., 221.
[10]Kain, *No Longer Immune*, 216.

CHAPTER 12

Marital Conflict

DURING THE 1980s, over 1.1 million marriages ended in divorce every year. Half of the first marriages begun during the 1990s will also end in divorce. Approximately 60 percent of all second marriages will collapse as well. This means that one out of every three children born during the past decade will most likely live in a stepfamily before they are eighteen.[1]

There was a time when divorce was considered the relatively happy alternative to a highly conflicted marriage. The common wisdom had concluded that, for the sake of the children, it was better to split than to stay together. More recent research is casting doubt on those assumptions. A substantial minority of divorced men and women feel rejected and angry at their former partners ten years after breaking up.[2] Recent research also shows that children may be significantly impacted by divorce as well.[3]

Divorce is normally the end result of protracted, unresolved marital conflict. While all marital conflict does not necessarily end in divorce, marriages filled with conflict are stressful and unsatisfying at best.

Marital conflict may originate from a number of different sources. Among the most common contributors are (1) faulty communication, (2) disillusionment, (3) ineffective conflict resolution, (4) lack of affirmation, (5) rules, (6) selfishness, (7) differences, (8) loyalty, (9) personal distortions, (10) infidelity, (11) parenting, (12) the blending of families. In this chapter we will briefly describe each source of conflict and suggest therapeutic goals and principles for reconciliation in each area of conflict.

It is highly recommended that the counselor regularly use the family genogram in cases involving marital conflict. The genogram provides a multigenerational family picture of *emotional themes* (anxiety, anger, depression), *relational patterns* (enmeshment, triangulation, cutoffs), *dysfunctional behaviors* (substance abuse, nonchemical addictions, eating disorders), *psychomoral rules* ("Don't fully commit yourself, keep your options open," "Take care of yourself first because you can't trust a man or woman to care about you," "If I get angry enough I'll be able to get what I want"), *secrets* (the discovery that a parent has been married before, an incestuous relationship, an adoption), *traumatic events* that have altered family patterns or self-perceptions (the death of a child, an act of violence suffered by a family member, a major economic or career reversal), *emotionally charged issues* (religion, independence and conformity), and *loyalty demands*.[4] Current issues can often be placed in the context of one or both partner's family systems and be more quickly and thoroughly addressed. And because the counselor's approach is more indirect, genograms frequently help a person or couple recognize significant patterns and face issues in a less defensive manner.

FAULTY COMMUNICATION

Human communication is an amazing phenomenon. There are approximately 600,000 words available in the English language. Of these, an educated adult uses about 2,000. According to standard dictionaries, there are about 14,000 different definitions for the 500 most-used words with some words having as many as 100 different meanings. Looking at this fact alone, the possibilities for miscommunication are astronomical. In addition, it is estimated that as much as 80 percent of communication is nonverbal, which is much more ambiguous than words. Nonverbal communication also carries the most weight in emotionally significant and intimate interactions. It is amazing, then, that we humans are able to arrive at any shared meaning given these factors!

One frequent flaw in communication is the tendency for spouses to assume that they either know in advance or know with minimal information what their partner is thinking or saying. Such "mind reading" is usually justified on the basis of the longevity of the relationship or the predictability of the spouse. Neither reason justifies the behavior, given the ambiguities inherent in verbal and nonverbal communication. It does not make sense to assume.

Furthermore, when we understand that the meanings arrived at through communication involve the interpretation or filtering of another person's intended message through our own mental and emotional screens, we would do well to assume little and to make a habit of confirming the meanings we assume. This is especially critical when a couple is under stress and dealing with emotionally charged issues. Each spouse needs to be sure to ask for clarification of their partner's messages, and to make sure that their intended meanings are being received as well. Learning to communicate assertively with each other is critical for accurate and healthy communication.[5]

> Peter and Sylvia were in the midst of major conflict when they sought out a counselor. At the heart of the conflict was Sylvia's conclusion that Peter was uninterested in her, never listened to her, and did not love her. Through counseling it became clear that Peter was verbally unsure of himself, felt intimidated in emotional exchanges with his wife, and failed to look at her or respond because of his nonassertiveness and resentment toward her emotionally insistent style.

DISILLUSIONMENT

Many marriages, in Western society at least, are composed of hopes and dreams and, often, unrealistic expectations. People decide to marry for any number of reasons. Some marry to escape unpleasant family situations. Others want to "change" their spouse. The problem is that when people marry out of need, their need-centered marriages rarely live up to expectations. In fact, more often than not, couples go through a period of disillusionment sometime during the first two years of marriage. Perhaps their partner's personality is not the way it was during courtship. Perhaps it turned out that the partner was not as interested in certain goals and pursuits as he or she appeared to be before marriage. Perhaps expectations about love and marriage are unrealistic. For example, some believe that if there is true love, there will never be any conflict. Others believe that if their partner truly loves them, the partner should know their needs without being told. Regardless of the reason, disillusionment is a big problem.

Counseling those in conflict because of disillusionment involves helping them to let go of need-generated fantasy and realize that all couples must adjust their initial expectations on their way to a mature and healthy marriage. It must focus on the positive characteristics of their partner and in their relationship, rather than the negatives. It must stress forgiveness—forgiving their partner for being less than their ideal and for failing to be the answer to all of their needs.

> Priscilla and Larry had been married for three years when they came in for counseling. They continually argued with each other. Larry had had several sustained episodes of impotence as well. Counseling revealed the underlying issue of Priscilla's disillusionment with Larry—he did not live up to her idealized recollection of a former boyfriend. Priscilla was thus encouraged to renounce romantic fantasizing and focus on the positive aspects she could sincerely identify in her husband. For his part, Larry was encouraged to be more assertive and to let go of the deep resentment that had interfered with his ability to perform sexually.

INEFFECTIVE CONFLICT RESOLUTION

A certain amount of conflict is an inevitable part of close relationships, especially in a world populated by finite and fallen creatures. Ineffective conflict resolution and thus marital conflict is manifested in several different ways. It frequently arises when a couple fails to clearly define the primary issue under discussion. A refusal by one or both partners to accept the validity of the other person's viewpoint is also an area of conflict. Still another type of conflict occurs when the partners fail to stick with the primary issue at hand, and begin to "kitchen sink," or bring all kinds of emotionally charged irrelevancies into the discussion in a kind of power play. In addition, are *ad hominem* arguments in which one or both partners attack the personality, character, or family history of their partner in an attempt to gain power through personal attack.

Counseling those who have excessive amounts of marital conflict or faulty ways of processing conflict initially involves helping them to set aside adequate and unpressured time to deal with emotionally significant issues. (On the way out the door to go to work is not the time to deal with such matters!) It also involves instruction in how to define the primary issue at hand, how to focus on one's partner as a friend rather than an enemy, how to brainstorm and evaluate possible solutions to the problem, how to contract and be sure that both partners have definitely agreed to the apparent solution, and how to subsequently review the solution to see if it is working.

It is very important that the couple be helped through several conflict resolution experiences with "live" issues so that they are able to gain the positive experience of constructive conflict resolution. The counselor should be sure to start with issues that have high potential for success in order to encourage the couple to use a constructive approach. Subsequent issues addressed in the counseling sessions can be gradually upgraded in difficulty as the couple gains experience, good feelings toward each other, and conflict resolution skills.

If difficulty persists, it may be that one of the partners is attempting to unilaterally control outcomes due to emotional insecurities or learned patterns of dominance and aggression. Too, there may be underlying mistrust because one partner has reneged on agreements in the past. In either case, the counselor will need to be sensitive to such hidden influences.

LACK OF AFFIRMATION

Close relationships are inherently unstable. They can either grow or wither and take place in a short period of time. The climate in which they are set is a key factor. To thrive, they must be regularly nourished with affection and affirmation. Some have suggested that relationships work on an exchange basis; that is, the more positive reinforcement received (compared to negative or nonexistent reinforcement), the more likely a relationship is to endure and to grow.

A big problem in ongoing relationships is the tendency for a couple to forget that their marriage must be intentional. The courtship period in most relationships is immersed in a lake of affirmation. There are many positive reinforcers for the relationship, from the thrill of looking deeply into a lover's eyes to sharing hopes and dreams. In the crunch of daily routines and responsibilities, however, it is easy to forget that specific attention must be paid to nurturing the marriage if it is to remain alive.

Marriages are killed by the lack of regular affirmation. Affirmation communicates verbally and nonverbally that one is glad to be in the relationship, is happy being married, and likes one's spouse. Conversely, active criticism or the lack of positive reinforcement signals disinterest and negative feelings toward the partner or relationship, and introduces bad feelings that cause the partners to pull away from each other. Because a spouse's evaluation and feelings typically carry heavy emotional weight, even small criticisms function as significant put-downs. The relationship begins to wither.

The counselor needs to encourage the couple to see affirmation in terms of a savings account for their relationship. The more regularly they put "deposits" of affirmation into their account, the better chance they have to build a positive and growing relationship. As long as the assets exceed the costs in the particular marriage, the marriage will be satisfying. If, however, they make few affirmational deposits while making regular and substantial withdrawals, their relationship will diminish until there is nothing left. It is then that separation and divorce typically occur.

Among the deposits or positive reinforcers available are such things as basic courtesy and politeness, responsiveness to a partner's needs, going out of one's way to do something significant for one's partner, spending time talking together, engaging in recreational and leisure activities that both enjoy, spiritual encouragement, regular and positive sexual interaction, and shared dreams and goals. Among the withdrawals or costs to the relationship are direct criticism and put-downs; failure to spend regular time together talking, praying, and playing; arguments and bickering; disagreements over parenting issues; and failure to show respect and care toward each other.

The counselor should instruct each partner to make a list of things that communicate to them their spouse's love. The items should be positively worded, specific, repeatable actions. Each item should be assigned a deposit value from 1 to 100. After the lists have been separately developed and screened in a session with the counselor, the couple should then be encouraged to make at least one intentional deposit per day in their partner's account, based on the partner's list.

RULES

Human beings are rule-oriented. We make rules, we enforce rules, and we break rules. A world without rules is frightening to consider. Because we are made in the image of God, we naturally look for order, but because we instinctively sense our fallenness, all human societies have rules for the purpose of avoiding utter chaos and destruction.

As we are socialized, each person acquires a complex set of rules. Some of the rules are explicitly taught by parents, adult authority figures, and peers. Others are implicitly taught as we observe those who are important to us and inferentially abstract principles or rules as we watch them. In one way or another, we learn that some things are "right" and some things are "wrong." Unfortunately what appears to be "right" may not actually be right. Rotten rules may be internalized and subsequently held onto with tremendous emotional intensity. Faulty rules are invariably destructive emotionally or interpersonally (or both).

Examples of rotten rules are, "Don't make waves, keep your troubles to yourself," "A wife should be submissive and do what I want her to," "Don't be selfish, take care of others' needs (exclusively)," and "You should do your own thing and develop yourself regardless of what your spouse thinks."

Each spouse inevitably brings rules into the marriage. Some of the rules may be good, and some may be rotten. Often we are not really aware of what our rules are until we try to operate with them and we find our partner balking. Or perhaps our partner tries to function by his rules and we discover he's not playing by the "right" (that is, "our") rules. Conflict is heightened if the partners do not understand that most of the rules they operate by are familial and cultural, not biblical. Although such rules *feel* like absolute biblical standards, they usually are not. The rules are emotionally based and defended as absolutes. Failure to understand this will lead to power struggles as one or both spouses attempt to impose their psychomoral standards on the other. The counselor must help each spouse (1) clearly identify his rules, especially the faulty ones; (2) de-absolutize (or let go of) the conviction that only his or her rules are right; and (3) negotiate a set of compromise rules acceptable to both partners.

Tanya and Stanley were having considerable conflict over the issue of rules. They had been married for about two years. Tanya came from a home where togetherness and mutuality were encouraged, and responsibility was an accented value (rule). Stanley, on the other hand, came from a divorced home without a father. His mother's job had left little time for them to spend together; hence, expectations of togetherness were minimal. Stanley was free to do what he wanted most of the time, as long as he did not get into trouble. Their differing backgrounds set the stage for conflict over rules. Tanya felt that Stanley should be home every night to spend time with her.

Stanley felt that it was important for him to develop his interests and abilities so that he could continue to grow as a person. He wanted to be out four nights a week taking continuing education courses, pursuing a model-railroad hobby, and playing basketball or baseball. Tanya also felt that they should be praying together and going to church twice on Sunday and on Wednesday night. Stanley, however, felt that his faith should be practiced in freedom rather than in legalism. He balked at the rules Tanya tried to enforce while, at the same time, trying to enforce his rules of liberty and independence.

SELFISHNESS

Selfishness is part of being sinful, egocentric beings. To some degree we all struggle with it, whether we face the truth or not. Allegations of selfishness within marriage usually arise when one partner feels neglected or not listened to. If his spouse constantly insists on having her own way and refuses to allow the offended spouse to express his viewpoint, accusations of selfishness will soon emerge. Therefore, it is essential that both spouses work hard to curb their selfishness or the relationship will break into warring camps with both parties primarily concerned about getting and guarding what they feel they need. Sometimes the partner who is accused of being selfish is not the selfish one; the accuser may just have learned how to use guilt and personal attacks to get the other person to give in. In these cases, the accuser is the one who is selfish.

Jill and Eddie were on the brink of divorce because Eddie felt that he should be the one to choose the car and the home they wanted to purchase. He also felt that he should not have to work full time, and since they were married they should live off the inheritance Jill had received when her parents were killed in an automobile accident. Eddie accused Jill of being selfish for not wanting to go along with his plans.

The counselor needs to help each partner put himself into the other's place. This can be done by very intentionally asking the person how he would feel if a similar (or even more emotionally relevant) situation confronted him. If the problem is rooted in a family system that has catered to the partner's selfishness (perhaps as a youngest or only child, or as a favorite), it will require considerable skill and perseverance to help the person adopt another viewpoint.

DIFFERENCES

Differences tend to threaten. Psychological security is largely based on unanimity. The more others are like us, the less anxiety we feel. The more others agree with us, the more assured we are about our identity, our worth, and our way of life. Marriage, however, often triggers intense and disruptive feelings, as one's very essence seems to be called into question in the face of a spouse's differences. Further, when one's differences are criticized because they are threatening to one's spouse, conflict erupts with full force. One secret to a successful marriage is to marry someone who has similar values and interests, and then to accept any differences as interesting opportunities to learn and grow.

Some of the more significant differences likely to surface in marriages are those involving gender, emotional style, values and preferences, biological rhythms, energy, and personality. Gender differences include variations between men and women in the emotion-centeredness of their communication, directness and indirectness of communication, and listening responses. Men tend to have a much narrower range of emotions and have more difficulty expressing feelings. Women tend to consider relationships when weighing decisions, while men are more likely to solve human-relation problems less personally. Women are more verbally interactive when listening and men give fewer cues to indicate that they are listening and responding.

Differences in emotional style include emotional pursuer and emotional distancer orientations. Emotional pursuers tend to look to other people, especially those they consider close, for comfort when under stress. They usually prefer to talk out their problems and arrive at solutions through the process of dialogue. Emotional distancers tend to pull away from others and seek their own counsel when under stress. After they have gained emotional strength by emotional withdrawal, and after they have formulated their basic solution, they may move back toward their partner and "announce" their decision. As a result, the pursuer spouse often feels abandoned, not realizing that, when they pursue, stress increases for the distancer. An emotional drag race commences— the pursuer pursues, causing stress, and the distancer distances, feeling hemmed in, smothered, and seeking escape.

Differences in values and preferences have to do with those things each person perceives to be important in life. One partner may highly value aesthetics and wish to invest significant time and resources in the pursuit of artistic preferences. Another may highly value recreation and wish to do the same thing in the pursuit of recreational activities. Obviously, the potential for conflict is great because of the necessary decisions regarding allocation of time, energy, and money.

Biological rhythms may differ between spouses and cause marital conflict. One of the most frequently encountered sources of conflict has to do with being a "morning person" or a "night person." If spouses are dramatically different, conflict will arise over when to talk with one another, when to have sexual relations, and when to have private space. Differing energy levels may lead to conflict as one partner may be "raring to go," while the other prefers fewer and more sedate activities. Finally, personality differences such as those suggested in the Myers-Briggs Type Indicator[6] may produce significant conflict.

LOYALTY ISSUES

John and Anna were on the verge of separation when they came in for marital counseling. Anna was frustrated by John's insistence on putting his mother's needs ahead of her and the children. His mother, who had been widowed for a year, had always put pressure on John and his brothers to visit at least once a week and spend holidays with her. With his father gone, John felt an added responsibility to check in on her. As a result, he would spend over an hour with her two or three nights a week and do maintenance work for her on the weekends. John also felt that he should attend the same church as his mother and pressured Anna to attend against her will. Lately, whenever John and Anna had any tension between them, John had gone to his mother's house and stayed there for two to three days.

Loyalty issues in relation to one's family of origin primarily involve a sense of obligation on the part of the child toward the parent. The message conveyed verbally or nonverbally is that the adult child owes some form of recompense to the parents for all they have done to rear him. As a result, the adult child feels pressure to place the needs, schedules, and traditions of his parents above those of his spouse and immediate family. Failure to do so may cause the adult child to feel like a bad son or daughter.

The stress of this conflict of loyalty may be extremely intense, depending upon the degree of family enmeshment and shaming that mark the family of origin. Certain cultural groups emphasize family togetherness and loyalty more than others. This was the case for John, who comes from an Italian culture. Typically, these pressures for loyalty create significant marital conflict. The spouse feels as if she is not the most important person in her partner's life, that he cannot be relied on to be there when needed, and that the marriage is not really the couple's own.

Counseling must show respect for each partner's family of origin, while drawing out the meaning of the biblical mandate to "leave and cleave" for their marriage relationship. A spouse who is exceptionally loyal to the family of origin too often has deep feelings of resentment because of the unnatural sense of obligation. The counselor should very cautiously help him express some of those feelings, while at the same time empathizing with his partner's feelings of being second in his life. The counselor should also point out any cultural values that conflict with family loyalty with the view to elevating responsibility to spouse and nuclear family over cultural values.

> Tanisha and John have three children. Since the birth of their firstborn, Jaylene, John had spent very little time with Tanisha or the children. He worked long hours. When he was not working, John felt that he deserved some relaxation doing things with male friends, so that is how he spent most of his free time. Over the years, because of her husband's absence, Tanisha had bonded very closely to her children and found herself with little affection or attachment toward John. As far as she was concerned, they were primarily business partners. John, though, had recently begun complaining that they never had sexual relations any more and that he felt he did not matter to the children.

Triangulation and coalition building is a second, equally damaging loyalty issue. It is often difficult to discern which comes first, a lack of commitment to one's spouse or a shift of bonding from parent to children. Regardless, the result is a weakening of the primary bond between husband and wife that reverberates throughout the family system. Helping both partners understand the emotional roots of the coalitions that have been formed, the immediate and probable long-range impact on the children (especially in their future marriages), and the benefits that both would enjoy by putting their relationship ahead of any other bonding (including attachment to work, success, money, and children) is a goal all can work toward.

PERSONAL DISTORTIONS

Because of the Fall (Gen. 2–3), all of us have some level of distortion or dysfunction. We do not perceive, think, feel, or behave in the most healthy ways possible at all times. As a result, emotional distortions such as latent anxiety, shame, low self-esteem, pessimism, depression, and perfectionism (among others) dynamically interact and affect marriage and family interactions. To a certain degree, a successful marriage might be defined as the ability of a couple to address and neutralize their respective dysfunctions. The more severe and chronic the dysfunction, the more difficult it will be to absorb the pathology. Paranoia, chronic lying, obsessive-compulsive disorder, clinical depression, and psychosis are typically too stressful for a couple to process successfully without substantial professional help. Without counseling, such problems will eventually lead to some level of disengagement or marital dissolution.

Even when a marriage suffers from less severe dysfunctions, counseling may be very helpful for enhancing the health and longevity of the marriage. Frequently, the counselor will call for both joint and individual counseling sessions so that couple-generated dysfunctions, as well as individual dysfunctions can be addressed. A failure to focus on the personal dimension usually results in an impasse in the marital counseling.

INFIDELITY

Infidelity is perhaps the most devastating conflict and becomes the greatest test of a marriage because it introduces feelings of mistrust and rejection, questions about commitment and loyalty, anxiety over sexually transmitted diseases, and struggles over bitterness and forgiveness. Infidelity may come about because of such sexual issues as impulsive lust and frustration over unfulfilled sexual desire. The highly sensual and sexual images that continually bombard men and women through the media are two of the prime "triggers" for this type of behavior. More often than not, however, infidelity is the result of unresolved stresses and emotional immaturity. For example, infidelity may be an expression of weak emotional bonding, a failure to have one's psychological needs met as expected by one's partner, an unsatisfying level of emotional intimacy, or the build-up of resentment and hurt that has greatly distanced the partners.

Leonard and Chris had been married about seven years and had been Christians for less than two years when they came for counseling. The event that prompted their visit had taken place at a revival meeting. There Leonard had gone forward in response to an altar call. Chris joined him, and sobbing, he asked her forgiveness for an affair he had been involved in until three months after his conversion. He had never mentioned this to Chris before, and he was genuinely repentant and deeply remorseful. For her part, Chris felt hurt and betrayed. She had trusted Leonard. Because Leonard's lover had been one of Chris's close friends, she felt that she had been made to look like a fool. Chris found it difficult to forgive not only in regard to the affair, but she felt she had taken a lot of "guff" from Leonard both before and after his conversion, and yet, even though she had had several chances to do so, had never betrayed him.

Counseling involved first examining Leonard's background to determine if there were other instances of infidelity or premarital promiscuity. Then the counselor evaluated the marital and family system to discern what particular stresses had led to Leonard's decision to triangulate with another person. Counseling also helped Chris forgive Leonard by examining the place of forgiveness and rule-keeping in her family experience. Finally, counseling helped them analyze their current relationship and develop ways to make changes in the problem areas that had contributed to the affair.

As Chris was able to see the depth of Leonard's remorse, and accept the fact that she had also committed sins that needed forgiveness, she was encouraged to focus on the future rather than on the past. She and Leonard began to address specific, continuing needs in their relationship, and Chris was able to let go of her hurt and forgive Leonard. She still needed reassurance from time to time that the affair was over, and Leonard was encouraged to answer her periodic questions about it as a way of helping her put the issue to rest.

PARENTING

Several studies of marital satisfaction have revealed that the child-rearing years are the time of least satisfaction with the marital relationship. Among the reasons is the sheer amount of energy required to keep up with children, work demands, and household management needs. This leaves little available time for marital focus and affirmation. In addition, however, marital dissatisfaction frequently arises as a result of conflict over parenting.

By its very nature, parenting requires making countless decisions. Each decision involves the value systems of the parents. Some level of conflict is virtually inevitable, because no two people will totally agree on everything. Decisions about what kind of discipline should be used and when, dress standards, schooling, snacks and meals, bedtimes, curfews, involvement in outside activities such as athletics and drama, academic choices, and friends are enough to overwhelm any couple. These decisions produce countless opportunities either to strengthen the marital bond or to cause tension and conflict. For example, if one parent dislikes conflict and tries to please the children, while the other believes that the children's preferences should not take precedence over parental decisions, marital conflict may arise and unhealthy parent-child coalitions may form.

It is wise for a couple to discuss child-rearing goals and methods even before marriage. If they have not done so, the counselor should help them establish two or three goals each in the areas of spiritual and moral development, and in intellectual, emotional, physical, and interpersonal development. When setting the goals, the couple should try to envision the kind of person they would like their child to be at age twenty-five, understanding that the child must be allowed to ultimately chose his own identity.

For each goal established, two or three methods for reaching that goal should be developed. For example, one interpersonal goal might be "to have healthy and positive relationships with members of the opposite sex." Two methods to facilitate that goal might be (1) to include friends of the opposite sex in play groups from early age, and (2) to have open and expressive communication with the opposite-sex parent.

The philosophy and practice of discipline is also an area of potential conflict.

> Emilene and Terrence were in constant conflict over the issue of discipline. Emilene had come from a large family in which her father was very harsh, even violent, in his discipline of her brothers. Based on her past bad experience in regard to discipline, she felt that Terrence was too harsh in his responses to their three-year-old son. Emilene felt that discipline should be instructive, while Terrence felt that its primary purpose was to correct, and that spanking was one way to get their son to

change his "bad" behavior. Terrence, therefore, did not feel he was harsh, though he admitted that he was sometimes impatient.

Discipline may be viewed primarily as an opportunity to teach a child standards of behavior, which involves the idea of correction but focuses more on instruction than on punishment. Other approaches lean more heavily toward punitive correction. The philosophy behind this is to cause the child pain so that he understands how negative his actions are and will stop those behaviors to avoid subsequent pain. Depending upon the degree of difference on these viewpoints, substantial conflict may result. Even when parents agree on their basic philosophy, conflict may arise over differing interpretations of the severity of an offense (and the appropriate level of disciplinary response), or on specific methods (withholding privileges versus grounding, spanking with one's hand or with a switch).

BLENDED FAMILIES

The potential for marital conflict is particularly high in blended families. These are newly formed families (most often including children from both marriages) that result from remarriage after death or divorce.

There are a number of significant emotional and interpersonal tasks to be worked out if the blended families through remarriage are to be relatively harmonious and successful. These include dealing with losses and changes, recognizing different developmental needs, establishing new traditions, developing a solid bond as a couple and forming new relationships, creating a new coalition as parents, and accepting shifts in the composition of the household.[7] The challenge is to develop new patterns of relationships within the newly composed family so that the unit progresses from minimum to maximum cohesion among new family members with a growing sense of trust and identity as a family unit.[8]

The most common areas of difficulty that stepfamilies tend to encounter are unrealistic beliefs, life-cycle discrepancies, power issues, loyalty conflicts, and boundary problems.[9] The major task of the counselor is to help the family members accept one another and bond with one another in a positive way. This process involves adjusting to differences in personalities, preferences, rules, and values. At the same time, the feelings triggered in each child by the breakup of his or her parents' marriage and the relationship with the custodial parent must be addressed. Many times there is resentment and jealousy at the intrusion of the stepparent if the child had enjoyed special parental attention and emotional closeness during the period between the divorce and the remarriage.

> Colleen was very angry about her stepfather. She resented his macho mannerisms, which reflected his Hispanic background. She considered him to be insensitive, harsh, and a "jerk." Colleen's mother had met Luis while traveling in Central America after her divorce from Colleen's father, Bob. She had been attracted by his good looks and apparent strength and stability. After marrying Luis, however, she discovered that he did not consider her his equal and was very rigid in his ideas about child rearing. She found herself agreeing with her teenage daughter about his attitudes and methods, and often felt torn between her roles as loyal wife and loving mother.

Counseling helped both Colleen and her mother become more assertive in relation to Luis. Surprisingly, they discovered that when they worked out agreements between them that were generally consistent with his values and assertively communicated their plans, he did not react or interfere. He mainly needed to be reassured that things were not chaotic and that Colleen would not get into any trouble that would cause problems for him.

NOTES

[1]Jerrold K. Footlick, "What Happened to the Family," *Newsweek* (Special Issue, 1990).

[2]Judith S. Wallerstein and S. Blakslee, *Second Chances: Men, Women, and Children a Decade After Divorce* (New York: Ticknor and Fields, 1989).

[3]Neil Kalter, *Growing Up with Divorce* (New York: The Free Press, 1990).

[4]Two very helpful books are Monica McGoldrick and Randy Gerson, *Genograms in Family Assessment* (New York: W. W. Norton, 1985) and Emily Marlin, *Genograms* (New York: Contemporary Books, 1989).

[5]See Robert E. Alberti and Michael L. Emmons, *Your Perfect Right* (San Luis Obispo, Calif.: Impact Publishers, 1986).

[6]The Myers-Briggs Type Indicator (Palo Alto, Calif.: Consulting Psychologists Press) is distributed by the Center for Applications of Psychological Type, P.O. Box 13807, Gainesville, FL, 32604. See also David Keirsey and Marilyn Bates, *Please Understand Me: Character & Temperament Types* (Del Mar, Calif.: Prometheus Nemesis Book Company, 1984).

[7]Emily B. Visher and John S. Visher, *Old Loyalties, New Ties: Therapeutic Strategies with Stepfamilies* (New York: Brunner/Mazel, 1988), 10.

[8]Ibid., 12.

[9]Ibid., 22.

CHAPTER 13

Domestic Abuse

HOME IS NOT ALWAYS the haven that it's supposed to be. In the United States alone there are between two and six million cases of physical, spousal abuse every year along with more than one million cases of child abuse. The House Select Committee on Aging has estimated that, in addition, about 4 percent, or 1.1 million of the U.S. elderly, may be victims of abuse each year. Abuse may be physical, emotional, or sexual in nature and it may involve passive neglect or active deeds. Its victims range from aborted fetuses to senior citizens in their eighties.

Counseling for people involved in domestic abuse typically involves the victim, but may also involve the abuser. Anyone can be either an abuser or a victim. Generally, however, in cases of violent spouse abuse, the victim is the wife with the husband being the batterer. In cases of child abuse, sons *or* daughters may be victimized by mother *or* father. In cases of elder abuse the mother, because of women's greater longevity, is most likely to be the victim with sons committing physical abuse and daughters, emotional abuse.

Due to space limitations, we will only focus on counseling for spouse abuse in this chapter.

CRISIS INTERVENTION

Because of the danger of serious injury, physical abuse may require emergency or crisis intervention by the urban counselor.

It was Tuesday. Susan was due for the initial visit at her counselor's office later that afternoon. First, though, she needed to make a trip to the post office. Unbeknown to her, Peter, her estranged husband, spotted her and followed her home. Susan had pulled into the driveway, but as soon as she realized that Peter was tailing her, she tried to back out to get away. Peter, however, not about to let her escape, rammed her compact with his station wagon. As Susan tried to get out of the car, Peter slammed the car door against her. Managing to free herself she jumped out of the car and tried to escape into the house. Before she was able to reach the relative safety of the house, Peter caught her and began to slap and kick her, and, then, ripping off a loose piece of the picket fence, beat her.

Finally, after escaping, Susan called her counselor from a pay phone, sobbing. The counselor managed to get her calmed down, and Susan was able to keep her afternoon appointment. When the counselor saw Susan, she had a smashed middle finger on one hand, and a reddened and bruised upper arm. She also had numerous other bruises that were hidden by clothing. Susan was positive that Peter wanted her dead and felt that it was only a matter of time before he either killed her with his car, like he had tried to do earlier in the day, or with one of the many guns he owned.

Crisis intervention consists of four phases: (1) gathering basic information about the episode; (2) initial assessment of the potential for further harm; (3) provision of needed emotional and physical support, including housing alternatives; (4) possible contact of appropriate legal authorities, as required by the law or by the abuse suffered.

It is extremely important to gather basic information about the violent episode. The basic information-gathering should include questions about the extent of physical injury. If it appears that there may be serious injuries, especially to the head or internal organs, the counselor should help make arrangements for immediate medical attention. In addition, the counselor should take detailed notes about the violence that brought the victim into her office. This information may, at some point, be requested by a court, so the record of events should be as thorough as possible.

Initial assessment of the potential for further harm is critical. It is especially important to gather information about the occurrence of previous violent episodes, the availability and use (or threatened use) of weapons, the use of alcohol or drugs in relation to abuse, other acts of violence committed by the abuser, a history of abuse experienced in the batterer's own background, the abuser's attitudes toward the law, and previous or current threats by the abuser to kill himself or family members.[1] The presence of one or more of these factors increases the likelihood that the victim is indeed in serious danger.

It is important to understand that abuse tends to increase in severity and frequency if it is ignored.[2] The CSR Abuse Index[3] is a helpful tool for estimating the level of danger for an abused spouse. Questions about past or present threats to children should be asked, even in situations that are not primarily focused on child abuse or neglect. Assessment for abuse of the elderly is aided by the use of tools such as the Ferguson-Beck H.A.L.F. Assessment Tool.[4]

Assessment of child abuse needs to be attuned to the age and sophistication of the child being evaluated. Questions and language should be kept very simple. In the case of suspected child abuse, a standard assessment technique is to have the child draw a picture of a person. Victims of sexual abuse frequently do not put hands, feet, arms, or even legs on people, suggesting their feelings of helplessness. Their drawings are often localized to the part of the body the abuser touched. Besides drawings, the use of dolls is also very helpful, especially with very young children. In any case, the counselor should not pressure the child, but instead ask open-ended questions using terms the child understands. "Why" questions should be avoided.[5] The counselor also needs to carefully assure the child that she is not being bad because she is telling things that the abuser may have termed a "secret," and should assure the child that she will not be harmed because of what she has shared. Then the counselor should take whatever legal steps are necessary to insure promised safety.

In Susan's case, abuse had started even before she and Peter were married. Peter had punched her during a disagreement yet Susan was the one who apologized to him for having upset him. Because she would not agree to a second abortion two years later, Peter punched and kicked Susan. About a year after this incident, while drunk, he slammed a door on her hand and broke two of her fingers. Another two years passed, at which time he broke her nose and eye socket, telling her she "deserved it." She had to drive by herself to the emergency room to have reconstructive surgery. He never visited her at the hospital or apologized for his attack. At this juncture, she did finally call a lawyer and had photos taken.

When encountering an abused spouse, child, or senior citizen in a crisis situation, it is important to provide emotional and physical support. In the case of an abused spouse the victim is likely to be highly agitated; and in the case of a child or an elderly person, the victim is likely to be withdrawn. Each one will be struggling with a mixture of fear, self-doubt, guilt, and self-recrimination. The counselor must provide a calm presence and a listening ear. The victim needs to sense that she is believed. The counselor should *never* dismiss reports of abuse, even if the perpetrator is a church board member or influential leader. If there is doubt, it can be explored in subsequent sessions but not in the initial one.

Physical support may come from providing safe housing for the abused person. For a battered spouse and family there are battered-women's shelters, which provide maximum safety, despite certain inconveniences such as a lack of privacy. These shelters may be preferable to staying with friends or family; they protect all involved from the harassment of an angry and violent man. Susan stayed in a shelter for a couple of nights before going to stay with relatives for several days, during which time she obtained from the court a restraining order against Peter, and questioned the wisdom of returning to her home.

Crisis intervention should also include consideration of possible contact of legal authorities. All states require suspected child abuse to be reported. Most states specifically include counselors and clergy among the professionals required to report abuse or themselves face misdemeanor charges. Those who report abuse are usually given immunity and can remain anonymous. However, information obtained in counseling sessions is not considered privileged and protected by the court in cases of abuse and neglect.[6]

When there has been moderate to severe physical abuse of a spouse or parent, the counselor should encourage the victim to weigh the possibility of legal involvement. Various options include obtaining a court order of protection, court-ordered counseling, assault charges, and an arrest warrant. This is especially true if there is a history of repeated violence and the indicators mentioned above suggest the likelihood of continuing, intensified violence. One study in conjunction with the Minneapolis police shows the wisdom of careful consideration. The study found that when legal action was taken and the abuser was ordered out of the house, 22 percent repeated the violence. But, of those who received counseling, only 16 percent repeated the violence. Only 10 percent of those arrested, who did not have counseling or were not ordered out, beat their wives subsequently.[7]

Unless the abused spouse is willing to press assault charges, however, there is very little the police can do. They cannot make a man leave his home. Temporary restraining orders obtained from a judge require the husband to stay away from the wife for a short period of time, but the most belligerent and violent husbands may only be further incensed by the action. Short of police protection or arrest, not much will stop a violent spouse who is bent on further harm, even when there is a restraining order.

Susan filed charges against her estranged husband two days after he tried to run over her with the car. She signed a formal complaint for his arrest, and obtained a court order of protection. Peter, however, contacted his lawyer and pressed charges against Susan for provoking him and ramming his car! Because of her husband's familiarity with the legal system, and his position as a police officer, the judge issued a summons against Peter instead of a warrant for arrest, and treated Susan as though *she* were the abuser!

CASE STUDY: RICHARD AND MARILYN

Marilyn had fallen asleep on the living room couch after an exhausting day. She awoke to hear her husband, Richard, yelling at her to come into the bedroom. When she did not immediately go, he went and dragged her to the bedroom insistent on having sex. Marilyn resisted, and incensed, Richard tried to choke her. She managed to break away, but he grabbed her and continued choking her. Finally, in response to Marilyn's screams, her three teenage children ran downstairs, freed her from their father, and took her upstairs to protect her. The next day she obtained a restraining order and her husband was not allowed to enter the home.

Richard came from a home with a highly critical and controlling mother and an emotionally absent father, totally dominated by Richard's mother. His parents were obsessive-compulsive perfectionists, who were also physically and verbally abusive. He remembers his mother choking him when he was four years old and breaking a milk bottle over his head when he was about ten. After he became a Christian as a teenager, Richard's mother went into an intense, year-long rage over having lost control of him. Her verbal assaults at this time were merely a continuation of the way she had always treated him. As a youngster, Richard remembers going into the bathroom and cursing his mother with every swear word he knew and his feelings had not changed much since then. Richard was still filled with resentment toward her and toward his emotionally absent father at the time he went for counseling.

Richard's relationship with Marilyn is marked by a curious combination of control and dependency. (Marilyn describes him as being highly controlling.) He wants Marilyn to nurture him and give the kind of supportive, noncritical, caring, accepting, and warm responses that he never received from his mother. Because of the depth of his emotional deprivation and the fear of being controlled by a woman, however, he *demands* Marilyn's caretaking on an almost constant basis. His demands are similar to those of a starving, emotional infant. By delivering his demands forcefully and incessantly, he is able to exercise almost complete control over Marilyn and by refusing to take "no" for an answer, he is able to avoid facing his feelings of rejection.

Richard has an explosive temper, although he comes across to the outsider as being very mild-mannered. Richard physically abused Marilyn by grabbing, holding, pushing, and hitting. His abuse of her began early in their relationship; he first hit Marilyn about a year after they began dating. Most of the abuse, however, is emotional or verbal. Throughout their courtship he was jealous and possessive. His jealousy showed even during their wedding reception—he became angry when he saw that Marilyn was talking to the best man.

There was no let up in the abuse on their honeymoon either. While making love Richard said to Marilyn, "I wonder what it would feel like to kill you?" After the honeymoon, Richard insisted on having sex with Marilyn two times every day, even during her period. Whenever he did not get sex or anything else he wanted from her, Richard would become verbally abusive. (He continually belittles Marilyn and has directed the same kind of verbal abuse toward one of his teenage sons.) Early in their marriage, they separated. After a brief separation they reconciled, but Richard told Marilyn that he would permanently shut her up if she ever told others or if they ever separated again.

In later years, Marilyn began to resist his various demands. She would involve Richard in screaming matches that seemed to calm him down. However, when he calmed down and backed off, she would then usually give in to what he wanted.

From almost the first day of the court-ordered separation, Richard began manipulating to get back into the home. He refused to honor commitments made during counseling to limit the number of times he called Marilyn. He insisted on coming to the house, initially with a policeman, but subsequently alone whenever he desired, to see the children. He wrote Marilyn love letters, begging to be allowed to see her and asking her not to tell the counselor of his actions. He continually tried to tell her that she was mixed up and really did want to see him (though during the counseling sessions, she denied wanting to see him). Over a period of several months, he showed up whenever he wanted to, and after wearing Marilyn down emotionally, managed to have sexual relations with her. Soon Richard and Marilyn took on a childish, coy, and even seductive air as they related to each other in the counseling sessions. The counselor sensed that Marilyn and Richard were playing a game of deception and it was then that Marilyn reluctantly admitted that they were again involved sexually.

Marilyn was a caretaker and a people-pleaser par excellence. She had been conditioned from early childhood to be the nurturing mother type that Richard demanded. This caretaker role came naturally—her maternal grandfather had been caretaker. Marilyn was born into a sickly family; her grandfather was dying and her older sibling was extremely colicky. When Marilyn herself was two years old, she became very ill, and though she was hospitalized she was not expected to live. Her parents, however, never visited her in the hospital because according to Marilyn, "they didn't want to upset me." At a very young age, Marilyn began to carry a little doctor's kit around to take care of anybody's hurts. At school, she gravitated toward kids who were distressed and needed her help. Then she would come home and help her parents with chores every afternoon. During their marriage, Richard continually tried to get her to take care of him by showing utter helplessness over the slightest "ouchie" (as he called a cut he incurred during a counseling session and begged Marilyn to "help").

By the time they began counseling, Marilyn was filled with resentment toward Richard, although she was at the same time highly dependent on him. She had been unable to maintain any independence of identity, thought, or action from Richard, even during the time of their court-ordered separation of several months.

Richard had concluded early in the counseling that the counselor was an "enemy." He felt that the counselor was trying to get Marilyn and him to separate emotionally. Counseling ended unsatisfactorily shortly after Richard finally managed to manipulate his way back into the home. The week he returned, Marilyn wrote a short note that had definite suicidal overtones to the counselor. Subsequent attempts by the counselor to continue counseling were unsuccessful.

ANALYSIS

In the following analysis, we will examine multimodal profiles for both Richard and Marilyn, since they were seen individually and jointly over a period of several months.

Richard

BEHAVIOR:	1.	Demanding and persistent.
	2.	Physically assaultive.
	3.	Deceptive.
	4.	Manipulative.
	5.	Relationally immature and self-focused.
	6.	Teasing and seductive toward wife.
AFFECT:	1.	Feelings of anger.
	2.	Feelings of helplessness.
	3.	Feelings of rejection.
	4.	Feelings of emotional deprivation.
	5.	Pining and feelings of loneliness.
SENSATION:	1.	Stress.
IMAGERY:	1.	Cursing at mother as a little boy.
	2.	Being hit by mother.
	3.	Being controlled by mother's rage, criticism, and coldness.
	4.	Dad is a wimp.
	5.	Parental demands for perfection and cleanliness.
	6.	Unclean house; wife not cleaning and keeping it in order.
COGNITION:	1.	My wife should be submissive
	2.	My wife should take care of my needs.

3. It is my wife's responsibility to respond to my sexual desire/need.
4. The counselor is trying to keep my wife away from me.
5. I just got a little angry; my anger is justified—I'm just trying to get her/them to do what they should.
6. I haven't really hurt anyone; I wouldn't hurt my family—I love them.
7. I'm the head of the household and I'm supposed to be in control.
8. It's not right for us to be separated.
9. Marilyn really wants me and needs me even though she's saying other things (because of the counselor).
10. Marilyn is defying me and blocking my goals.

INTERPERSONAL RELATIONSHIPS:

1. Jealous of wife.
2. Resentful and critical of strong women.
3. Scapegoating and abuse toward middle son in particular and children in general.
4. Verbally abusive toward wife.
5. Immature; inappropriate affect at times.

DRUGS/ BIOLOGY:

1. Recurrent stomach difficulties.

SPIRITUAL:

1. Identifies self as evangelical.
2. Sees no discrepancy between foul language, physical abuse, and his professed faith (simply makes no connection).

Marilyn

BEHAVIOR:

1. Caretaking, nurturing.
2. Contradictory—distancing from, but "inviting" toward husband.
3. Tells husband one thing and then agrees to his contradictory interpretation.
4. Nonassertive, passive.

AFFECT:

1. Feelings of fear.
2. Feelings of helpless, powerless.
3. Feelings of weariness.
4. Feelings of hopelessness.

	5.	Feelings of depression.
	6.	Feelings of being burned out, overwhelmed.
	7.	Feelings of failure.
SENSATION:	1.	Physically and emotionally exhausted.
IMAGERY:	1.	Excessive and angry sexual demands by husband (marital rape).
	2.	Parents not there when in hospital.
	3.	Implied threats of murder by husband.
	4.	Being dragged off couch, choked and struggling for breath before passing out.
	5.	Sounds of husband's belittling words.
	6.	Husband with arm around neck and Marilyn being split in two with stick of dynamite in her stomach.
COGNITION:	1.	It's my duty to take care of those in need.
	2.	In order to honor God, I must submit to Richard's needs, wants, and demands.
	3.	I am his masturbating post.
	4.	I'm trapped.
	5.	I'm not strong enough to resist him.
	6.	Ending it all might be the only way out of this.
	7.	I can't say no.
	8.	I am a failure.
INTERPERSONAL RELATIONSHIPS:	1.	Generally healthy (with other women).
	2.	Positive relationship with children.
	3.	Skewed toward those who are needy in some way.
DRUGS/ BIOLOGY:	1.	Significantly overweight.
	2.	Difficulty sleeping.
SPIRITUAL:	1.	Identifies self as born-again Christian.
	2.	Cannot understand why God allows husband to mistreat her, but is not angry at God.

GOALS: THE VICTIM

Primary goals for assisting the spouse through longer-term (noncrisis) counseling include:

1. Deciding whether or not to remain in the relationship.

2. Overcoming passive and codependent relational patterns.
3. Building positive self-esteem.
4. Facilitating genuine and healthy forgiveness.

Decision Regarding the Marriage

Should an abused spouse remain in the marriage? How much abuse warrants termination of the marital covenant? Does biblical submission include the possibility of fatal abuse for the wife or the children? Is legal separation an acceptable alternative for those suffering significant physical or emotional damage? How much fear and anxiety should a child living in an abusive home be expected to suffer? Are the limits of suffering different for physical, sexual, and emotional abuse?

The counselor must help the abused wife thoroughly consider the spiritual, psychological, relational, economic, and parental implications of any decision regarding the continuation of the marriage. If the husband is willing to enter intensive therapy, if the abuse is comparatively moderate and is not life-threatening, if the abuse pattern has not been deeply ingrained in the relational dynamics of the marriage, if drug or alcohol addiction is not involved, and if children have not been the targets of either physical or emotional abuse, there is a good probability that the marriage can therapeutically benefit and continue on a healthy, non-abusive basis. The likelihood of sustained change is much lower if drugs or alcohol are involved, if the abuser refuses therapy or is resistant, if there is a well-established pattern of abuse, and if the abuse is severe.

Overcome Codependent Patterns

Abused wives frequently have nonassertive and codependent interactional styles. They tend to be very loyal to the abuser and their relationship, to blame themselves for any difficulties, and to excuse the behaviors of the abusing spouse (who usually blames them). Often abuse victims are governed by inner rules that make it a virtual moral crime if they make another person unhappy, rock the boat, or respond in any way that can be considered noncooperative and selfish. They not only have typically learned to put the needs and wishes of others first, but to negate their own.

The abused wife needs to differentiate herself from the

abuser. She is not meant to serve as an extension of the abuser's ego while ignoring, repressing, and crushing her own identity and valid needs. She needs to distinguish between biblical submission and the elimination of her identity through the intimidation and assault of an aggressive husband. She needs to gain the sense of dignity and self-respect that is her right as a person made in the image of God. She needs to see that God does not sanction abuse as a legitimate form of marital or parental interaction.

Specific training in assertiveness skills is suggested.[8] Once basic concepts and principles of assertiveness are understood and memorized, she should be encouraged to make and log assertive responses daily. She should be guided in role-playing assertive responses to problem situations that have led to violence in the past. The nonnegotiable communication that abuse will no longer be tolerated must be the starting point for establishing assertiveness in the abusive relationship. Carefully considered consequences should also be clearly communicated to the abuser, for example, an arrest warrant will be issued if any further abuse takes place.

It is also recommended that the counselor and the client work through the dynamics of codependency as they are expressed in the abused spouse's relationship with her husband. There are a number of excellent sourcebooks and workbooks available (see Resources p. 323ff.) to facilitate the process of self-understanding and change.

Building Self-Esteem

Because of low self-esteem brought about by victimization and abuse, it is likely that, without intervention, an abused girl will become an abused wife. That is to say, they think of themselves in disparaging, negative terms. In the extreme, they are willing to accept abuse because an abusive marriage is at least a marriage, and the abuse is a form of attention.

Healthy self-esteem is built on biblical standards that are rooted in an accurate self-image and that do not involve comparison with others (Gal. 6:3–4). The Christian needs to see herself as having been created in God's image as a responsible and valued being (Gen. 1:31), as having been redeemed (Rom. 8:1–2), and as having been spiritually gifted (1 Cor. 12:1–11). Careful examination of Scripture indicates that the God-given standards for human interaction involve gentleness, compassion, kindness, forgiveness, the absence of wrath, and love (Eph. 4:29–32; Col. 3:12–17). These standards are clearly incompatible with both arrogant self-esteem and abuse. The biblical guidelines for marriage (Eph.5:21–33; 1 Pet. 3:1–7) also are clearly incompatible with self-denigration or abuse in any form. Abused spouses need to understand that they *do not deserve* to be verbally or physically assaulted. As they come to accept their treasured status in God's eyes, they gradually are able to believe that they deserve to be treated as someone special.

Forgiveness

Perhaps the most difficult goal to achieve is genuine forgiveness. It is important to understand that forgiveness does not necessarily mean that the abused spouse will choose to continue living with the abuser. It does mean that she is able to pray for her husband, to not wish evil on him, and to let go of the emotional and spiritual wounds caused by his abusive behavior.

Forgiveness is not granted because the abuser deserves it. It is not given because the victim has been able to convince herself that he really did not mean or could not help the abuse. Forgiveness clearly sees the wrong and chooses not to hold it against the one who is genuinely guilty. Even though our sense of justice is often warped by sin, human nature is justice-centered. We find it much easier to demand retribution once we have accepted the inexcusable reality of another's offense than to forgive.

To reach the point of being able to forgive, then, the abused must stop making excuses and blaming herself for the abuser's behavior, acknowledge and express her anger over the abuser's violation of her being, and move beyond anger and *choose* to forgive. However, failure to stop making excuses will only insure the continuance of the abuse. Failure to acknowledge and express anger will most likely result in depression, despair, a martyr orientation, emotional numbness, purposelessness (giving up on life), and aggressiveness toward weaker people, such as children. Failure to choose to forgive will most likely result in bitterness that poisons not only self, but others (Heb. 12:15). Perhaps the single greatest "secret" of the late Corrie Ten Boom's magnificent ministry was the fact that she chose the way of grace and forgiveness over the path of justice and bitterness.

Three problems facing those who are trying to forgive are (1) the feeling that they will become vulnerable and defenseless once more if they forgive, (2) the feeling that they are surrendering themselves (they will experience an emptiness when giving up a bitterness-centered identity), and (3) the desire to see the abuser receive the treatment that he deserves. Although these feelings are extremely difficult to overcome, they can be defeated. When the victim identifies with Christ and the full teaching of Scripture regarding relationships, she can be reassured that God will be her defender, that submission is not a biblical license for marital assault, that the Holy Spirit will fill the void with love if she gives up a bitterness-based identity, and that God will one day dispense full justice, if the abuser does not repent.

GOALS: THE ABUSER

There is an understandable reluctance on the part of some nonprofessional counselors to counsel batterers. It is easy to have negative feelings toward them. However, the counselor should remember that in a sizable majority of cases, the abused spouse will choose to return to the abusing partner. It is vitally important, therefore, for the abuser to receive counseling so that he might change his destructive patterns.

The counselor should focus on the following ten objectives when counseling the abusive spouse:

1. Taking responsibility for one's abusive behavior.
2. Understanding consequences.
3. Controlling anger.
4. Correcting distorted thinking.
5. Managing stress.
6. Improving communication skills.
7. Increasing emotional awareness and articulation.
8. Managing conflict.
9. Controlling jealousy and dependency.
10. Decreasing interpersonal isolation.

Taking Responsibility

Many abusing spouses will rationalize their violent behavior by blaming their partner for provoking them, "pushing their buttons," "refusing to back off," or "asking for it." In so doing, they are both denying responsibility for their own behavior and blaming the victim. The counselor must assertively, but without attacking, confront the batterer so that he sees that *he* is the one who chooses to act; that he is not forced by his spouse's behaviors to react with violence. This may be especially difficult for those who have themselves been abused or whose parents modeled spouse abuse. In a very real sense they may not be aware that there are alternatives to violence in situations of conflict and frustration. The counselor must help the abuser identify these alternatives by presenting a number of typical conflict situations and then brainstorming possible nonviolent responses. This can then be followed by counselor-abuser role play, and finally by guided spouse-spouse interaction on difficult issues.

Understanding Consequences

The counselor should describe to the abusive spouse the effects that his behavior has on his wife and children. The husband must see that abusive behavior destroys his wife's sense of safety, her trust, and her self-esteem, while producing anxiety, fear, and alienation. He must also see that physical abuse introduces chaos into the entire family system and predisposes his children to become either abusers or abused spouses.

The counselor must assist the wife in deciding the consequences of any future violence and in communicating these consequences to her husband. These consequences may include the involvement of the law, physical and legal separation, and public disclosure in one's church. After the abused spouse has carefully considered her options and role-played the communication of her choice with the counselor, that consequence must be clearly and firmly communicated to the batterer. A similar process may be followed by those who are victims of emotional and verbal abuse. Communication of consequences should not occur unless the victimized spouse is absolutely committed to following through.

Controlling Anger

Perhaps the most crucial type of therapeutic intervention is anger management. This begins by exploring how the abuser's family expressed anger. What did family members do when they were frustrated? How did they handle conflict? How was anger expressed? The abuser must be helped to see that there does not have to be a direct connection between feelings of anger and acts of violence; one can be angry without being violent or verbally abusive. He *can choose* to act nonabusively.

Control of anger also includes helping the abusive spouse see that the words or actions of his spouse do not directly cause anger. Nor are violence and abuse a necessary result of anger. Rather, his anger is triggered by his interpretation of her actions and by his inferences that her intentions and attitudes are insulting or intolerable. For the abuser, anger, as a result of past modeling and reinforcement, has become paired with violent actions. Usually the anger and violence are then "justified" because of some perceived evil perpetrated by the other spouse ("She deserved it;" "She's supposed to be submissive and she challenged my authority;" "Her behavior was unbiblical and inflammatory.").

The abusive spouse should be taught ways to recognize anger, and he should communicate his feelings with some kind of verbal cue to his spouse ("I'm starting to get ticked;" "Time out for a bit;" "I need some space;" "Please don't pressure me."). An agreement must be worked out so that whenever the abusive spouse says one or two of these phrases, his partner will stop the interaction. The discussion can then be resumed within a day or two when the abusive spouse feels more in control of himself.

Correcting Distorted Thinking

The counselor must help the abuser identify some of the faulty filters and rotten rules that trigger anger. These filters and rules usually involve the perception of being diminished or put down. For example, he may have learned that to be a "real man" he should exercise total control; appropriate efforts by his wife to influence him may then be interpreted as insubordination or emasculation. The justified result is to fight for his masculinity or for domination through anger and violence, thus intimidating her into submission.

It is critical for the abusing spouse to become aware of what he is thinking before, during, and after a violent episode. Among the types of distorted "self-talk" that typically accompany anger are the use of dehumanizing labels, thinking "should" thoughts, assuming one knows the other person's motives, and thinking the worst. The husband must learn to describe his wife's behavior in positive terms and use her name instead of reducing her to an object, and consider alternative explanations instead of making assumptions. He must also avoid using "always," "never," "you should," and "I can't take it any more" statements.[9]

Managing Stress

Stress management involves making a decision not only to prevent the build-up of stress, but also the reduction of stress when one feels tense and angry. Preventive management is critical in abusive relationships because it is often the build-up of stress in the abuser's life that promotes inner disturbance, frustration, irritability, and loss of self-control. As stresses in one's life compound, it is easy for the abuser to feel that he is at the mercy of circumstances, which bring on feelings of helplessness, feelings of being overwhelmed, and feelings of being battered himself. Relatively minor incidents and actions by a spouse then become major. Preventive stress reduction should include skills training in time management, decision making, goal setting, as well as, practical responses to areas of recurrent frustration. Preventive stress management also must include teaching the abuse cycle (tension building, explosion or acute violent episode, loving contrition or remorse).[10]

Often several stressors at a time cluster together and have an impact on the abuser. Corrective stress management lowers this built-up stress and should primarily focus on relaxation training and choosing how to lessen the number of stressors.[11] Fred and Belinda came in for counseling after arguing rancorously for a month. A study revealed that a cluster of over twenty major sources of personal and relational stress had been affecting them in the weeks prior to their visit. However, with the instruction of the counselor, they began to plan their weekly schedule together and to write their commitments on the calendar. Thus, they were able to make better joint choices. Their stress levels—and the level of conflict—were significantly reduced.

Improving Communication Skills

Effective communication in an emotionally and physically intimate relationship requires self-discipline, assertiveness, careful listening, and editing, among other qualities. Many abusers have never seen or experienced these essential elements of mature communication because they come from dysfunctional or broken-family backgrounds. Abusive patterns are built on power and put-downs, whereas healthy communication is built on a foundation of caring and mutual respect.

It is essential that each partner develop self-discipline, learning to hold emotions in check when feeling threatened, ignored, misunderstood, or opposed. Instead of exploding in frustration, mature partners discipline themselves to think well of the other partner's motives. They also recognize that time will be required to sort out differences and come to a point of shared meaning.

Assertiveness involves "speaking the truth in love" (Eph. 4:15). When defined in terms of speaking the truth in love, assertiveness means learning to think in partnership terms, rather than in power-play terms. It involves learning to identify and express one's true emotions and thoughts instead of hiding them behind a mask of intimidation or confrontation.

The ability to check one's initial tendency to react on the basis of what one *thinks* has been said is the basis of careful listening. It involves knowing one's faulty filters well enough to ask, "Am I hearing this correctly?" It also involves asking the communicator the same kind of clarifying question ("Am I hearing you say. . . ?" "Do you mean. . . ?" "What I seem to hear you saying is. . ."). Making the choice to respond to one's spouse in "soft" or courteous language rather than in harsh or blaming terms is what editing is all about. Editing aims to build up one's partner rather than to tear her and the relationship down with defensive verbal punching.

Increasing Emotional Awareness and Articulation

Male socialization typically allows only the expression of feelings of anger, and "outlaws" feelings of weakness and vulnerability. Perhaps that is why many male batterers have great difficulty identifying and expressing emotion appropriately. They frequently feel overwhelmed by the kind of emotional intensity that many women consider essential for intimacy. As a result, they tend to act out rather than talk out their feelings. Anger is often used by men as a defensive mask to cover intense inner feelings of powerlessness, helplessness, and inadequacy. It acts to drive the other person away when interaction has become too threatening. This is why a macho attitude often corresponds with abuse. It is an attitude that is essentially defensive because it places women in a subordinate position to keep them from getting close and threatening the male. It is a power orientation aimed at keeping one's self protected from emotional hurt. It is an orientation that sees women as threats because of their ability to fight effectively with emotions.

Counseling an abusive male, then, requires a process of resocialization whereby he is able to see that identifying and expressing emotions will not make him weak. Rather, emotional expressiveness will aid his ability to interact in a satisfying and competent way with his spouse. Constant defensiveness, distancing (isolation), and conflict are not needed. Emotion and intimacy that result from such sharing must come to be seen as allies rather than enemies.

The counselor should lead the man through the process of emotional identification suggested in chapter 9, and introduce the task of sharing feelings. A daily scheduled time to share feeling with his wife is a must for the husband who wants to be emotionally aware and articulate. Discussion of "risky" topics should be restricted and gradually introduced into the counseling session where the counselor can monitor and guide the interaction to assure relatively positive outcomes for both spouses. Because of previous verbal or physical abuse, the abused spouse will also have to be gently encouraged to talk about her real thoughts and feelings. It is often a good idea for the husband and wife to sign a contract guaranteeing that they will in no way punish their partner for things said during counseling sessions.

Managing Conflict

Conflict management begins with perception. The abuser must learn to avoid seeing his partner in me-versus-you terms. As he learns assertive interaction techniques, his orientation will shift from power to partnership. The emphasis in conflict management is on dialogue and self-control. The abuser needs to view problems as normal experiences, as opportunities to collaborate and grow together in a mature way.

Other principles of conflict management that need to be

discussed and dramatized in guided interactions include the following:

- Each partner's commitment to change appropriately without demanding that the other partner make the first move.
- The decision to approach problem solving in terms of two distinct phases: problem definition and problem solution.
- The commitment to discuss only one problem at a time.
- The commitment to consciously look for and explicitly verbalize points of agreement and appreciation for the partner's interaction.
- The recognition that conflict management usually involves some form of negotiation and compromise.
- The agreement to emphasize communication patterns that express mutual respect.
- The avoidance of interruptions and criticism of the partner.
- The use of brainstorming as a means to resolve conflict.
- An agreement to specifically summarize each partner's understanding once it appears that agreement has been reached.

If the issue is one of historical conflict, it might be good to write out and sign the agreement to avoid subsequent difficulties.[12]

Controlling Jealousy and Dependency

A feeling of jealousy is basically a statement of insecurity. It is the irrational, strong feeling that one might lose one's spouse to another. An abusive man is filled with mistrust and anxiety. He may demand absolute loyalty, and usually will systematically cut his spouse off from her family and friends. Although it may appear otherwise because of his controlling and abusive behaviors, an abuser is highly dependent on his spouse. He is frequently blatant in his attempts to control all of her interactions, relationships, and activities in order to prevent her from being tempted to infidelity; be it emotional or sexual.

Both partners in a marriage need to see that jealousy is mainly a response to a *perceived* threat, and they must understand the part that interpretation plays. For example, they need to understand that the marriage relationship involves a normal pattern of fluctuation between closeness and distance that has nothing to do with the potential loss of a partner. Rather, fluctuation is part of the inherent tension in *all* human relationships. On one hand it represents our need for individuality and identity, while on the other it represents our need for intimacy and mutuality.

Ultimately, of course, jealousy is an issue of trust. The counselor must be prepared to help the abuser understand the roots of his underlying mistrust and accept the fact that his attempts at total control may very well create the loss that he most fears. The abuser must understand that love is something that is given, not demanded, and that marital loyalty is a matter of inner commitment, not external constraints. He must see that the problem lies primarily in his perception and interpretation, rather than in his spouse's behaviors (assuming that this is objectively true). He will have to be encouraged to experience moments of anxiety and helplessness in order to courageously and experientially learn that these feelings do not mean that he has lost his spouse's affection or loyalty. Little by little, he needs to come to the realization that he actually "gains" his spouse by letting go of her.

Decreasing Interpersonal Isolation

Finally, the abusive spouse should be encouraged to develop relationships with other people, especially males, in which he can be genuine and open. Often men who abuse have no close friends. Any relationships they have are frequently kept on a very superficial, impersonal, acquaintance level. This, of course, is even true of their marital relationship, as we have seen. The counselor should encourage the abuser to become a regular part of a support group, which is especially critical is he is a also a substance abuser (alcohol, drugs) or is nonchemically addicted.

The counselor should also utilize extensive role playing to help the abuser learn relationship skills. A variety of situations should be imagined and the counselee taught "scripts" and encouraged to act out socially appropriate behaviors conducive to the building of healthy relationships.

NOTES

[1]Grant L. Martin, *Counseling for Family Violence and Abuse* (Waco, Tex.: Word, 1987), 54–56.

[2]Peter H. Neidig and Dale H. Friedman, *Spouse Abuse: A Treatment Program for Couples* (Champaign, Ill.: Research Press, 1984), 39.

[3]William A. Stacey and Anson Shupe, *The Family Secret* (Boston: Beacon Press, 1983), 122–27.

[4]Doris Ferguson and Cornelia Back, "H.A.L.F.—A Tool to Assess Elder Abuse Within the Family," *Geriatric Nursing* (September-October 1983), 301–5.

[5]Martin, *Counseling for Family Violence and Abuse*, 183–91.

[6]Ibid., 200.

[7]Cited in *Newsletter* (New York: The American Jewish Committee, Institute of Human Relations, Summer 1983).

[8]One very helpful book which emphasizes practical assertiveness skills is *Your Perfect Right: A Guide to Assertive Living*, by Robert E. Alberti and Michael L. Emmons (San Luis Obispo, Calif.: Impact Publishers, 1986).

[9]Martin, *Counseling for Family Violence and Abuse*, 108–10.

[10]Lenore Walker, *The Battered Woman Syndrome* (New York: Springer, 1984), 24–25.

[11]For helpful suggestions refer to Dorothy H. G. Cotton, *Stress Management: An Integrated Approach to Therapy* (New York: Brunner/Mazel, 1990), and Martha Davis, Matthew McKay, and Elizabeth Robbins Eshelman, *The Relaxation and Stress Reduction Workbook* (Oakland, Calif.: New Harbinger Publications, 1982).

[12]Neidig and Friedman, *Spouse Abuse: A Treatment Program for Couples*, 170–71.

CHAPTER 14

Divorce Recovery

HALF OF THE PEOPLE who marry this year will be divorced within five years. But, since 79 percent will remarry, the divorce rate for all marriages is about 40 percent.[1] On a scale that measures stress in the lives of individuals, divorce ranks as the second most stressful event behind death.[2] In the urban center, divorce and marital separation appear to be more frequent than in suburban or rural areas.[3] Thus, the urban Christian worker will often find himself faced with this problem.

Divorce and marital separation affect more than the spouses involved; they have an adverse effect on the children and other family members as well. They also affect friends and acquaintances, who find it awkward to relate to a once-married couple as separate nonmarried individuals. The tendency for friends is to take sides as to who was right and who was wrong. In short, marital breakup has a convulsive effect on all of the former couple's relationships.

Regardless of which spouse initiates the rupture, significant emotional distress often follows. During the first year of separation especially, many will feel inadequate and view themselves as failures. Divorced men go through a great deal of pain being separated from their children.[4] Women go through a severe period of depression, self-doubt, and fear of abandonment.[5] In addition, there are many bizarre reactions to the breakup such as alcoholism, drug abuse, sexual promiscuity, and child abuse.

CASE STUDY: LIZ

Liz is an attractive woman in her late thirties. She came in for counseling because her husband had announced that after fifteen years of marriage he wanted a divorce. Liz was devastated. They had had some disagreements over the years but she had never really expected their marriage to end even though she had, in moments of anger over the years, told him to divorce her if he was dissatisfied. She had never intended, however, for him to take her seriously.

In Liz's own words the major concern in coming for counseling was that "I have always been Bill's wife and I have no identity of my own." She had never developed an identity of her own because, until the day she married, she had lived with her mother. Although she admits that she did not love Bill at first, she grew to love him as the years went by and he is a good father to their two children.

Bill attended one session promising to return, but he never did. During that session, he not only recited a long litany of Liz's faults, he also insisted that she was not a real wife to him and was not loyal to him in the way he wished her to be. He spoke in vague generalities about his expectations. His tone was dictatorial and pontifical, which gave the counselor a fair amount of insight into the nature of their relationship. Liz admits to being strong-willed, which has often produced negative reactions to his tirades—to the point of physical retaliation on a few occasions. In spite of his catalog of complaints, Bill still attempts to have sex with her, which she refuses.

The separation has had a negative effect on everyone. Liz says the two children are "always at each other's throats." Bill has moved out, but sees the children on alternate weekends. At those times, he does not seem to do anything special with them. They apparently just sit around the apartment, although he sometimes takes them out to eat.

Liz feels ashamed of the separation. She feels that if she had acted differently, Bill would not have left even though she admits that he was not much of a support to her either emotionally or economically. He had worked only sporadically and had not contributed very much to the household budget. When her mother died, Bill did not comfort her but acted very distant. Thus, Liz had to look elsewhere for her support, which came from her girlfriends, with whom she is very close. Despite the fact the Bill never supported Liz emotionally, he resented Liz's relationships with her friends and often ordered her to sever the relationships. At one time she had been willing to do this but realized that if she did, she would have no emotional support at all.

The whole situation has affected Liz's health and job productivity. She has had headaches and insomnia off and on since Bill left. She does not want her friends and coworkers to know about the separation and the impending divorce (only some of her very close friends know). She feels very much supported by her close girlfriends, who invite her on weekends to stay overnight and accompany them to church. But, she feels that her employment, which is very critical, is suffering because she is just going through the motions. Bill's family has been affected too, and they are very angry with him because they see no reason for his actions.

ANALYSIS

Divorce recovery is a process. There are certain predictable phases, with some variations, through which individuals pass. This is important to note as we analyze Liz's case.

A multimodal analysis of this case might look as follows:

BEHAVIOR:
1. Trying desperately to devise ways to get Bill back. Using the children to manipulate him.
2. Feeling the need for support from friends but ambivalent about asking for it, and feeling guilty when they do help her.

AFFECT:
1. Repressed anger.
2. Feelings of helplessness.
3. Feelings of abandonment.
4. High level of stress.
5. Feelings of loneliness.
6. Depression.
7. Feelings of inadequacy as a woman.
8. Jealous of husband's female relationships.

SENSATION:
1. Constant headaches.
2. Insomnia.
3. Need to eat to control stress.

IMAGERY:
1. Husband criticizing her.
2. House seems empty.
3. Driving aimlessly around the city.
4. Husband paying attention to other women.

5. Family berating her for having married Bill.

COGNITION:
1. I'm a failure.
2. I always have helped others but few will help me now.
3. People are laughing at me.
4. I'm at Bill's whim—if he wants to, I'll take him back.
5. I'm not doing my job properly.
6. I'm not any good to my children like this.
7. People are pretending to be interested in my situation but they just want to pry.

INTERPERSONAL RELATIONSHIPS:
1. Both angry at and subservient to estranged husband.
2. Angry at the children.
3. Alienated from family.
4. Abrupt with those whom she supervises at her job.

DRUGS/ BIOLOGY:
1. Overweight because of "nervous eating."
2. Psychosomatic headaches.
3. Constant feeling of fatigue as a result of poor sleeping.

SPIRITUAL:
1. Finds it difficult to accept that God is working something out in her life as a result of his present discipline.
2. Feels that she is not fit for ministry because she has failed to remain married.
3. Unable to trust Christian friends who are willing to help her.

GOALS

The primary goals for helping those who are going through divorce recovery are to:
1. Help them accept the reality of the marital breakup.
2. Help them overcome the feeling of failure.
3. Help them deal with the criticism of insensitive relatives and friends.
4. Help the custodial parent deal with the children.
5. Help them overcome loneliness.
6. Help them overcome depression.
7. Help them to be able to love again.

Process

Whenever human beings are faced with a traumatic experience, the first line of psychological defense is denial.[6] Denial is the individual's refusal to accept the reality of the situation. The denial usually takes the form of deceiving one's self into believing that the former mate will return. Typically people who are in denial hold onto articles of clothing, books, golf clubs, or anything that will support the denial.

Acceptance of Reality

Liz was clearly not accepting the fact that Bill had left for good, so, initially, counseling focused on getting her to accept the reality of the marital breakup. Because she was denying reality, that denial had an affect on what she believed and said. For example, she said that she had read that a man will go through a "midlife crisis" and although he leaves his wife, he soon returns. The counselor, at this point, asked her to look at what she was saying and compare it to reality. He pointed out that Bill had moved all of his belongings and had purchased a house in another city. He had become involved with another woman and finally had filed for divorce. Liz, however, decided to ask her husband to return to her. He let her know in no uncertain terms that he was never going to return. She was devastated, but in the next counseling session the counselor was able to use this experience to help her realize the truth of her situation. He questioned her about what she was feeling when Bill had told her he was never going to return. She wept as she spoke of her feeling of abandonment. He asked her what images she had of the incident and she replied that she felt as though he had slammed a door in her face.

The counselor used her own imagery to help her face reality. "What kind of door was it?" She replied, "It was a huge door like those in a medieval castle with a gigantic bolt." The counselor used the door as a metaphor for the marriage. It was closed and bolted, never to be opened again. Liz wept uncontrollably, unable to talk for a few minutes. When she was able to talk again, she said that she realized the marriage was indeed over. This, though, was but the beginning. Denial often returns over and over again, but usually with diminishing intensity, and this case was no exception.

Overcoming the Feeling of Failure

We live in a society that respects those who achieve and criticizes those who fail. These attitudes affect our entire lives—in school, at play, and at work. As children, most of us have felt the criticism of our parents and others not only toward what we have not been able to achieve, but also toward our inner being—who we are. Then, when we become adults, we see *ourselves* as being a failure when we should see the *action* as being a failure.

This is true also in marriage. Liz saw herself as being a failure because she felt that there were many things she should have done, that Bill would not have left if she had done them. The counselor went through her list of "should have dones" one by one, asking at strategic points how that particular "failure" would have saved the marriage. Liz began to see that it was not necessarily any of these failures that ended the marriage. She had indeed committed misdeeds, but other marriages had weathered similar trials without ending in divorce. The counselor was able to get Liz to turn her attention away from her perceived failures and to focus on the marriage's persistent problems including poor communication and her husband's poor self-image, which he masked by belittling her.

Insensitive Relatives and Friends

As we have noted, everyone seems to feel that they should have something to say about a broken marriage. The counselor encouraged Liz to talk about the criticisms leveled at her. He then evaluated them dispassionately with her. She saw that they were, for the most part, untenable. One relative had suggested that her failure to spend enough time with Bill was the "reason" for his departure. The counselor asked her to evaluate this remark. It became clear that Bill was either studying (he was a graduate student), playing golf with his buddies, or socializing at one of their houses. He only came home to eat and sleep. Liz gradually came to see that the remarks of others are often a projection of their own needs and life situations. As a believer, she was encouraged to prayerfully consider her *real* contributions to the marital difficulties, confess them to God, seek his forgiveness, and trust him for her healing.

Dealing with the Children

When children are involved, the divorce issue is infinitely more painful for everyone. The custodial parent, however, bears the brunt of the children's resentment and anger. In most cases, the custodial parent is the mother, although the courts sometimes award custody to fathers. Often the children are angry at both parents for disrupting their lives, but the custodial parent is more available and must absorb their anger.

Guilt, fear, and anger are other reactions experienced by children. They will feel guilty that "Dad left because I was bad," or some variation of that theme. It is crucial to reassure the children that the divorce involves Mom and Dad and has nothing to do with them and it cannot be stressed enough that they must be absolved of any guilt. Often children will begin fighting among themselves after a divorce. Much of this fighting stems from fear and anger that they displace onto each other.[7]

The counselor can help the child identify the source of her anger. "You're really angry at your parents for separating, aren't you?" This is often all that is needed to unleash a torrent of angry accusations such as, "They didn't think about me, only themselves." It is very effective to have the children attend some counseling sessions to deal with their needs, as well as to help them deal with the new family constellation. Often the father had been the disciplinarian, and now the mother has had to take on that role.

The counselor must be on guard and not let the custodial parent use the children in order to manipulate the noncustodial parent. Using the children to get at the estranged spouse is very inconsiderate and may be "dangerous." Children may feel imposed upon and may retaliate or, at least, not cooperate. Children should not be expected to "spy" either. They should not be asked questions that imply that they are required to bring back information.

Both the custodial parent and the noncustodial parent need to be on their guard against using money to manipulate their children. Children are masters of manipulation and will play on guilt! The custodial parent must not give in to the child's demands as a way of comforting the child for his or her suffering. Nor should the noncustodial parent (usually the father) give in to the child's whims out of a feeling of guilt; buying anything asked for.

Finally, the custodial parent (usually the wife) must deal with a greatly reduced income. The counselor may be called upon to assist her in setting up a budget. All too often, in the case of inner-city households, budgeting has not been the norm. Most just live from "paycheck to paycheck" in a haphazard fashion. The counselor should suggest some of the very helpful books on budgeting available, such as *The Practical Money Manager* by Robert H. Persons.

Overcoming Loneliness

Loneliness is one of the most common aftereffects of marital dissolution. Two individuals who have married have been part of each other's lives for a number of years and have bonded together, even if the marriage was not the happiest it could be. Now they must operate separately, and loneliness frequently sets in. It has been pointed out that loneliness is more than aloneness. Loneliness is *feeling* alone;[8] it is a longing for companionship. Liz felt very alone. Although Bill had put her down and had had frequent arguments with her, she longed for his companionship.

The divorced woman must focus on the positive and the counselor can help her recognize that loneliness at this point is a normal reaction.[9] This knowledge goes a long way in helping her cope. Too often, however, loneliness is accompanied by self-pity, which is not healthy. Self-pity, therefore, should be discouraged because it intensifies the feelings of loneliness.[10] The divorced woman must recognize that *she, alone, is responsible for her own loneliness.*[11] In Liz's case, she had always wanted to do many things, such as attending plays and concerts, that Bill would not allow her to do. The counselor pointed out that now was her opportunity to do these things. In other words, she was not to focus on what she had lost but on what she could gain from her divorce.

Intense loneliness has a limited life and does not last forever, but divorced people have a very bleak outlook and often feel that the intense feelings will never end. However, they are the ones who must do something about those feelings. All of the counseling sessions in the world will not cure loneliness. A powerful antidote to loneliness is to recognize that "God loves you and accepts you as you are."[12] Divorced people typically feel unloved because they are not receiving love from a mate. Liz was greatly helped to focus on the love that God has for her—unconditional *agape* love! Taking active, positive steps to decrease loneliness will also help cure loneliness. One step is to reach out to others.[13] This gets the divorced person's mind off of herself and onto others. She might begin a ministry to shut-ins or start a clothing cooperative where mothers share, with others, good, used clothing. The divorced woman who does this probably will find, as Liz did, that the feeling of loneliness will begin to lift. Loneliness never goes away completely, however. Thus, she must be ready to *actively* deal with it when it recurs.

Overcoming Depression

Depression, like loneliness, often follows divorce. The counselee will report having thoughts of worthlessness such as, "I'm a failure," or "I mess up everything," or "Nobody cares about me." The person may have many somatic complaints such as poor appetite (or increased appetite), insomnia (or sleeping too much), and other physical symptoms that have no physiological basis. These symptoms are the manifestation of depression.

Depression is either endogenous or reactive. The former has no precipitating event but seems to come "out of the blue." Depression of this kind is very difficult to treat and is best handled by a psychiatrist qualified to prescribe the type of medication necessary to cure it. The kind of depression one feels when going through a divorce is usually the reactive type—there is a direct cause and effect between the divorce and the depression. Counselees will typically recite a long list of "failures." They have a "cognitive triad of depression" in that they have a negative view of themselves, of their environment, and of the future.[14] The emphasis here is on cognitive; that is, they have negative thoughts that make them feel depressed, which leads to more negative thoughts, which deepens the depression. The counselor and the counselee should evaluate these thoughts.

Liz felt like a failure because she was not able to hold onto her husband. She saw her financial situation, the ridicule of her friends, and the prospect of spending life alone as circumstances that were overwhelming. During counseling, her counselor asked her what she could have done to have kept her husband. When she realized that she could have done nothing to keep him, and that she was putting a burden on herself that was unrealistic, she began to feel less depressed. As the counselor helped her evaluate the reality of how she viewed her circumstances and she was able to see the irrationality of those thoughts, she began to feel better about her circumstances also. She was encouraged to write down any further thoughts of failure and decide how valid they were. This led to continued improvement in her outlook.

Help Them Love Again

Perhaps one of the most difficult problems a divorced woman has to deal with is learning to love again. Most of the time, she does not even love herself at this point.[15] She feels unloved, acts unloved (and unloving), and soon other people do not act lovingly to her. One divorced woman stated that she was looking for "a man to love me," to which her counselor replied, "You will not find him until you love yourself." The counselee must see that her ability to love need not be dependent on a man's loving her. She needs to be reminded, however, of God's love for her. She should be encouraged not to look to others for love but to *give* love—to her children, to those at work, to those in the neighborhood, to those in the church. Love begets love. Just as God receives love from his children because he demonstrated his love first, so, we will receive love, if we first give love.

SUMMARY

Divorce is one of life's most wrenching experiences. It involves the tearing apart of two people who were bonded together. Anger, pain, and feelings of rejection inevitably follow in its wake. The counselor must minister the balm of healing in a loving, caring, yet firm manner so that the divorced person will recover with a minimum number of residual fears.

NOTES

[1]R. L. Atkinson, R. C. Atkinson, and E. R. Hilgard, *Introduction to Psychology* (New York: Harcourt Brace Jovanovich, 1983), 98.
[2]Ibid., 446.
[3]P. Blumstein and P. Schwartz, *American Couples: Money Work and Sex,* (New York: William Morrow, 1983), 29.
[4]V. J. Derlega and L. H. Janda, *Personal Adjustment, the Psychology of Everyday Life* (Morristown, N.J.: Silver Burdett Company, 1978), 305.
[5]R. S. Weiss, *Marital Separation* (New York: Basic Books, 1975), 49.
[6]A. Brock, *Divorce Recovery: Piecing Together Your Broken Dreams* (Fort Worth, Tex.: Worthy Publishing, 1988), 17.
[7]Weiss, *Marital Separation,* 211–15.

[8]C. W. Ellison, *Saying Good-bye to Loneliness and Finding Intimacy* (New York: Harper & Row, 1983), 28.

[9]Ibid.

[10]Ibid., 153.

[11]Ibid., 154.

[12]Ibid., 156.

[13]Ibid., 162.

[14]A. T. Beck and J. E. Young, "Depression" in D. H. Barlow, ed., *Clinical Handbook of Psychological Disorders* (New York: Guilford Press, 1985), 207.

[15]Brock, *Divorce Recovery*, 152–53.

CHAPTER 15

Single Parenting

IT IS ESTIMATED that 13.4 million children under the age of eighteen now live in one-parent households, an increase of 66 percent in ten years. While these statistics represent a national concern, the percentages cause even more alarm in the urban centers.[1] In urban centers fifty-eight percent of all black children live with one parent,[2] and twenty-two percent of all children are born out of wedlock, one-third to teenaged mothers.[3]

Parenting is one of the most difficult developmental tasks a human being can undertake. Other developmental tasks move fairly smoothly from one stage to another, but not parenting. A two-parent situation is usually difficult, and a single-parent role is doubly difficult. A single-parent, having no one with whom to share the problems that arise in the difficult job of child rearing, must assume the tasks and gender roles of both parents.

The financial strain that most single parents feel adds another difficulty to the role of single parenting. On the average, women earn 60 percent of what men earn for the same work.[4] Since 95 percent of all single custodial parents are female, it is not difficult to see what a problem this can be. Although many have been awarded child support by the courts, most do not receive it on a regular basis and some never get it at all.[5] In 1985, the average divorced or separated mother received only $1800 in child support. In addition, fourteen percent of women were awarded alimony, but very few received it.[6]

In this chapter we will discuss three types of single parents: (1) divorced or separated, (2) never married, and (3) widowed. The divorced or separated form the largest group of single parents. The growing group of never-married singles is next largest. The widowed make up the smallest group because, in most cases, by the time a person reaches an age where they are likely to be widowed, her children are grown.

CASE STUDY: ROSA

Rosa is a very attractive, intelligent Puerto Rican woman who works as a case aide for a social service agency. She is a single mother who has three children—two girls and one boy. Her husband, from whom she is separated, is in state prison serving a seven-year sentence for being an accessory to a crime—he acted as lookout for the burglary of a plumbing-supply store.

Rosa's parents raised their family in a section of the city that was populated by Puerto Ricans and blacks. She describes her upbringing as being extremely unhappy. Her father was very cruel to his children. Often, especially when drunk, he would grab Rosa or one of the other children by the hair and slap them across the face for the slightest infraction. Rosa's mother, terrified of her husband, never intervened, but always justified his actions.

Rosa did very poorly in school, both academically and socially. Even though she often knew the answers, she never volunteered to verbalize them. During high school, she began to hang around with girls who had a reputation for being delinquent. Because of Rosa's behavior, her parents were often called to school. They did not speak English very well, however, and because of that they were not really able to understand the seriousness of Rosa's situation. Foolishly, the school authorities had Rosa translate and, of course, she completely distorted what was said. Therefore, Rosa continued behaving as she always had before.

In her junior year in high school, Rosa met Dito. Three months later she was pregnant. Rosa's mother, though promising to keep the pregnancy confidential, instead told Rosa's father who kicked Rosa out of the house with just the clothing on her back. She and Dito lived together, but Dito never held a regular job. His employment consisted of illegal activities such as stripping cars and selling marijuana, and of dead-end, low-paying jobs. Soon after their third child was born, Dito began seeing other women, though Rosa now suspects that he had been doing so all along. When confronted, he first denied any involvement with another woman, but soon began to stay away from home for several days at a time. Finally he left altogether, was eventually arrested, and subsequently incarcerated.

Shortly after Dito left her, Rosa was invited to an evangelical service where she accepted Christ. She then joined a local Pentecostal church. Dito wrote to her from prison and asked her to visit him, which she did. He, too, professes to have accepted the Lord and has promised to go back to Rosa when he is released. In the meantime, in addition to regular visits, Rosa has conjugal visits with him. These visits are humiliating to Rosa—she and Dito are given an hour alone in a trailer with a prison guard standing outside the door.

Rosa, believing Dito's conversion to be real, is prepared to wait for his release. In the interim, however, a single male neighbor asked her out to a church social (he is a believer). Although she was attracted to this man, Rosa realized that she was committed to Dito, and, thus, refused the invitation.

Dito's incarceration has been difficult not only for Rosa, but also for her children, especially her son, who misses his father terribly much. Rosa's oldest daughter does not say much about her father but does draw pictures of families that do not have a father present. The middle child, a daughter, is having difficulty in school and is seeing a counselor who believes that Dito's incarceration is at the bottom of the child's difficulties.

With Dito in prison, Rosa's financial situation is precarious, at best. At one time she received public assistance but found it too humiliating to continue. She also realized that she was vegetating at home, but wanting instead to use her mind, she found a job. She earns barely enough as a case aid to pay rent and buy some of life's essentials. At work, however, she is a "nervous wreck." Because of low self-confidence she believes that the social workers do not value her work and consider her incompetent. Thus, she experiences chest pains almost every morning just as it is time to go to work. Her work evaluations have all been satisfactory thus far; so there is no objective evidence for her feelings. At the end of the day her nerves are "shot" and she finds herself yelling at her children for very minor offenses.

ANALYSIS

Rosa's family of origin was, to say the least, problematic. Her father was abusive, her mother weak and unsupportive. She was never given any positive reinforcement for anything she did. This type of dysfunctional family invariably produces offspring with serious problems such as poor self-image, poor ability to relate, and distorted relationships with authority figures.[7] Her family background did not provide Rosa with the psychological coping skills she needed to handle the adverse circumstances in which she found herself. She lacked self-confidence, which hampered her career and thus her financial situation. Because of poor self-confidence she was reluctant to take charge of her children, and they were beginning to get out of hand. The success of the single parent in coping with a tremendously demanding situation is related to the skills acquired in her family of origin.

Multimodal analysis of this case might look like this:

BEHAVIOR:	1.	Fear of failure at work.
	2.	Inability to conduct her household adequately.
	3.	Inordinate concern with her parent's attitudes toward her.
AFFECT:	1.	Feelings of helplessness.
	2.	Feelings of fear.
	3.	Feelings of inadequacy (at home and at work).
	4.	Feelings of loneliness.
	5.	Feelings of stress.
	6.	Insomnia.
SENSATION:	1.	Chest pains that have no physiological origin.
	2.	"Morning anxiety" before going to work.
IMAGERY:	1.	Father slapping her and calling her "dirty" names.
	2.	Mother betraying her confidence.
	3.	Father arriving home drunk.
	4.	Being anorexic as a teenager.
	5.	Guard standing outside the trailer door during conjugal visits.
COGNITION:	1.	All of the social workers think that I am a poor case aide.
	2.	My children do not respect my authority.
	3.	Deep down I don't think that Dito is going to be any different after his release.
	4.	My parents don't respect me.

	5.	I don't have a life outside of taking care of my kids.
	6.	I feel very alone in the world.
	7.	I hate having to scrimp all of the time.
INTERPERSONAL RELATIONSHIPS:	1.	Cannot trust her parents—especially her mother.
	2.	Desperately wants her father's approval.
	3.	Wants to believe that her husband has changed but has some doubts.
	4.	Difficulties establishing herself as authority over her children.
DRUGS/ BIOLOGY:	1.	Ambivalence about taking antianxiety medication.
SPIRITUAL:	1.	Needs to allow the Holy Spirit to be the power to help her overcome feelings of lust.
	2.	Needs to understand that God has the answer to the dilemma of whether to trust Dito again.
	3.	Does not yet see that her lack of control over her children is related to the paucity of spiritual guidance she is giving them.

GOALS

The primary goals for helping single parents are to help them to:

1. Feel like whole, worthwhile people.
2. Take charge of their households and be the "executive."
3. Be able to depend on family and friends for help without being dominated by them.
4. Handle their needs for love relationships.
5. Satisfy their own needs as persons.
6. Handle financial matters adequately.

Process

Single mothers often feel overwhelmed, especially if they have been married or had a mate. The never-married single mother, on the other hand, may also feel overburdened, but she more easily learns to cope because she has never had a male on whom to depend. Single mothers deal with an avalanche of emotional issues, and they sometimes resent their children, whom they blame for their predicament. They are enraged at the mate who has left them and yet often still have feelings for him. They both need and resent family and friends whom they look to for emotional and other kinds of support. They must learn to handle their sexual needs. Often the single parent resents being both mother and father. Very often people who end up as single parents were themselves raised in single-parent households; they bitterly resent reliving the experience they found so painful.

Rosa sought counseling because of these and other issues. Her most pressing problem was the anxiety she felt each morning as she prepared for work. Her chest pains were acute even though she had been thoroughly examined at a very competent medical facility, and they had found no physiological basis for her condition. They recognized that her pain was a conversion symptom[8] and prescribed an antianxiety medication. She did not like taking the medication because she felt that taking it meant that she was not "depending on the Lord."

Feeling Like a Worthwhile Person

Rosa, because of her childhood experiences, never really felt like a worthwhile individual. For as long as she can remember, her father had called her a *puta* (whore), along with other similarly denigrating terms. Her older brother, who is a civil engineer, always the "prince" of the family, could do no wrong. While it is a cultural norm in Puerto Rican culture to cater to the male child, Rosa felt that it was carried to the extreme in her family.

Finding herself as a single mother further reinforced her feelings of unworthiness. She especially hated the welfare system. The social workers treated her like "dirt." Even though her section of the city is populated by low income people, and welfare assistance the norm, she felt horrible having to pay for groceries with food stamps. Her feelings of worthlessness were compounded when she had to fill out forms that required her to reveal that her husband was in prison.

To help Rosa with her feelings of inferiority, the counselor focused on her major complaint, that of feeling inferior at work. A careful analysis of her work situation was done. When did she most feel anxious? What triggered the feeling? Did she see the relationship between these feelings and feelings she might have felt while growing up and being verbally abused by her father? As the counseling proceeded, Rosa saw, by analyzing her work situation, that while *everything* at work made her anxious, only certain situations triggered an anxiety attack. The major triggering situation was any conference with the social worker about cases she was handling. Rosa was able to see that these conferences reminded her of the times when her father would yell at her and call her names. She had "connected" two events that had no objective connection. However, once she realized that her total job situation did not make her anxious, her anxiety began to subside. In addition, she was instructed in "thought stopping." She was told to think about the conference and, as soon as she felt the anxiety begin to build, to tell herself to STOP! Through the counseling, she also was able to see that her ongoing relationship with her father reinforced her feelings of inferiority. (Her father picked up her children from school.) To remedy that problem the counselor pointed out that they were now old enough to go home by themselves and call her at the office each day to let her know that they were home safely.

Taking Charge

Rosa readily admits that Dito was the disciplinarian, that the children had listened to him but not to her. Now that she is a "solo" parent, there is virtual chaos: beds are not made, fighting and arguing is the norm, and she finds herself "yelling her head off" every day. The children are fourteen, twelve, and nine—old enough to be reasoned with. The trick is to get their attention and set the rules down.

The counselor suggested that in order to get the children to understand that she is now in charge, Rosa should use the "shock" method to get their attention. Upon arriving home, instead of the usual yelling and screaming, she was to say nothing, go to her bedroom, and sit in a chair in silence. The children were indeed "shocked"—petrified might be more accurate. Once they had each, in turn, gone to the bedroom with the query—"Mom, are you all right?"—they sat in stunned silence in the kitchen. When she felt the time was right, she went in and very calmly yet firmly established the "new order." The method that a single parent will use to establish authority will vary depending on the ages of the children, but the principle is the same. The custodial parent *must* establish herself as the "executive."

Dependence on Family and Friends

Rosa needed her parents to babysit while she worked full time and pursued her degree in social work. A problem arose, however, when her parents began to interfere in her life and undermine her authority. In order to deal with the problem, Rosa needed to set very clear territorial boundaries in regard to the children's discipline. After she was able to communicate to her parents her concern that, although she was a grown woman, they were treating her as if she were a child, she was able to set the boundaries.

Rosa explained to her mother that she did not want her children to grow up feeling intimidated the way she had. Fortunately, Rosa's father did not physically abuse her children, but they said that he was "grumpy." The counselor and Rosa agreed that Grandpa was not going to change. Together, they were able to help the children ignore his grumpiness, and when he no longer escorted the children home, their contact with him was minimized. Grandma was more the problem. She allowed the children to do things that Rosa had forbidden, which forced Rosa to firmly introduce her mother to the "new order." Although timid about this at first, Rosa grew bolder as she saw that nothing terrible happened as a result. The counselor had pointed out to Rosa that Grandma so much wanted to be with the children that she would "toe the line, " which she did.

Love Relationships

The handling of love relationships is often difficult, and in Rosa's case this was one of the most difficult areas for her. On one hand, she wanted to wait for Dito to be released, but on the other, she was struggling with physical and emotional needs for intimacy. These needs were only heightened after a few chance encounters with Gonzalo in the community laundry room. The first step for the counselor in dealing with this issue was to confront her. The counselor realized that she was denying her attraction to this other man and the subsequent sexual feelings that were being aroused. After pointing out to her that her face flushed and her breathing increased when she talked about Gonzalo, Rosa admitted to the counselor that she had these feelings but had been unaware of how strong they were. Once she had admitted her attraction, she was reminded of how vulnerable she was at this particular time and how she needed to provide other outlets for her needs, such as physically active sports to reduce her sexual desires. She also recognized that she should not go out with Gonzalo, or any other man because that might prove to be more than she could handle.

Rosa's major problem had been that she could not decide whether she wanted to wait for Dito. Toward the end of her treatment, however, she decided that she did want to wait. She was then able to handle her physical and emotional needs better. Albeit, the counselor had some grave misgivings about her decision to wait for Dito—his past behavior did not indicate that he could be relied on. Rosa was, however, firm in her resolve.

Satisfying Her Own Needs

This area is of prime importance for single parents. Too often the needs of the children are placed first, but it has been stressed by workers in the field of single parenting that if the emotional and psychological needs of the custodial parent are not met, they will be of little use to their children.[9] One of the issues counselors must deal with is the guilt that the single parent often feels when she is involved in an activity that does not directly relate to her children. They must see that their recreation *does* relate to their children in that they are better parents if their personal needs are satisfied. Rosa needed a lot of prodding in this area, especially. In Puerto Rican culture, the mother typically "sacrifices" everything for the sake of her children. They are her paramount concern. It was not until Rosa felt as though she were "coming apart" that she recognized the need for a life away from her children. Again, she had to deal with her parents who felt that a "good mother did not go off to roller-skating parties," but fortunately, Rosa's church provided plenty of social activities, which gave her a wide range of choices.

Handling of Finances

Since the vast majority of single parents are female and earn less than men, finances are a major problem. Few single mothers—and even fewer inner-city single mothers—receive regular alimony or child support. The financial picture is bleak indeed. Help with finances for the single mother does not begin with the amount of money available, but with the single mother herself.[10]

Money has *psychological* meaning for each one of us. For some, money is equal to status or security. For others, it may have been used as a weapon. This is especially true in divorce situations where the former husband wants to get back at the ex-wife and does so by withholding the support payments, or the wife wants to be sure that he has no money for dating, so demands exorbitant support. The counselor needs to understand these dynamics so he must begin the counseling from the standpoint of the counselee's *attitude* toward money.

Rosa grew up in a household where the lack of money was always a problem. Her father often spent much of his paycheck at the bar on payday. Because of this, she recalls having to "make do." She feels powerless when money is lacking and it was this feeling of powerlessness that she had to confront. Once she realized that she need not feel powerless, she was able to take charge. The next step was to begin a budget. Again, her cultural upbringing had to be challenged: budget did not equal restrictions. On the contrary, budgeting was liberating. She could plan for her needs so that the quip, "There is too much month left at the end of the money," would not apply to her.

The well-informed urban counselor should be equipped with a file of information on financial aids, including food cooperatives, clothing exchanges, and babysitting co-ops. Also, the counselor must be on the lookout for opportunities that will allow counselees to upgrade their skills in order to earn more money. Through her counselor Rosa learned that some graduate schools of social work offer scholarships to needy minority students. Most importantly, however, show your counselee that no matter how bleak the financial picture, God has the answers.

SUMMARY

The urban counselor may find that the single mother is the rule, rather than the exception, in his ministry. This raises a host of issues he will have to confront. "To be forewarned is to be forearmed" is never so important as in the area of single parenting. The single mother needs all the support you can give her, especially in the early stages. If you can get her off to a good start, the rest will be much easier. If you find that you have a sufficient number (five is plenty), begin a "Single Parent Group" that will meet at regular times to provide mutual support. This can be extremely helpful and will take a lot of the burden off you, the counselor. Above all, the single parent must see that all is not lost—she can make it, and triumph!

NOTES

[1]A. S. Skilnick, *The Intimate Environment: Exploring Marriage and the Family* (Boston: Little, Brown, 1983), 126–27.

[2]A. Bustanaby, *Being A Single Parent* (New York: Ballantine Books, 1987), 1–2.

[3]"The 21st Century Family," *Newsweek* (Winter/Spring 1990 Special Edition).

[4]Bustanaby, *Being A Single Parent*, 237.

[5]Ibid., 14.

[6]Ibid., 14.

[7]P. Solomon and V. D. Patch, *Handbook of Psychiatry*, 3d ed. (Los Altos, Calif.: Lange Medical Publications, 1974), 216.

[8]A conversion symptom is a physical complaint brought on by psychological stress. In the conversion symptom there is no tissue damage. Even though there is no tissue damage, the symptoms are real. Psychosomatic illness is similar, but there is tissue damage, such as in ulcers.

[9]F. Dodson, *How to Single Parent* (New York: Harper & Row, 1987), 3.

[10]K. McCoy, *Solo Parenting: Your Essential Guide* (New York: Signet Books, 1987), 125–37.

CHAPTER 16

Crisis Pregnancies

PREGNANCY, by its very nature, creates a certain amount of anxiety, even when planned and desired. Two psychologists compiled life changes that cause stress in an individual's life, and ranked them high to low. Pregnancy ranked very high as a stressor, along with serious health problems, loss of job, and death of a family member.[1] The development of a human being brings many emotions to the surface. There is the parents' anxiety that the child will be born healthy. There is the stress of added expenses; the couple may have to live on one income for a time. It may be a "back-to-back" pregnancy, where the couple had just had a baby the previous year and is still adjusting to that life change.

In this chapter, the term "crisis pregnancy" describes those pregnancies that create stresses beyond those of a normal pregnancy. A crisis pregnancy is a pregnancy that psychologically convulses those involved. The pregnancies described in this chapter are teenage pregnancies, aborted pregnancies, back-to-back pregnancies, and adult unwed, unwanted pregnancies. While each creates an enormous amount of stress on those involved, each has its unique features. The ensuing discussion will center on Paula, an unwed woman who did not plan on becoming pregnant.

CASE STUDIES

Wilma

Wilma is a black sixteen-year-old high-school student who is one of the top ten students in her class. She has maintained a straight "A" average for four semesters. In addition, she is a member of the girl's basketball team and has won honors for the most points scored by a girl in the history of her school. She is attractive and highly articulate. Wilma lives with her mother and stepfather in a comfortable, middle class section of the city. Her mother is an executive with the local telephone company and her stepfather is an electrical engineer. Wilma was born out of wedlock when her mother was fifteen.

Wilma's mother took her to the counselor after she overheard a telephone conversation between Wilma and her boyfriend that made it clear that Wilma was pregnant. Mrs. P. (Wilma's mother) was irate. She berated Wilma in front of the counselor for being so "stupid" as to allow herself to get pregnant. "She's making the same stupid mistake that I made," she stormed. "I told her even before this happened what a horrible life I've had being a single mother and this is what she's done. Tell me, Doctor, what's wrong with her?"

When Mrs. P. stopped to take a breath, the counselor was able to ascertain the circumstances surrounding the pregnancy and the plans which they, as a family, had made. Mr. P. was not involved at all. When the counselor asked that he come for a session with Mrs. P. and Wilma, Mrs. P. made it clear that under no circumstances would he come. He felt that the unplanned pregnancy was an issue between Mrs. P. and Wilma.

Although both were Christians, Wilma and her mother decided that Wilma should get an abortion. The counselor presented the moral and psychological issues involved, but their minds were made up. After the abortion Wilma came back for one session. She had no regrets. "The idea of walking around with a big belly did not appeal to me," she stated.

Wilma's case is somewhat out of the ordinary because it is unusual for there to be unanimity in decisions involving a teen pregnancy. This is true even when the family is Christian. Usually, there are five possible scenarios:

- The girl wants to carry the pregnancy to term, both parents agree, and they want the girl to keep the baby.
- The family and the girl agree that she should carry the baby to term, but give it up for adoption.
- The girl wants an abortion and both parents disagree.
- The girl wants an abortion, one parent agrees, but the other disagrees.

● Both parents want her to have an abortion and she disagrees.

Seldom do both the girl and her parents agree to an abortion, as in Wilma's case.

Families facing teenage pregnancies must make decisions regarding three areas: the initial shock, anger, and disappointment of the parents; the guilt and shame of the girl; and the plans for the future. The input of the counselor is crucial in all three areas and must, therefore, be active in the counseling. That does not mean that she does not allow the family to participate, but they have come for information and she should give it, understanding all the while that counselees will ultimately do what they wish to do.[2] The counselor's hope is that they will make well-informed decisions based on the issues and the consequences.

It is very important to allow the parents to express their feelings about the teen's pregnancy. They have had plans, hopes, and dreams for their daughter and now they see them dashed to pieces in one fell swoop. Counseling will help them see that this is an opportunity to open the lines of communication. The girl also needs to express her needs at this time. Often girls who engage in premarital sex are looking for affection and confuse affection with sex.

However, let us return to the five possible scenarios and see how they could possibly be handled.

In the first scenario, both parents and girl want the pregnancy carried to term with the girl keeping the baby. This is the option that is frequently chosen in the inner city. The counselor's function in this situation is to help the family consider some practical issues, such as working out space for mother and child, dealing with the need for public assistance if needed, and discussing the role the grandparents will play. Often because of family dynamics, the children of teenage mothers do not see the teen as a mother but as a sister, which can raise problems of authority. The teen girl must be counseled about sexuality, because she is likely to get pregnant again.[3] All this counseling must be done within a moral context that includes love, warmth, and understanding.[4]

When the family agrees that the daughter should carry the baby to term and give it up for adoption, the counselor needs to help the girl understand that she may feel differently once the baby is born. The parents, too, may decide to change their minds. The counselor needs to be forthright about this. If the baby is to be given up, it is best done immediately after birth, before the inevitable emotional attachment takes place.

In the case where the girl wants an abortion and the parents disagree, the counselor must be sensitive to everyone's needs. Without being judgmental, she needs to ask the girl her reasons for wanting an abortion, but need not be neutral with regard to abortion. She can state very clearly her position while she respects the girl's. The counselor can point out to the girl that she may bear emotional scars for the rest of her life. Sometimes women are damaged physically through abortion, and will have those scars as well. Finally, the girl must understand that she is terminating a human life. We cannot emphasize enough that abortion counseling must be done in love and understanding. Nothing will be gained by "preaching" at her.

When one parent disagrees with the abortion decision, you have a "two against one" scenario. Very often this conflict between the parents is only an outgrowth of a deeper, long-term conflict that may also have influenced their daughter's behavior. Again, let each parent and the girl have their say. Listen sympathetically. Point out the parents' differences and help them resolve them.[5] Let them all know that you understand their feelings. "You both have Mary's interest at heart. It's just how best to help her at this time that's an issue." A statement like that will set the agenda positively. As in the previous situation, let them know your feelings regarding abortion.

The last scenario is very difficult because the two adults are against a child. She is already feeling vulnerable and will find it difficult to oppose them.[6] Often the parents' reasons for wanting the abortion have to do with their needs and not those of their daughter. They may be embarrassed to have an illegitimate grandchild. They may not want the burden of raising another child. The counselor must point out that they are not looking at God's plan for their daughter's life, or that of her unborn child. Let them know that you respect their position as parents and that it is difficult for their child to oppose them. It is vital that they do not see you encouraging their daughter to show them disrespect. You might say, "Mary is beginning to think like a parent; she must have learned a great deal from you both." This is not mere flattery. The fact that she wants to keep and care for the child says a great deal about how she herself may have been reared. Once you "break the ice" by letting the parents know that you hold them in high esteem, you can begin to help the family resolve their differences.

Teenage pregnancy is a very difficult matter to handle, but if you remember that the girl belongs to a family and that the family has a stake in what happens, you will be in a better position to deal with this thorny issue.

Raquel

Raquel is a thirty-one-year-old Puerto Rican woman, who looks older than her years. She entered the counseling room with shoulders stooped and head hanging, as if apologizing for being in the world. She complained of feeling depressed, sleeping too much, and overeating. The counselor doing the intake interview and trying to identify some events that might have led up to this point, had the distinct impression that there was something Raquel was not telling him. She told him that she was an officer in a bank that catered to Hispanic people, had an M.B.A. in finance, and made a good salary. She lived at home with her mother and sister. They owned the house, and she owned a late model car and travelled extensively.

During the interview Raquel blurted out, "I shouldn't have any problems, but I feel lousy! Last Saturday I went to a baby shower for one of the girls at church and had to leave in the middle of it, pretending to feel sick. I couldn't even drive, I was crying so much." The counselor asked, "What could there have been about a baby shower that would upset you so? What comes to mind when you think about a baby?" There was a silence that seemed to last forever. Raquel's shoulders began to shake; then her whole body was heaving. A sob seeming to come from her innermost being escaped her and she whispered, "The baby that I let them kill!"

Raquel had been enrolled in a demanding MBA program at a prestigious graduate school of business when she had become pregnant. She had not dared tell her family and she felt that it was impossible to leave the program. After all, she had been the first person in her family to go to college, let alone to graduate school. Her older sister who had become pregnant in her last year of high school had ended up working as a nurse's aide for low wages, and had struggled for years to raise her son alone. With this pregnancy, Raquel could only see herself taking the same road.

The father, a fellow student, blamed the unplanned pregnancy entirely on her: she should have known "how to protect herself." He had offered to pay half the expenses of an abortion, but had not accompanied her to the clinic and had had nothing more to do with her. After several years, Raquel was still consumed with guilt and shame. She was still in mourning for her dead child.

A female psychologist, who went through an abortion herself, delineates nine steps for the healing of past abortion trauma (PAT):[7]

- Awareness of the unfinished business. The counselee, like Raquel, is aware of sadness and depression but does not link it to the abortion.
- Link to abortion identified. The counselor gently suggests to the counselee that her sadness may be related to her abortion. Allow her to respond. Do not *tell* her what her experience has been.
- General catharsis of details. This is the purging process. Allow the counselee to describe the details of the abortion: the doctor's office or clinic, what it looked like, what it smelled like, what the various clinicians said to her, the feeling of lying on the table with her feet strapped in the stirrups—everything she remembers. This will help the counselor know what to focus on in the healing prayer that comes later.
- Spiritual frame of reference. At this point the counselor makes an assessment of the counselee's conception of God. Is he a loving father or a punitive judge? Lead the counselee through God's Word to see that God stands ready to forgive the worst sin (1 John 1:9). It may take time for her to take this in; be patient.
- Blending of psychology with Christianity. Psychology offers adjustment of emotional difficulties; Jesus offers healing. Use guided imagery to lead the client to see Jesus as the healer of her broken heart.
- Client chooses to forgive or not. The client must choose whether or not to forgive all those connected to the abortion. Raquel did not get real freedom until she was able to forgive Carlos for his callousness toward her after fathering her unborn child.
- Prayer of healing. Beginning with prayer to Jesus as Healer, pray with the counselee, asking the Holy Spirit to give her a real sense of having been healed. Bind Satan and

his emissaries in the name of Jesus. Thank him in advance for healing the counselee, and give God the glory.

- Healing of the abortion memory. In step 3, the client purged herself of the abortion experience. In this step, through guided imagery and the power of the Holy Spirit, she relives the experience for the healing of her emotional scars. You can say something like this: "Raquel, I want you to allow the Holy Spirit to take you back to that abortion experience. Allow him to be with you as you remember whatever you wish about it." Tell her that you will be with her as she closes her eyes and lets the Spirit of God minister to her. The counselor is also in prayer as she goes through the experience. Invariably, she will weep at this point—Raquel sobbed audibly as she went through the experience, and saw her baby in Jesus' loving arms. Finally, the counselee is led in prayer to receive God's unconditional forgiveness. She places all the emotions of hurt and shame at his feet and hears his words of forgiveness. Guide her through this in soft, gentle tones, remaining quiet at strategic points to allow her to commune with the Lord. Pray silently that the Holy Spirit will guide her into the presence of the Lord.
- Committal service for the baby. Ask the counselee to share what she has said to the Lord and what he has shared with her. Write down the counselee's words verbatim and give it to her to read at home as often as she needs to. Pray and commit the aborted baby to the Lord for eternity. In doing this, ask the woman if she had ever thought of a name for the baby; often, she has. Use the name in committing the baby to the Lord.

This last step puts closure on the experience.

Belle

Belle was overjoyed when the doctor confirmed that she was pregnant. She and Sam had been trying for three years without success to have a child. Little Sue Ann was born and they began feeding, diapering, and "walking the floor" at night with her.

When Sue Ann was about three months old, Belle began to feel tired. She attributed it to the arduous schedule of mothering, but when she felt sick in the morning, she knew better. A doctor's visit confirmed it: she was pregnant again! Sam was upset. He loved his little daughter, but realized that her birth had put a strain on their already meager budget. Belle had planned to return to work when Sue Ann was six months old, but this was now impossible. Throughout the pregnancy, Sam became increasingly irritable and one day did something he had never done—in a fit of anger over the lack of money, he slapped Belle. Belle was shocked and angry. She called her best girlfriend who suggested that they see a counselor.

The counselor first showed them that they had a strong marriage and had had, up to this point, a loving relationship. Subsequent counseling sessions uncovered the fact that Sam's model had been his dad who had worked twelve hours a day, six days a week all of Sam's life. Sam had been raised to believe that a "real man" provides for his household. The counselor pointed out that he was not "Superman," and Belle confirmed that she did not expect him to be.

The counselor then showed them how to take some practical steps to handle their situation. They converted their basement into a studio apartment that they rented out. The rent helped their budget considerably. Sam, who was a teacher, found a job tutoring on evenings and Saturdays, which further beefed up their income. Sam also took a more active part in helping with the household chores, which greatly helped Belle. They still had some rough times ahead, but were fortified to face them.

In counseling parents with back-to-back children, the following are important considerations:

- Assess the strength of the marriage.
- Carefully investigate their respective role expectations. How does he see his role? How does she see hers?
- Have the couple carefully assess their monetary resources.
- Allow them to express anger or dismay at the prospect of another baby so soon. They need to know that they do not need to feel guilty for these feelings. If they do not go through this step, they may harbor resentment toward the unexpected baby, which may result in his or her mistreatment.
- Help them learn to distribute the household chores as evenly as possible so that neither is saddled with too much.

Paula

Paula is a charming black woman of twenty-three who was born in Trinidad, West Indies. Because of strict class distinctions, Paula's mother had not married her children's father—he was upper-middle class and Paula's mother was from a poor working-class family. At the age of fourteen, Paula came, with her mother and her younger brother, to the United States. They had high hopes of escaping the grinding poverty of Trinidad and making a new more prosperous life. As Paula says, "In this country, a nobody can become somebody, but in Trinidad you remain a nobody."

Paula entered high school, had some initial adjustment problems, but soon acclimated to her new country. She graduated and went on to a state college to become a teacher. In her sophomore year of college she met Tory, a handsome, athletic soccer star. Like Paula, he had migrated from the Caribbean. His home had been Grenada. Paula recalls that the relationship was "one-sided"—she was madly in love with him, but he was rather distant with her. She attributed his behavior to his Caribbean upbringing; men are not supposed to show their emotions. After several months of dating, they began having sex. Two months later Paula was pregnant, and terrified. She knew that if her mother found out, she would be devastated. Myra, Paula's mother, was working at a backbreaking job to support herself and her children, but Paula knew that her mother had loftier aspirations for them. To add to the pressure, Paula dared not let her grades drop or her mother would suspect something.

Paula went to the campus health services office, which referred her to a clinic. There she had an abortion. She recalls that she had gone through the whole ordeal like a robot, not allowing herself to feel anything. Finally, the school year was over and she went home. She lapsed into depression, but could not share her secret with anyone. She stayed in her room and cried for a week. Fortunately, a neighbor girl helped Paula obtain a job, which took her mind off her predicament during the day. However, her gloom returned as soon as her mind was unoccupied—even commercials about diapers upset her.

The neighbor girl, who was a believer, told her about a loving Savior. Paula had gone to church in the past, but had only thought of God as someone who is far away and uninterested. Nevertheless, she knew that she needed forgiveness, and, after listening to her friend, accepted Christ as her personal Savior. She began to feel her emotional hurt healing, but still had some "flashbacks."

For his part, Tory remained distant, but still wanted to have sex with her. She wanted to have sex with him, too, but felt that she should not because of her conversion. She was not strong in her new-found faith and, little by little, she drifted back to Tory, and began to sleep with him. Then instead of treating her better because he had gotten what he wanted, Tory now treated her worse. He would "forget" to call her, and refused to return her telephone calls except when he wanted sex. Paula knew she was being used but could not resist her need for Tory. She went to see one of the elders of her church and confessed her sins. He prayed with her and she felt forgiven. The elder had told her to call on the Holy Spirit for the power to resist sin, and she was able to do so. For two years after that she was able to refuse Tory's advances. As time went on, however, she began to feel lonely. She stopped praying and reading the Bible. Against her better judgment, she called Tory and resumed a physical relationship with him, which resulted in her getting pregnant again.

ANALYSIS: PAULA

Paula was raised in a culture that was highly stratified according to social class. Because she was female and poor, she had a low self-image, which moving to the U.S. did not change. Her mother, though ambitious, was not a warm, loving person. Paula had not seen positive male-female relationships growing up and she somehow felt that a sexual relationship was the only relationship that men and women had. The fact that Tory's family was upper-middle class made any attention he paid to her a compliment. She had come for counseling because she felt depressed, worthless, and had some suicidal thoughts.

A multimodal analysis of Paula's case might be as follows:

BEHAVIOR:	1.	Long periods of uncontrolled crying.
	2.	Staying in her room with the door locked for days at a time.
	3.	Trying to devise ways to get Tory to love her.
	4.	Thinking of ways to commit suicide.
AFFECT:	1.	Feelings of depression.
	2.	Feelings of anger.
	3.	Feelings of loneliness.

| | 4. | Feelings of being used. |
| | 5. | Feelings of being abandoned. |

SENSATION:
1. Pain in the pit of her abdomen.
2. Never felt rested (slept all day and night).

IMAGERY:
1. People laughing at her for being "used."
2. Tory thinking of her as an object.
3. Mother demanding that she "be the best."
4. Dream that Tory called her a whore.
5. Seeing her father stopping at the house in a Jaguar, practically throwing money at her mother, and driving off.
6. Feeling "dirty" after sex with Tory.

COGNITION:
1. I am a loose woman.
2. I don't deserve to live.
3. God will never forgive me.
4. I respond to Tory's every whim and fancy.
5. Why can't somebody love me?
6. My brother gets all the recognition.
7. Nobody is going to want me.

INTERPERSONAL RELATIONSHIPS:
1. Not able to confide in mother.
2. Taken advantage of by Tory.
3. Brother thinks that she is an "airhead."
4. Traumatized by the prospect of her mother finding out that she is pregnant.

DRUGS/ BIOLOGY:
1. Gaining excessive weight.
2. Morning sickness.

SPIRITUAL:
1. Difficulty believing in the full, unconditional forgiveness of God.
2. Alternates between believing that she has been made worthy by the work of Christ and feeling that she is not worthy of his love.
3. Just beginning to accept the love and support of godly women in the church.

GOALS

The primary goals for counseling single women with unplanned pregnancies are to:

1. Restore their broken relationship with the Lord.

2. Identify the psychological needs that got them into this situation.
3. Help them deal with shame.
4. Lead them to see that God can bring good out of their situation.

Process

There are many issues that must be addressed in regard to unplanned pregnancies. Women who are believers and who become pregnant outside of wedlock often feel ashamed. They feel they have failed the Lord. Many evangelical churches reinforce this feeling of shame by forcing the woman to make a public confession. This is not to say that fornication is to be condoned, but the church needs to correct in love not judgment. These women also feel abandoned. Often the fathers, especially if the couple is from the inner city, do not want to accept responsibility for their children. Another issue is the feeling they have that the future is very bleak and that their lives are ruined. Some of these women have not had fathers in the home while growing up and long for a warm, loving relationship with a man. The counselor was able to help Paula see that, because she did not have a father, her involvement with Tory was an expression of her need for the love she had missed. The counselor was eventually able to steer her into a healthy relationship with a man for the first time in her life.

Restoring a Broken Relationship with the Lord

Tory had shown his disrespect for Paula on many occasions. For example, one stormy night after being with him, he refused to get out of bed and drive her home. She had to go out in the rain and wait fifteen minutes for a bus to take her home. Still she went back. During counseling, she saw, in retrospect, that the Lord was using Tory's disrespect for her as a way of showing her just how bad her situation was. It was then that Paula began to feel that, by carrying on a sexual liaison with Tory, she had failed the Lord and could not be forgiven.

The counselor asking why she felt that she could not be forgiven, received the reply, "I just see it that way." After all, she had prayed and wept over her failure, and had asked the Lord to forgive her—why did she not *feel* forgiven? The counselor pointed out, from God's Word, that forgiveness is not a feeling, but a fact based on God's Word. He also pointed out that Satan was at work in making her *feel* that she had not been forgiven. The counselor assigned Scripture passages dealing with forgiveness, which Paula was to read and memorize. Because of 1 John 1:9, she now has a real sense of the forgiveness of God.

Identifying Psychological Needs

Paula began counseling with the idea that it was her physical need that precipitated her sexual relationship with Tory. The counselor agreed that she was probably right, but probed further, asking her to think about what else there was that made her return to Tory after he treated her with such disrespect. One day she came into a session and, without even taking off her coat, began, "I know. I wanted someone to love me and care about me. I thought that by giving him what he wanted, he might love me in return." Paula had to see that by giving in to him, she had lost his respect. She also saw that he had not ever loved her. This revelation came to her like an uppercut to the jaw, jarring her to the realization of how faulty her thinking had been. Paula began to see that God loved her more than any man ever could. As she believed this and experienced his love, she began to learn to love herself. With her self-esteem on the rise, Paula began to see that she did not need Tory's affirmation—God had affirmed his love in giving Jesus to die for her.

Dealing with Shame

In the church Paula attended there were some legalistic individuals who felt that unmarried pregnant women should be required to make public confessions. Paula felt humiliated as it was, and a public confession certainly was not going the make the situation any better. She was prepared, however, to make a public confession, if need be, but a wise pastor and sensitive elders were able to handle the matter in the privacy of the pastor's study. (The counselor had spoken to the pastor previously and had his word that she would not be publicly exposed.) From the Word they showed her that, like the woman caught in adultery (John 8:1–11),

God did not condemn her either, and that she should go and sin no more.

Seeing the Good That God Can Bring

Often these young women believe that God is going to punish them for the rest of their lives. But God's Word clearly teaches otherwise. David, after he had committed adultery with Bathsheba and murdered her husband, experienced God's forgiveness. More than that, he was blessed with Solomon, whom God named Jedidiah ("beloved of the Lord," 2 Sam. 12:25) to confirm to David that he was more than forgiven—he was blessed.

All we have said here presupposes that the counselor's attitude will itself be an instrument of healing. There are still many problems a woman will face as a single mother, but she can now face them with the peace of God. Susan Stanford, a Christian psychologist, arrived at that peace when she wrote, "Jesus' healing brings with it an inner peace and happiness that far surpass any human understanding. No money or riches or fame of this world can ever bring the kind of peace and tranquility that a personal relationship with Jesus can bring to our hearts."[8]

NOTES

[1]T. H. Holmes and R. H. Rahe, "The Social Readjustment Rating Scale," *Journal of Psychosomatic Research* 11: 213–18 (1967).

[2]E. Worthington, Jr., *Counseling for Unplanned Pregnancy and Infertility* (Waco, Tex.: Word, 1987).

[3]T. Coombs-Orme, *Social Work Practice in Maternal and Child Health*, (New York: Springer Publishing, 1990), 167.

[4]Worthington, op. cit., 104–5.

[5]Ibid., 100.

[6]Ibid., 99.

[7]S. Stanford, *Will I Cry Tomorrow? Healing Post-Abortion Trauma* (Old Tappan, N.J.: Revell, 1986), 161–71. Also, a very useful step-by-step manual for post-abortion victims is N. Jones, *A Therapy Model of Crisis Intervention for Post Abortion Syndrome* (published by the author, 124 Sheffield Drive, Vacaville, CA 95687).

[8]Ibid., 159.

CHAPTER 17

Sexual Abuse

SEXUAL ABUSE HAS BECOME a greater social problem in the last ten years than ever before. The McMartin child-molestation case in Los Angeles was the longest, most expensive, and most publicized case in U.S. history.[1] Since then there have been several other cases that have also been widely reported in the press. Besides being reported in newspapers and magazines, sexual abuse is being reported on television news and talked about on television talk shows, which feature women who were the victims of sexual abuse as children. Sexual abuse, however, is nothing new. We know from the story of Tamar's rape in the Bible (2 Sam. 13: 1–20) that sexual abuse has been around for a long time.

Sexual abuse has been defined by D. Allender in *The Wounded Heart* as "any contact or interaction (visual, verbal, or psychological) between a child/adolescent and an adult when the child/adolescent is being used for the sexual stimulation of the perpetrator or any other person."[2] It takes the form of fondling, improper sexual talk, exposure of the genitals, and penetration of body orifices. There are many variations, but this definition indicates the parameters of the problem. We should also point out that these practices may be carried out in combination with each other. That is, more than one form of sexual abuse may take place.

The person who has been sexually abused may experience guilt, shame, depression, and sexual maladjustment, which will be discussed later in this chapter.

Bill is a forty-two-year-old urban pastor who came for counseling because of an addiction to pornography. He could not resist "girlie" magazines, and he also frequented adult movies. He is married and the father of two children. From the age of eight through his late teens, his mother's bath time was their talk time. Bill remembers being sexually aroused by these encounters with his mother.

There appeared to be a very clear relationship between this early experience and Bill's addiction to pornography. Bill was seduced without any physical contact—a visual seduction. Later he recreated that sexual experience with pornographic material. In Bill's case, the sexual abuser was female and the abused, male, which is the reverse of the vast majority of cases that the urban counselor will encounter.

What is clear from the study of sexual molestation is that the sexual abuse will engender pathological sexual adjustment later on in life.[3] A woman who had been sexually abused as a child writes:

"My husband thinks there's something wrong with me, because I don't enjoy sex. But the thought of it turns my stomach. I feel so guilty because my father did those things to me. . . . I have so many conflicting feelings."[4]

While there are many problems caused by the trauma of sexual abuse, there is no question of the psychological problems later on in life. These problems range from transitory sexual adjustment problems to major psychiatric illness that requires hospitalization.

CASE STUDY: CARMEN

Carmen is a bright, articulate eighteen-year-old high school senior who was referred to the psychologist because of a suicide attempt. After being seen at the local hospital, she was released to the care of one of the members of the church. Up to this time, Carmen had lived with her mother and her stepfather. The attempt at suicide was Carmen's cry for help. From age eight to age fifteen, she had been sexually abused by her stepfather.

Carmen's mother worked as a live-in domestic, leaving Carmen alone with the stepfather. In the beginning, the sexual contact between Carmen and her stepfather was innocent enough. He hugged Carmen and held her close, which made her feel special. He always told her that their relationship was their "secret" and that she was not to tell anyone. It soon disintegrated into ugly sexual abuse.

However, before Carmen's stepfather had started abusing

her, he had fathered two children with her older sister, Irene. The girls' mother would not believe that her husband had impregnated Irene, but rather blamed Irene's boyfriend for the pregnancies. Later, Irene decided to begin legal proceedings for statutory rape against her stepfather. Her mother attempted to dissuade her from doing so, but Irene persisted and as a result was thrown out of the house. The stepfather was convicted and spent a year in prison. While her stepfather was in prison, Carmen and her mother moved to another part of the county. However, Carmen's mother eventually reconciled with her husband supposedly because she was afraid that he would harm her if she didn't.

Carmen had never told her mother about the sexual abuse she had undergone. Her mother had not believed Irene. How could she expect her mother to believe her? Carmen had been able to repress most of the memories of her sexual abuse until the issue of sexual abuse came up in her high-school health class. Shortly thereafter, she became clinically depressed and made an attempt at suicide. The first person Carmen confided in, after being released from the hospital, was a Christian Bible teacher, who contacted a Christian psychologist who attended the same church.

Very cautious at the beginning of counseling, Carmen was especially concerned that there be absolute confidentiality. She had had her confidence betrayed on a previous occasion and did not want that to happen again. She was tearful and angry over the abuse. Her hurt was especially painful because she had so badly needed to be loved, but the love she had received turned out to be something ugly and dirty.

ANALYSIS

Carmen's sexual abuse is a classic case—a case of a weak mother and a domineering father who demands obedience from everyone in the house.[5] The mother often aids and abets the abuse unconsciously. In this case, Carmen's mother denied that her daughters had been abused, even though Irene had two children to show for it.

A multimodal analysis of this case might look like this:

BEHAVIOR:	1.	Attempts to repress the feelings of anger and resultant depression.
	2.	Self-blame and resultant suicide attempt and gestures.
AFFECT:	1.	Feelings of anger.

	2.	Feelings of betrayal.
	3.	Feelings of hatred.
	4.	Feelings of depression.
	5.	Feelings of rejection.
	6.	Feelings of fear.
	7.	Feelings of being misunderstood.
	8.	Feelings of loneliness.

SENSATION:
1. Fitful sleep.
2. Unable to eat.

IMAGERY:
1. Cutting of wrist.
2. Stepfather calling her to his bed.
3. Mother denying sexual abuse.

COGNITION:
1. It was all my fault.
2. Nobody will believe that this happened.
3. Nobody really cares about me.
4. I feel unprotected.

INTERPERSONAL RELATIONSHIPS:
1. Distant from mother.
2. Exploited by perverted father.
3. Unable to trust adults.
4. Unable to have normal relationships with the opposite sex.

DRUGS/ BIOLOGY:
1. Taking L-Tryptophan.
2. Refusing antidepressant medication prescribed by doctor.
3. General feeling of malaise.

GOALS

The primary goals for helping victims of sexual abuse are:
1. To work through the experience.
2. To realize that she is not at fault.
3. To recognize that the abuser is a sick individual.
4. To release the feelings of anger toward the abuser.
5. To establish healthy relationships with the opposite sex.
6. To forgive and let go of the past.

Process

One feature of the family when the father (or stepfather) is the abuser is the fact that he often isolates its members by his behavior. He does not want anyone to know what is transpiring and thus keeps everyone away. The victim is not allowed to have girlfriends, talk on the telephone, go on dates, or have any healthy relationships with boys. She is often lonely and isolated. In addition, she does not feel like a child. (Adults who have been abused often speak of having been robbed of their childhood.) Even at school, she feels at odds with her peers because she harbors a secret her friends would never understand. To add to the burden, she is sometimes told that she dare not share what is going on because her father (the abuser) might go to jail and the family would then be without financial support.

Initially, Carmen was confused, angry, and in severe emotional pain. She did not feel that any good could come out of counseling. An added difficulty was the fact that the counselor was an older male, like her stepfather. The initial goal of therapy, therefore, was to build a therapeutic alliance with Carmen. The counselor did this by discussing the few things in her life that brought her pleasure. She is very bright and excelled in school. The counselor discussed her academic achievements with her. She also excelled at sports, which provided another opportunity for mutual sharing. The counselor himself had had an abusive mother and was thus able to establish an alliance with Carmen by sharing his own childhood experiences. This provided something of a breakthrough in building trust with her.

Work Through the Experience

Carmen was encouraged to talk about the experience in as much detail as she wanted. All of the pent-up feelings that she had never shared poured out of her. She told of the psychological and the physical pain she had experienced from her stepfather. She recalled the fear that would seize her whenever her mother left for work, knowing that her stepfather would call her into his bedroom. As she spoke, the hurt and anger continued to overcome her. She wept and needed to be reassured that she was free to express her feelings in any way she wished. She apparently felt safe enough to do this and continued to recall the many instances of pain and humiliation she had experienced.

To help the victim work through the experience, the counselor should encourage the counselee not only to recall the events but to *experience* again what transpired. Have her visualize where the abuse took place and how she felt in as much detail as possible. A catharsis then takes place and the counselee can release the "poison" that has lain dormant for a long time. This purging may take more than one session, because it is a very painful though necessary process. Be as reassuring as possible; let the counselee know that you are there with her as she takes this journey back into a painful past. Encourage her by letting her know that there will be sunlight at the end of her dark tunnel.

Realize That She Is Not At Fault

This was one of the most important aspects of Carmen's counseling. She was convinced that somehow she had brought this behavior on herself. Her stepfather had intimated that she was at fault and that she had wanted him to abuse her. She had believed that since he was an adult, he must have been right. The counselor led her to see, however, that as an eight-year-old, there was nothing she could have done to precipitate the sexual abuse. Gradually she began to see how irrational her thoughts had been and recognized that the abuse was solely a product of her stepfather's sick mind.

The victim must absolve herself of the slightest hint that she is at fault. Have her think back realistically and ask herself what she possibly could have done to provoke this behavior. Let the answers come from her. The counselor should elicit the responses rather than give them. A possible question might be, "What could you have done at ten (or whatever the age) to provoke this abuse?" Questions like these will usually help the victim recognize that her feelings of guilt are erroneous.

Other erroneous thoughts are often uncovered during sexual-abuse counseling. For example, one woman said that she should have told her mother. The counselor asked, "What was there about your mother that made you keep quiet?" "She always blamed me for everything that happened," was the reply. Even as an adult, her mother blamed her. She recalled that whenever she visited her mother and stepfather (the abuser), her mother cautioned her to be sure not to wear a short dress, implying that the short skirt was provocative. Recalling this helped this woman see that her mother would never have supported her as a small girl nor would she do so now that her daughter was an adult.

Recognize That the Abuser Is Sick

While this phase of counseling is related to the previous one, it is a separate part of the treatment. The abused person must see that her abuser is a sick individual who perpetrated a horrendous deed. But, his actions should not be generalized to all men. Carmen was fearful of all men and would not allow herself to trust them. Indeed, she wondered about all adults since she could not even depend on her mother for protection. Finally, she was able to begin to trust the counselor and thus realized, on an emotional level at least, that she could begin to trust other men. This is an important milestone for the future sexual adjustment of the abused person. *The abused must place the blame where it belongs—on the abuser.*

To help the victim place the blame on the abuser, have the counselee reflect on what a real father or caring older male ought to be and do. Ask her to think of one of the most caring males that she knows. "What is he like? Compare him to your father (or whoever the abuser was) and think about the differences." Allow her to detail as many differences as she is able. Support her as she does this, helping her see that a normal, caring adult male would not sexually abuse a ten-year-old girl. Be prepared to "walk her through" this several times before it is effective.

Release the Feelings of Anger Toward the Abuser

In order for the abused person to free herself of the pent-up anger she feels toward the abuser, it is necessary to confront the abuser. If that is not possible, or if the victim feels unable to do so, another tactic is in order. In Carmen's case, the counselor used the "empty chair" method. He had Carmen pretend that her stepfather was sitting in the chair and instructed her to tell him how she felt. She was able to vent her feelings of anger and betrayal toward him, even though he was not there. There is no question that it is best to confront the actual person, but this alternative technique can be very effective.

Establish Healthy Relationships with the Opposite Sex

When a girl has been victimized by an older man, she will usually view other males guardedly. This can have serious negative effects on her relationships with men even when such relationships are proper. This is the point at which it will be beneficial for the male counselor to make sure he is building a healthy, positive relationship with the counselee. Carmen and her counselor were able to build a healthy, positive relationship, which she successfully transferred to other male members of the church. She is now able to carry on a healthy, satisfying relationship with a special young man.

The key here is the counselor himself. This is not easily explained. As the counseling proceeds, the supportive manner in which the counselor works with the abused person should engender a positive relationship, potentially acting as a corrective emotional experience. This is not so much a technique as a positive presence.

Forgive and Let Go of the Past

As long as the poison of sexual abuse festers, healing cannot take place. Anger is an appropriate response to this type of abuse, but it needs to be vented. The counselor must allow the victim to release her feelings in whatever way she wishes—banging on a table, punching a pillow, crying, screaming—anything to release her feelings of rage. Then the next step toward healing can take place—forgiveness.

As long as the victim continues to hold onto angry feelings about the abuser, she continues to have him as an object in her psyche—a presence in her life. For the believer, the way to sever that relationship is forgiveness. Forgiveness is not to be forced on the abused person but rather the counselor should gently lead her to the realization that this is an integral part of the healing process. If she continues to hold on to the hurt that has been perpetrated upon her, she will have to also live with the incident and its attendant pain. Forgiveness is not a feeling but an act of the wills energized by the Spirit of God. It is not in us in the flesh to do such an unnatural thing. Secular counselors see forgiveness as an option while for the believer it is not. The victim can not count on the faithfulness of God to heal if we obey his will (Mark 11:25–26).

Admittedly, the process is a long and painful one. The counselor can aid in the process by showing her that the abuser is ⁻ick sinner who needs God's grace just as she does. In addition, pathetic creature if he needed to take advantage of a defenseless child. The counselee may have to close her eyes, take three deep breaths, and imagine relaxation flowing down over her body. In this relaxed state have her visualize the abuser not as the powerful figure who took advantage of her but rather a really frightened, insecure, and pathetic creature who desperately needs God's grace.

Some victims may find that they can more easily write about this experience. If that is her wish, she may write a letter to the abuser expressing her forgiveness (whether she mails it or not) telling him that while what he did to her was a most reprehensible thing, that God would have her forgive him and as an act of her will she is doing so, counting on God to do the work of healing in her life.

Many communities have groups for incest victims and the counselor should have a list of these on hand. Many victims find great relief in being able to share their feelings in a group of persons who have had similar experiences. The victim should be strongly encouraged to attend a group for as long as she feels it is necessary.

The act of forgiveness has the potential to lead to a therapeutic cleansing in order to help her put the experience in the past but she may need the help of the counselor in this. Again, the counselor should go through the relaxation procedure with her. While she is in the relaxed state, have her imagine the experience is receding into the past as if she were looking out of the back window of a car and the road stretched longer and longer until she could no longer "see" the experience. This is a exercise that she can do on her own every time she begins to think about the abuse.

Carmen, through the warm counsel of a Christian worker, accepted Christ as her personal Savior and was able to forgive this man and is a changed young woman. Her countenance is beaming and she is counseling other young people through their problems. The road was not an easy one. There were stops and starts but the net result was victory.

SEXUAL ABUSE OF YOUNG CHILDREN

One of the most painful problems confronting the urban Christian worker is the sexual abuse of young children. The small child often cannot or will not tell adults what is going on. Sometimes the adult will threaten the child with harm if she reveals the abuse. In some cases, the adult will excuse the abuse as punishment for the child's misdeed.

The following list outlines some signs that sexual abuse may be taking place.

Behavioral Indicators of Sexual Abuse in Infants and Preschoolers[6]

1. Being uncomfortable around previously trusted persons.
2. Sexualized behavior (excessive masturbation, inserting objects into real or imaginary body cavities, explicit sex play with other children, etc.).
3. Fear of restrooms, showers, or baths (common locations of abuse).
4. Fear of being alone with men or boys.
5. Nightmares on a regular basis or nightmares about the same person.
6. Abrupt personality changes.
7. Uncharacteristic hyperactivity.
8. Moodiness, excessive crying.
9. Aggressive or violent behavior toward other children.
10. Difficulty in sleeping or relaxing.
11. Clinging behavior that may take the form of separation anxiety.
12. Passive or withdrawn behavior.

Any of the above behaviors may be present without necessarily indicating the presence of sexual abuse. But in combination over a period of time, they may indicate that sexual abuse is the cause.

Patty was a bright, trusting three-year-old girl brought to the counselor because she had been sexually abused by an uncle. Her mother had noticed changes in the child's behavior but did not know to what she should attribute them. One day she found Patty trying to force a pencil into the anal area of one of her dolls saying, "You're bad, you're bad." When her mother asked her about this, she told her that this is what her uncle said when "he tried to put his thing into me."

Counseling in this case involved Patty and her mother together. The primary aim was to relieve Patty of any responsibility for what transpired. She was told that this uncle was a bad man who had no right to do what he did and that it had nothing to do with her misbehaving. It helped her to see that Mommy treated her misbehavior in a very different way. Indeed, no one had a right to touch her or do any of those things to her at any time.

As with all treatment of young children, the counselor established a working relationship with the child. The counselor told her that he, too, had a little girl and allowed Patty to ask questions about her. Toward the end of the counseling, Patty wanted to hug the counselor in her mother's presence, which indicated that trust in adult males had been re-established. Parents whose children have been abused should watch the child carefully and return for counseling if any changes in behavior occur. Whether the abuse is new or recurs, the child should be brought in for counseling as soon as possible after the abuse has been discovered.

The cases presented have been those in which the abuser was a family member. This is not always the case. Other "trusted" adults such as teacher, scout masters, and clergy have abused young children. Parents and/or caregivers should be alert to the signs of abuse as outlined earlier in this chapter.

What to Do When a Child Reports Sexual Abuse

A policeman and sexual abuse consultant offer excellent advice to those who receive reports of child abuse.[7]

1. Temper your reactions. Remember, children will evaluate your responses. Do your best not to overreact or display shock or horror.
2. Above all, believe the child. Children rarely lie about sexual abuse.
3. Commend the child for telling you and convey your support.
4. Reassure the child that he or she is not to blame. It is of paramount importance to alleviate self-blame.
5. Let the child know what you are going to do.
6. Report the abuse to the proper authorities.[8]
7. Do not promise not to tell.

SUMMARY

Only those who are comfortable dealing with the issues involved in sexual abuse should counsel those who have been abused. Individuals who are uncomfortable will only serve to make the abused person feel distressed and perhaps more guilty. Sexual-abuse counseling is emotionally demanding work, especially in the case of young children. When properly done, though, it is rewarding—especially as the hurt heals and real growth takes place. While in our experience the gender issue seldom arises, it may be necessary (and is usually preferable) to have someone of the same sex counsel the abused person. In Carmen's case, the Christian worker functioned as a "co-therapist." A male therapist and a female co-therapist counseling team is ideal because the female victim is then able to establish a wholesome relationship with a male while having the support of an understanding female.

NOTES

[1]"Second Trial Begins in Child Molestation Case," *The New York Times* (April 9, 1990).

[2]D. B. Allender, *The Wounded Heart* (Colorado Springs: Navpress, 1990), 30.

[3]C. W. Wahl, *Sexual Problems: Diagnosis and Treatment in Medical Practice* (New York: The Free Press, 1967), 122.

[4]P. Vredervelt and K. Rodriguez, *Surviving the Secret: Healing the Hurts of Sexual Abuse* (Old Tappan, N.J.: Revell, 1987), 18.

[5]Ibid., 46–48.

[6]D. P. Peters, *Betrayal of Innocence* (Waco, Tex.: Word, 1986), 90.

[7]Vredervelt and Rodriguez, *Surviving the Secret*, 183–84.

[8]Some states require that the sexual abuse of children be reported. The counselor is liable for criminal charges if it is not.

CHAPTER 18

Victimization

NIGHT AFTER NIGHT, our television screens are filled with the lurid details of crimes: robberies, rapes, burglaries, and scams, to name the most common. The urban dweller is much more likely to be the victim of crime than his suburban or rural counterpart. In 1984 the rate for violent crime was 6.3 percent for the city, 4.9 percent for the suburbs and 3.7 percent for rural areas. For every rape in the rural sections of the country, there are three in the city.[1] Minorities, while often portrayed as perpetrators of crime, are more often its victims with blacks much more likely to be victims of violent crime than whites.[2]

The urban dweller has been so inured to crime that the term "bystander apathy" has found its way into our vocabulary. It began with an incident in New York City in 1964. A young woman, Kitty Genovese, had been stabbed and lay screamed for help for over half an hour. Forty people admitted that they had heard her cries for help but did nothing, not even attempting to call the police. Kitty Genovese died of her wounds.[3]

There is so much crime in the city that the average person tries to protect his psyche by ignoring it. Somehow, that is less painful than concerning oneself with each horrible event. Also, because of the enormous amount of crime, the victim is often neglected in the urban center. For example, a large narcotic "bust" is often described in terms of the drug's street value rather than in the number of lives it destroys. This chapter will deal with healing for victims of crime.

CASE STUDIES

Geraldine

Geraldine is a black girl who looks older than her twelve years. She is one of eight children. Her mother is single and the family lives in a housing project. A deaconess from her church took her to a counselor after she had been raped by four neighborhood boys. As she sat in the counselor's office, she held tightly to the deaconess's hand and only looked furtively at the counselor, who was male. She spoke almost in a whisper. At one point the deaconess asked if she wanted to speak to the counselor alone and Geraldine almost shouted, "Oh, no!"

Geraldine related that one of the boys had invited her to go for ice cream one evening. She was flattered. He was an older boy and she felt "grown up" to be in his company. On the way, he told her that he had to stop to see a friend, and asked if she would accompany him. They went into an apartment building, which was only partially occupied, and proceeded to the basement where they found three boys drinking beer and smoking marijuana. The four of them stripped her, and while three held her down, each raped her in turn, leaving her naked and screaming for help that never came. She managed to get dressed and went to the church, where she found the deaconess cleaning up for Sunday service. Ms. B., the deaconess, took her to the local emergency room where she was treated and released.

At that point, Geraldine did not want to go home, nor did she want her mother to know. "She always blames everything on me," she blurted through her sobs. Ms. B. thought of the serious ramifications of withholding such a matter from Geraldine's mother and convinced her to tell her mother, promising to go with her. True to Geraldine's prediction, her mother began to berate her and even went so far as to accuse Geraldine of voluntarily having sex with the boys. Ms. B. was shocked, but tried to maintain her composure. She explained Geraldine's condition when she had come to the church, and stated that it was not possible for Geraldine to have voluntarily engaged in such a heinous act. Geraldine's mother had grudgingly admitted that her daughter probably had been raped.

The boys, rounded up by the police, were placed under arrest. At their trial, the defense attorneys put Geraldine through a grueling cross examination and, like Geraldine's mother, blamed her. They told her to "admit that she did it for money." The upshot of the case is that the boys were treated as youthful offenders and were remanded to a youth facility. Geraldine was referred to a rape counseling agency run by the police department and staffed by female police officers and social workers. Her recovery has been slow but steady.

Tiffany

Tiffany is a twenty-nine-year-old, black, aspiring actress newly arrived in New York City from a small town in Maryland. She was on her way to an audition, dressed elegantly, including hat and gloves. She went into the subway and asked a young man, also black, if he could give her directions. He told her that he would go downstairs to a lower platform to see if the train she needed was there. After a few minutes, Tiffany followed to see for herself, since he had not returned. When she reached the lower platform, he reached out and grabbed her by the neck with one hand and placed a knife to her throat with the other. "Give me your purse!" he demanded. She gave it to him, telling him that there was no money in it. He rummaged through it and, finding no money, demanded that she must have some money elsewhere. She showed him a subway token and explained that she had nothing else. (While he looked through her purse, she had been able to place a five dollar bill in her armpit.) Angrily, he slammed the purse into her chest and ran off.

When the train arrived, Tiffany was standing on the platform, dazed by her experience. The conductor asked if she wanted to board the train. Ashen faced, she boarded. The conductor asked if she was all right, and offered to call the police after she had told him what had happened. Tiffany, very much upset and unable to keep her appointment, went back to her apartment. After this, she has been very cautious about where she travels.

Carmela

One bright summer day, Carmela, a young Puerto Rican student, strolled down a street, window shopping. A young man with a heavy Spanish accent walked up to her and asked if she spoke Spanish. When she answered in the affirmative, he told her that he had found an envelope with a great deal of money in it. He explained that he could not use the money because it was in large bills, and because he was not a citizen, he might be suspected if he tried to change them in a bank. While they were talking, another Hispanic, a young woman joined the conversation, affirming that it was difficult for foreigners to exchange large bills. The man told Carmela that if she would give him twenty-five dollars, she could have the envelope with "a lot of money." Carmela could not resist such an apparent good deal and agreed. She hurried home, opened the envelope, and found that it had been stuffed with newspaper. The only "money" in the envelope was a counterfeit hundred dollar bill that the man on the street had flashed in order to get Carmela's attention. Carmela, who was already in counseling, wept as she related how stupid she felt at allowing herself to be so duped.

Marian

Marian, a black eighty-two-year-old widow, lived alone in a very dangerous section of the city. The area had been a sedate, middle-class neighborhood in years past, but had fallen on bad times. One morning about three o'clock, she awakened to strange sounds. To her horror, she realized that a man was in her bedroom searching through her dresser drawers. Realizing that her life would be in danger, she suppressed an impulse to scream, and pretended to be asleep. She had no money in the dresser, but she did have a fair amount of valuable jewelry, which apparently satisfied him because he soon left through the bedroom window.

Once the burglar had left, Marian became hysterical, screaming so loudly that her next-door neighbor came over to investigate. The neighbor called Marian's daughter and son-in-law, who lived about thirty miles away, and the police. The police made a perfunctory investigation and left. Until that time, Marian had been reluctant to live with her daughter and son-in-law but now, with counseling, agreed to do so.

Dan

At about one o'clock in the morning, Dan's telephone rang. It was his neighbor. Dan's new car, in which he had had a cassette deck installed, had been broken into. The thieves had spotted this equipment, had broken the window on the passenger side, and had opened the door. They pried out the radio and tape deck, and cut the speakers out of the back of the car, leaving gaping holes in the dashboard and rear deck. The police, who arrived two hours after they had been called, asked a few questions, and left. Dan was outraged. Not only had his radio and cassette deck been stolen, he would now be forced to pay a huge bill for the damage.

ANALYSES

In previous chapters, we have done multimodal analyses on individual cases. Victims of crime face many significant, common issues. This is not to say that all types of victimization result in the same emotional consequences. A victim of a rape is certainly more traumatized than someone who is the victim of a pickpocket. Both, however, feel outrage and a sense of loss, as well as other emotions with which we will deal later.[4]

A multimodal analysis of these cases might be as follows:

BEHAVIOR:
1. Expressions of anger, rage, and revenge.
2. Avoidance of places or situations that remind them of incident.

AFFECT:
1. Feelings of rage.
2. Feelings of shame and guilt.
3. Feelings of hatred toward perpetrator.
4. Feelings of anger toward callousness of police.
5. Feelings of being personally invaded.
6. Feelings of being dirty (rape victims).
7. Feelings of depression.
8. Feelings of alienation.
9. Feelings of morbid fear.

SENSATION:
1. Unexplained pains: abdominal, joints, muscles.
2. Actual pain from the assault.
3. Jittery, unable to relax, insomnia.

IMAGERY:
1. Perpetrator's voice (in the case of personal attack).
2. Coming home to find house has been ransacked by burglars.
3. Knife or gun used in the crime.
4. Uncaring look on police officer's face.
5. Broken glass on the street (car window broken).
6. Man in bedroom.

	7.	Envelope full of newspapers and fake money.
	8.	Leering boys.
	9.	Mother accusing her of complicity in rape.
COGNITION:	1.	I'm a whore (rape victim).
	2.	I'm a real dope (scam victim).
	3.	I should have known better than to follow him (robbery victim).
	4.	I was stupid to park the car where it was dark.
	5.	I feel helpless.
	6.	My feelings are of no concern to the police.
	7.	Police don't care what happens to minorities.
	8.	Nobody really understands how I feel.
	9.	I want to kill the people who did this to me.
	10.	This city is a jungle.
INTERPERSONAL RELATIONSHIPS:	1.	Alienated—people don't say it but think the victim is somehow at fault.[5]
	2.	Further victimized by legal system.
	3.	Feelings of isolation—don't want to socialize.
	4.	Fear of males (rape victim).
DRUGS/ BIOLOGY:	1.	Victims sometimes need medication for trauma.
	2.	Emergency medical care for assault victims.
SPIRITUAL:	1.	God must not be protecting me if he allows this to happen to me.
	2.	Unable to separate the fact of being in a sinful world from their personal experience as a victim.
	3.	Difficulty seeing that vengeance belongs to God and not to them.

GOALS

The primary goals for helping those who have been victimized are to:

1. Help them deal with feelings of vulnerability and helplessness.

2. Help them as they alternate between denial and acceptance.
3. Assist them in dealing with feelings of revenge.
4. Help them put their lives back in order.
5. Encourage them to incorporate Romans 8:28 into their lives, "And we know that in all things God works for the good of those who love him. . . ."

Process

Crime victims typically feel personally violated, especially in the case of rape, but even in cases when they were not physically attacked. The fact that a stranger had entered their space awakens feelings of personal invasion and vulnerability. Human beings develop proprietary feelings very early in life. It does not take the small child long to learn to say, "Mine!" When we are personally attacked or when something is stolen from us, our feeling of security is breached.

There is no way to prepare for crime, and the suddenness of it further traumatizes the victim. No amount of television coverage prepares us for the crime that happens to us.[6] The victim must not only deal with the suddenness of the crime and the loss of a sense of security, but must also deal with the aftermath by allowing the reality to sink in, and then coping with the inevitable anger and rage that comes. The individual must come to terms with the crime and then get on with the rest of life.

The counselor who is aware of these steps will be better able to assist the victim. As in all human behavior, the counselor should not expect the person to go through the stages smoothly, but should anticipate both advances and regressions. With care and empathy, the victim can recover without undue fear and anxiety. In cases where there has been personal assault, especially rape, residual effects may last for a lifetime. Most of all the counselor must help the victim to lean hard on the One who heals: Jehovah-*Rophe* (Exod. 15:26).

Help Them Deal with Feelings of Vulnerability and Helplessness

A person who has been victimized will often be in a state of shock. A rape victim may walk around aimlessly, stare into space, withdraw, or sob uncontrollably, all in response to the crime. The counselor must listen carefully to the victim and identify the aspect of the painful experience that hurts the most. The counselor should not assume that he knows what the person is feeling. Let her tell you. Earlier we stated that the person may need to use words that are not exactly "Christian" to convey their feelings. We need to allow her to use them if that will help her purge herself of her feelings of rage and helplessness. A recent article about a rape victim stated: "Like countless other rape victims she felt humiliated, scared, angry, and finally helpless."[7] During one counseling session a rape victim screamed, "I feel so dirty!" "What do you think would make you feel clean again?" the counselor asked. She thought for a moment and blurted out, "Lysol!" The counselor encouraged her to put some Lysol in her bath water. Somehow, this helped her feel clean again. When the counselor allows the victim to point to where it hurts, the person begins to feel less helpless as she participates in her own healing.

The point is that the counselor is there to listen to and help the victim as needed. The victim who is able to take practical steps to insure his or her safety will feel less helpless. Marian, the widow, asked for help to nail shut the window through which the burglar had entered. Now she lives with her daughter. Tiffany is very careful about where and how she travels. Dan purchased another radio and cassette deck but made sure they were portable so that he could remove them.

The counselor should also avoid saying anything that will make the person feel as though she were at fault. One friend asked a woman whose purse had been snatched why she was walking on such a dark street, and furthermore, why she was carrying so much cash. Such statements come under the heading of "blaming the victim." Even if the person was doing something imprudent, this is *not* the time to bring it up.

Finally, the victim ought to resume his or her activities as soon as possible. A man whose camera equipment was stolen did not want to buy more; he was too angry. The counselor pointed out that he was punishing himself because he had left his equipment in the car in a dangerous part of town. As soon as he began to repurchase camera equipment, he felt less helpless. A rape victim was encouraged to resume sexual relations with her husband even though she felt reluctant to do so. He, in turn, was instructed to be gentle and not push her. The first few times he just held her close and caressed her until she felt comfortable.

Help Them As They Alternate Between Denial and Acceptance

Denial is a defense mechanism necessary for our emotional survival. It is not a sign of weakness for the crime victim to act as though the crime never happened. When a person arrives home and finds her home in shambles and just stares in disbelief, denial is at work. He will need time to allow the reality of what has happened to sink in. There will be times when he will accept the reality and other times when he won't. The counselor must be patient. It expresses empathy to say, "It must be painful to accept the fact that your brand new car has been stolen." You are then letting the victim know that you understand his feelings while leading him to accept the loss.

People need to mourn the loss of things that were precious to them. Allow them to do that. Let them talk about the bracelet Grandma left them that they will never see again. It is often difficult for men to cry. If you notice that they seem to want to, it may help to say, "It makes you want to cry, doesn't it?" This is an indirect way of giving them permission to cry if they wish.

Many people accept the loss when they realize that they are still alive. Even though the body has been violated or property taken, their lives have been spared. Believers often realize that they are able to put possessions in their proper perspective after they have been stolen. They realize that they have been putting "things" ahead of the Lord and that God has allowed this loss to occur. One man found this verse of a hymn encouraging:

"Our times are in His hand, why should we doubt or fear?
A father's hand will never cause his child a needless tear."[8]

Helping the victim look away from himself and help others is also useful in the healing process. Rape victims can be extremely effective in counseling other women who have been raped or sexually abused as children. Mothers Against Drunk Driving (MADD) was started by a woman whose child was killed by a drunk driver.

Above all, the Christian must come to the point where he realizes that God, as the Giver of all we have, may take it away if he feels that this is what we need for our spiritual growth.

Assist Them in Dealing with Feelings of Revenge

One common response to victimization is the desire to get revenge on the criminal. A person who feels violated, will be full of rage and will want to strike back. This is probably a universal response. The crime victim will fantasize about getting even; one rape victim wanted to find her attacker and castrate him. A man who had been attacked carried a lead pipe in his car and cruised the neighborhood for days, looking for his attackers.

As a counselor, allow your counselee to fantasize without censoring him. Avoid saying, "Don't think that way," or making similar judgmental statements. Fantasizing is a necessary phase of recovery. One victim took his scarf and wrung it in his hands to show the counselor what he would like to do to those who had mugged him. After the person has vented his feelings you might say, "I understand how you must feel. You have been through a horrible ordeal and you have a right to those feelings. Remember, though, that vengeance belongs to God (Deut. 32:35). Allow him to handle it." Encourage them to forgive their attackers and release their angry feelings to the Lord. Pray with them to this end. It is necessary for their healing.

Help Them Put Their Lives Back in Order

After going through these stages, the victim will be ready to reorganize her life. The more serious the crime, the longer it will take to reorganize. It may take rape victims as long as a year to get back to their former levels of functioning.[9] Encourage the person to join a victim's support group, many of which are run by police departments. When you see them beginning to revert to earlier stages, gently encourage them to get on with their lives. For example, one person was greatly helped when the counselor asked, "Do you think that the man who mugged you is sitting and brooding about you? Why then are you brooding about him?" The victim should allow herself to be ministered to by godly people. A well-functioning fellowship of mature believers along with loving family members, contributes significantly to a lasting recovery.

Adam's fall unleashed sin on the world. Rape, robbery, burglary, and scams are the direct result of Satan's influence on the hearts and minds of unregenerate people. Often believers will ask the counselor, "How can God allow this to happen to me?"

The counselor must remind them that crime is of Satan, not of God. Believers are subject to all of the ills of fallen humanity and we must suffer along with it. In fact, we should be thankful that things are not worse than what they are now, given the wickedness of the Devil.

It is not enough just to help the victim through her trauma. God's Word states that trials are not pleasant: "No discipline seems pleasant at the time, but painful. Later on, however, it produces a harvest of righteousness and peace for those who have been trained by it" (Heb. 12:11). She must see that her suffering is, from God's standpoint, for a purpose. One purpose is that she may be able to help someone else who has passed through similar circumstances. Paul states this basic truth: ". . .the Father of compassion and the God of all comfort, who comforts us in all our troubles, so that we can comfort those in any trouble with the comfort we ourselves have received from God" (2 Cor. 1:3-4). It may take the counselee some time to get to the point of being able to help someone else, but the counselor must have this as the primary goal. Then, the victims of crime will have peace—*shalom*.

NOTES

[1]"The World Almanac and Book of Facts, 1986," *Newsday*, 791.
[2]Ibid.
[3]R. L. Atkinson, R. C. Atkinson, and E. Hilgard, *Introduction to Psychology* (New York: Harcourt Brace Jovanovich, 1983), 566.
[4]M. Bard and D. Sangrey, *The Crime Victim's Book* (New York: Basic Books, 1979), 15.
[5]Ibid., 96-98.
[6]Ibid., 4.

[7]J. Schroeder, "A Rape Victim Speaks Out." *Readers Digest* (August 1990), 69.
[8]W. Lloyd, "Our Times Are in Thy Hand," in *Hymns and Spiritual Songs for the Little Flock* (London: The Dunbar Trust, 1979).
[9]Bard and Sangrey, *The Crime Victim's Book*, 46.

CHAPTER 19

Stress

STRESS[1] GENERALLY has a negative impact upon human functioning. Our sense of well-being decreases as stress increases. The staggering use of prescription drugs (over 230 million per year) to relieve feelings of stress and anxiety is a graphic commentary on both the pervasiveness of stress and our difficulty in managing it. Other results of our stress-filled age include over 25 million Americans who suffer from high blood pressure, over 1 million who suffer from heart attacks each year, over 8 million who suffer from stomach ulcers, over 12 million who are alcoholics, plus those who suffer from the exploding use of illegal drugs such as crack.[2]

As we discussed in chapter 1, stress may be caused by overload, developmental deficits, personality orientations, social-psychological factors, environmental conditions, and bioecological variables. In the urban context it is common for a person to experience stress from a combination of these stressors.

Stress intervention must begin with an identification of the primary symptoms and sources of stress. Much of stress counseling typically focuses on instruction and skills training. This involves helping the counselee recognize indicators of excessive stress and implement a variety of self-management strategies. Intervention may occur in the physiological, cognitive, behavioral,[3] or spiritual domains.

CASE STUDY: RALPH

Ralph is a man in his early forties who comes from a dysfunctional family. Ralph's mother always blamed her husband for having failed to meet her financial and emotional needs. They are now divorced. When Ralph arrived at the counselor's office the first time, his long-term feelings of worthlessness, helplessness, and hopelessness were being manifested in migraine headaches and depression.

As a youngster Ralph struggled with severe dyslexia, which made any progress in school a major achievement. He persevered though, and completed two years of community-college education before obtaining a position as a guard in a medium-security prison. After seventeen years on the job he has grown increasingly dissatisfied and fears that he will have to endure another twenty years in the same dead-end position. However, the thought of having to complete his college education, which would enable him to get a better job, is, due to his dyslexia, thoroughly overwhelming.

Ralph is married to the daughter of a highly respected surgeon and they have two daughters whose ages are seventeen and ten. Ralph's marriage and family life are not exactly problem-free. His wife clearly dominates him and conveys her "superiority" over him in various ways. She has made it clear that she regrets having married him. During the last few years Ralph's teenage daughter has become increasingly rebellious and has recently announced that she is pregnant. Because Ralph and his wife are devout Catholics, they are opposed to abortion, but the sense of shame and the anticipation of additional expenses and responsibilities for their daughter's baby (the father is unwilling to marry her) have created an extremely tense home atmosphere and high levels of stress. Ralph's wife blames him for Lydia's having become pregnant; if he had been the strong father and respected role model their daughter needed, she would not have become involved with a "loser."

ANALYSIS

The sources of Ralph's stress were developmental, environmental, social-psychological, and bioecological. A multimodal analysis of Ralph's difficulties revealed:

BEHAVIOR:
1. Withdrawal from interaction with his family (working extra hours, not present at dinner).
2. Occasional outbursts of anger toward his wife and children.

3. Two episodes of reported violence against prisoners.
4. Irregular attendance at church.
5. Increased work absenteeism.

AFFECT:
1. Feelings of depression, hopelessness.
2. Feelings of intense feelings of inadequacy.
3. Feelings of helplessness.
4. Feelings of stress.

SENSATION:
1. Tension in his back.
2. Feeling of a tightening band around his head.

IMAGES:
1. Mother yelling at father for being inadequate.
2. Not being able to read when teacher called on him and being laughed at.
3. Wife's belittling of his manhood, his ability, and his intelligence.

COGNITION:
1. I'll never amount to anything.
2. I'm a complete failure.
3. I can't stand being blamed for everything.
4. I don't have any options, I'm trapped.
5. Maybe I should just end it all.
6. There's no way that I can make a career change.

INTERPERSONAL RELATIONSHIPS
1. No close friendships.
2. Dominated by wife.
3. Treated with disrespect by teen daughter.

DRUGS/ BIOLOGY:
1. Severe migraine headaches.
2. Early stages of ulcerative colitis.
3. Occasional brief episodes of chest pains.
4. Dyslexia.

SPIRITUAL:
1. Identifies self as believer.
2. Doesn't believe that God has any special purposes for his life.
3. Feels God really doesn't want much to do with him.

GOALS

Counseling goals for people suffering from high levels of stress include:

1. Identifying the primary stressors and evaluating their stress impact.
2. Selecting appropriate interventions to lower general stress and helping the counselee to better manage specific stressors.

Identification and Evaluation

A stressor is anything that is perceived as a threat. Stressors may be internal (biological, cognitive, and spiritual) or external (environmental and social-psychological). They range in impact from relatively minor daily "hassles," which affect people differently depending on their interpretation, to major traumas likely to be stressful to any person who experiences them (rape, unexpected and violent death of a loved one, loss of one's belongings by fire).

Normally no single stressor produces a breakdown. It is the accumulation of stress over time that wears people down to the point where their physical, emotional, spiritual, or interpersonal functioning is impaired. The risk of stress exhaustion is increased, however, by repeated patterns of such things as:[4]

- *negative perception* (pessimism, looking at the negative side of things);
- *helper mentality* (always trying to meet the needs of others while ignoring one's own);
- *negative coping patterns* (using behaviors that give short-term results but ultimately create more problems than they solve, including addictive behaviors, overwork, and temper tantrums);
- *broken compass* (confused internal guidance system; lack of purpose, goals, and values), and
- *undeveloped stress management skills* (rigid use of the same coping style for different stressors, ignorance of possible self-management techniques).

Other risk factors include family pressures, environmental demands, work problems, responsibility without authority or gratitude, and personal tragedy.

Stressors that have an impact on the counselee may be

assessed in two general ways. First, the counselee may be asked to identify those things in current and past experience that are stressful to him. He should then be asked to rate each stressor on a scale from 1-10, with 10 representing an extremely high source of stress.

Second, the counselor may use several of the available "paper and pencil" instruments that measure stress levels. The Social Readjustment Rating Scale[5] and life events questionnaires[6] measure major life events. The Hassles Scale,[7] the Stressful Situations Questionnaire,[8] and the Fear Survey Schedule[9] all provide a measurement of life's hassles. General cognition is measured by the Rational Behavior Inventory[10] and the Dysfunctional Attitude Scale.[11] Finally, both the Spiritual Well-Being Scale[12] and the Health and Stress Profile[13] give general measures of stress and well-being.

The assessment of counselee responses to the stressors may include direct and paper-and-pencil measurement of physiological responses,[14] measures of cognitive distortions and impact,[15] direct and self-report behavioral evaluation,[16] and a multipurpose measure of five dimensions of stress.[17] These will help the counselor to plan his stress management intervention more precisely.

For Ralph, the most chronic, long-term factors contributing to his high levels of stress were his distorted cognitions (see Analysis), his negative perception orientation, his lack of appropriate stress management skills, and his nonassertive (passive) interpersonal patterns. Both chronic family pressures (the message of inferiority from his wife) and the immediate crisis of his daughter's pregnancy compounded and intensified his stress.

Appropriate Intervention

The counselor's ability to teach a range of coping skills to the counselee is crucial in counseling for stress management. Figure 1 presents a planning grid to be used to categorize the stressors and to organize specific treatment strategies in response.[18] In order to categorize stressors, the first question to raise is whether the stressor can be changed or whether it must be tolerated. Those that must be tolerated are assigned to the emotion-focused categories; those that have the possibility for change are placed in the appropriate problem-focused categories.[19]

In order to categorize stress management strategies, possible interventions related to the categorized stressors are then inserted in the grid. After the stressors and interventions have been placed in the grid, the counselor and counselee need to establish the primary goal of the stress counseling and prioritize the strategies and steps necessary to reach the goal.

	Physiological	Cognitive	Behavioral	Social
Problem-focused				
Emotion-focused				

Figure 1. The basic planning grid. Adapted from Dorothy H. G. Cotton, *Stress Management: An Integrated Approach to Therapy*, 112.

- *Problem-focused strategies* focus on attempts to alter the nature of the initial stressors so that they are not received as stressors.
- *Emotion-focused strategies* aim at changes in the various levels of response to stress that have been self-defeating, maladaptive, or nonproductive.
- *Physiological strategies* deal with physiological processes that either produce stress or respond to it.
- *Cognitive strategies* attempt to modify thoughts, underlying beliefs and assumptions, and values that are either triggering stress or showing up as companions to stress.
- *Behavioral strategies* focus on the learning of new behavior patterns that either modify the stressors or allow better adaptation.
- *Social strategies* address interpersonal patterns that either stimulate stress, such as conflict or the fear of displeasing someone, or are used to cope with external stressors that cannot be changed.

Figure 2 displays a variety of stress management interventions in the grid. In addition to the categories listed, *Spiritual Strategies* such as prayer, meditation on Scripture, anointing for healing, fasting, and even deliverance may be employed either as problem-focused or emotion-focused interventions.

In the following pages, we will briefly examine each of the interventions (see Figure 2) that are most likely to be used by a nonmedically trained Christian counselor. For more detailed instruction regarding specific interventions the reader should refer to other resources given in the end notes. It should be noted again that the goal is not the complete removal of stress; only dead people are totally stress-free! Rather, the goal is to reduce high levels of stress that are negatively affecting the counselee's ability to function healthily. The goal is stress management.

	Physiological	Cognitive	Behavioral	Social
Problem-focused	Drug treatment Surgery	Thought stopping	Skills training	Assertiveness
	Therapeutic exercise	Hypothesis testing	Time management	
Emotion-focused	Relaxation Exercise Nutrition	Reframing Modifying beliefs	Learning new behaviors Leisure time	Anger management

Figure 2. Potential stress management intervention strategies.

Physiological Strategies

Exercise is a valuable component of stress management. When exposed to a series of psychosocial stress situations, people who regularly engage in aerobic exercise recover more quickly than those who are not physically fit.[20] Aerobically fit people are more resistant to the negative effects of stress as well.[21] Research shows mixed results with regard to a relationship between aerobic fitness and improvement in mood[22] but, levels of anxiety and depression have consistently been found to have been reduced.[23] As part of a more comprehensive stress-management program, regular aerobic exercise appears to have value for at least some individuals.

To be maximally effective, though, aerobic exercise should be done three or four times per week for a minimum of twenty-five minutes each time. Aerobic exercise options include jogging, rapid walking, brisk bicycling, and swimming. Also, any aerobic program should be entered into gradually and only after medical clearance. Success of the formal exercise program depends largely on the counselee's motivation to exercise, the availability of convenient and affordable facilities, the presence of reinforcement for the exercise (social support from others who exercise), and the relationship of the exercise to other behaviors that he is trying to change at the same time. In addition to, or as an alternative to, formal exercise, a reduction in stress may be realized by increasing activities that involve brisk walking (using stairs, walking the dog farther and more frequently, parking in the far corner of the store parking lot, walking instead of using a golf cart).

Relaxation exercises basically involve the pairing of incompatible responses. The goal is to reduce stress by producing physiological responses that are contrary to stress. It is impossible for a person's body to be both relaxed and tense at the same time. These exercises are especially helpful for reducing tension in specific muscle groups. Progressive muscle relaxation (PMR) training[24] teaches people to relax the major muscle groups of the body through an alternating pattern of tensing and relaxing the focal muscles.[25] In order to be effective, these relaxation methods must be practiced daily; they are skills that improve with practice.

In addition to PMR, there is a shortened relaxation format that involves recall rather than the generating of tension. Counselees are taught to concentrate on letting go of any tension, then to focus on their breathing and repeating the word "calm" to themselves as they exhale.[26] Variations include training the counselee to imagine and focus on a particularly relaxing scene from their experience at the first sign of any tension and to continue until the tension goes away.

Nutrition is increasingly recognized as being an ally in stress management.[27] The reduction of salt, sugar, caffeine, saturated fats, and cholesterol appears to relieve the body of the stress that is induced by those substances. Proper nutrition also keeps the body in its most stress-resistant physiological state. Further, obesity appears to decrease resistance to disease and therefore increase the negative physiological impact of stress.

Cognitive

Cognitively based stress management focuses on the alteration of underlying assumptions and thoughts that interpret internal and external stimuli as stressors. Stress is both produced and intensified by our cognitions.

Thought stopping is designed to eliminate persistent negative thoughts. The counselee is taught to say "Stop!" (or think it if she is in a social situation) whenever a recurrent stress-producing thought occurs. Often this is combined with the behavioral reinforcer of snapping a rubber band worn on the wrist. After saying "Stop!" and snapping the rubber band, the counselee should be instructed to replace the negative thought with a positive one that counters it.

Hypothesis testing sets up an experiment with the counselee to test an underlying belief. Perhaps the person believes that "people will get mad at me if I am assertive, so I must do my best to suppress my own thoughts and desires and please others." Until tested and shown to be inaccurate, it is unlikely that this belief will be changed. Thus, the key hypothesis to be tested is that people will respond to the counselee's assertiveness with anger. A test period of two months (preceded by assertiveness training) in which the counselee records her assertive interactions and the response of others would provide the base for an empirical test that may lead to change.

Reframing reinterprets events or interactions in terms radically different from those typical for the counselee.[28] It is a therapeutic attempt to help the counselee take a different point of view. For example, for thirty-five minutes, one husband and wife took turns complaining about their relationship without the counselor's saying a word. They were experiencing great stress in their relationship and couldn't get out of the cycle of blaming each other for their lousy marriage. Toward the end of the session, when they finally ran out of steam and looked at the therapist for a response, he replied, "This is terrific! I'm really hopeful about your marriage." Their initial reactions were of total disbelief. The counselor explained that they sounded as if they were both longing for greater intimacy and friendship, and didn't like the distance between them. The couple began to view each other differently. That was the turning point of therapy; from then on they became increasingly motivated to make changes.

Modifying beliefs involves the identification and change of underlying assumptions that govern a person's responses to life.[29] These controlling beliefs act as interpretive filters. Depending on the beliefs they hold, people will respond differently to potential stressors. One person will interpret an interaction and become highly stressed while another is nonplussed. Underlying assumptions act as a framework for response toward relationships, oneself, God, and life in general. For example, if a person has a strong underlying assumption that "life ought to be perfect, without problems or hassles," the likelihood of stress is high. Likewise, if a person believes that "I just don't have what it takes to make it; I'm a loser," every inadequacy will become magnified and will create tremendous inner stress as the negative assumption appears to be verified.

Related to the modification of false, stress-producing assumptions is the modification of self-statements.[30] Human beings are constantly engaging in inner speech or self-talk that is based on controlling beliefs. Self-statements are responses to potential stressors that affect our emotional states and our subsequent behaviors. Negative self-statements ("I'll never finish college;" "I'll never get that job;" "I can't stand up in front of people and give a report;" "I'll look stupid if I ask a question") typically create or intensify stress. They do this because they frequently involve *overgeneralization* ("always," "never"), *catastrophizing* ("horrible," "awful," "terrible"), *black-or white thinking* ("all" or "none," extremes), and *self-pressure* ("I should," "I should never have," "I've got to").[31] Counseling intervention begins with attempts to help the counselee identify the most significant and frequently rehearsed of these various stress-enhancing habits. From that point, intervention involves the development of counter-truths or more accurate beliefs and self-statements.

Behavioral

Behavioral interventions positively reinforce alternatives to habitual patterns of action. Because they gain immediate rewards of some kind, people become trapped in stress-producing behaviors. The immediacy of the reward makes it difficult for the person to drop the behavior in favor of one with more constructive (less stressful), long-range consequences. The counselor must either help the counselee generate powerful positive reinforcers that are immediately stress-reducing, or help him identify and experience the negative reinforcement that follows stressful behavior.

Skills training may include teaching a person how to initiate interaction when with a group of strangers, how to prepare a public speech, how to study more effectively, and how to solve problems. The focus is on practical behaviors that can be taught, rehearsed, and positively reinforced.

Time management helps the counselee analyze his use of time and employ several standard techniques to use it more effectively, thus reducing stress. Most time management programs include having to determine priorities. This requires a hard look at all of the person's roles and responsibilities, goals and desires. After that, goals are established and plans are developed to achieve the goals. Common approaches to time management include learning to delegate responsibility, learning to say no, learning to schedule creative endeavors at the best time of day, learning to identify time wasters, and learning to make daily plans.[32]

Learning new behaviors refers to the analysis of client behaviors that either trigger or intensify stress. Counselees then learn to counteract that stress by learning a new way of doing something. For example, new behaviors may include laying the family's clothes out and setting the breakfast table on Saturday night to avoid Sunday morning conflict on the way to church. Or it may involve learning how to use a word processor to simplify preparation of work materials.

Leisure time is usually considered a luxury by stress-ridden and stress-driven individuals. Apart from the benefits of physical exercise, a regular period of leisure time each week can give fresh perspective on stress-promoting situations. Leisure involves play and play frees a person temporarily from the burdens and cares of adult life. It is an important ingredient of stress management and needs to be scheduled, especially by Type A persons and workaholics. Work productivity is generally enhanced if a person makes time for regular exercise and leisure, though the most common excuse is "I don't have time, I have too much to do." It's exactly at that point that the stress-filled person needs to relax. Paradoxical, but true.

Social

Assertiveness has been discussed in detail in chapter 10. Assertiveness is a key component in the management of the number one stressor in life—other people. It reduces stress because it encourages self-expression, is based on good communication, is oriented toward problem solving, and promotes constructive relationships.

Anger management involves examining the sources of anger (disillusionment with parents, violation of one's space, negation of one's being or worth, etc.). It also involves the development of anticipatory strategies to curb it. Essential components of anger management include role playing and rehearsal of assertive skills; the revision of anger-stimulating assumptions; the development of communication skills such as checking out and reflection; the modification of negative self-talk and perfectionism; the ventilation of feelings that have been bottled up over time; and the development of problem-solving skills.

Spiritual

Perhaps the most significant spiritual factor that aids in stress management is a deep level of trust in God's love and personal care. This enables one to "let go" and relax, instead of being anxious and frenetically working to keep things under control. The Scriptures are filled with invitations to place one's trust in the Lord and commit one's ways to him, with the promise that God will lovingly shepherd and provide (Ps. 37, Prov. 3). Passages such as 1 Peter 5:7, Philippians 4:6–7,12–13, and Matthew 11:28–30 invite us to place our anxieties and burdens (stresses) on the Lord because he cares so deeply for us. In an urban world filled with unpredictability and chaos, it is vitally important to encourage counselees to stretch in faith and see that God is ready to respond.

ANALYSIS AND INTERVENTION FOR RALPH

Analysis and intervention planning in Ralph's stress-saturated life is presented in Figures 3 and 4. Figure 3 portrays some of the more significant stressors that are having an impact on Ralph's life.

	Physiological	Cognitive	Behavioral	Social
Problem-focused	Dyslexia Tension	Failure Worthless Inadequate Shame		Passive Violence With-drawal
Emotion-focused	Migraines Colitis		Irregular	Daugh-ter's Preg-nancy

Figure 3. Grid of stressors in Ralph's life

Figure 4 indicates possible interventions that could reduce his stress and help him gain a healthy control over his life.

A systematic combination of these interventions helped Ralph revise his self-perception, and gave him a greater sense of control and choice over his life. He saw more of God's purposes for his life, which led to a significant lessening of stress.

	Physiological	Cognitive	Behavioral	Social
Problem-focused	Remedial Reading	Correct Assumptions Problem-solving		Asser-tivness Training
Emotion-focused	Relaxation Exercise	Reframing		Anger Manage-ment

Figure 4. Planning grid for counseling intervention

NOTES

[1]Stress is being used in the sense of *dis*tress as compared to the more positive form of stress, *eu*stress, which may be thought of as basic stimulation necessary for human motivation and functioning. In this chapter we are focusing on distress.

[2]Keith W. Sehnert, *Stress/Unstress: How You Can Control Stress at Home and on the Job* (Mineapolis: Augsburg, 1981), 14.

[3]These intervention categories are suggested by Dorothy H. G. cotton in *Stress Management: An Integrated Approach to Therapy* (New York: Brunner/Mazel, 1990) as part of a planning grid. The conceptualization for intervention given in this chapter relies significantly, though not exclusively, upon Cotton's suggestions.

[4]Nancy L. Tubesing and Donald A. Tubesing, eds., *Structured Exercises in Stress Management* (Duluth, Minn.: Whole Person Press, 1983), 33–34.

[5]Thomas H. Holmes and R. H. Rahe, "The Social Readjustment Rating Scale," *Journal of Psychosomatic Research* 11 (1967): 213–18.

[6]E. A. Marzaili and P. A. Pilkonis, "The Measurement of Subjective Response to Stressful Life Events," *Journal of Human Stress* (Spring 1986): 5–11; P. A. Pilkonis, S. D. Imber, and P. Rubinsky, "Dimensions of Life Stress in Psychiatric Patients," *Journal of Human Stress* (Spring 1985): 5–11.

[7]A. D. Kanner, J. C. Coyne, C. Schaefer, and R. S. Lazarus, "Comparison of Two Modes of Stress Measurement: Daily Hassles and Uplifts Versus Major Life Events," *Journal of Behavioral Medicine* 4 (1981): 1–39.

[8]W. F. Hodges and F. B. Felling, "Types of Stressful Situations and Their Relation to Trait Anxiety and Sex," *Journal of Consulting and Clinical Psychology* 34 (1970): 333–37.

[9]J. Wolpe and P. J. Lang, "A Fear Survey Schedule for Use in Behavior Therapy," *Behavior Research and Therapy* 2 (1964): 27–30.

[10]C. T. Shorkey and V. L. Whiteman, "Development of the Rational Behavior Inventory: Initial Validity and Reliability," *Educational and Psychological Measurement* 37 (1977): 527–34.

[11]A. N. Weissman, "Assessing Depressongenic Attitudes: A Validation Study," (Paper presented at the Fifty-first Annual Meeting of the Eastern Psychological Association, Hartford, Conn. 1980.)

[12]Craig W. Ellison, "Spiritual Well-being: Conceptualization and Measurement," *Journal of Psychology and Theology* 11 (1983): 330–40.

[13]David H. Olson and Kenneth L. Stewart, "Multisystems Assessment of Health and Stress [MASH] and the Health and Stress Profile [HSP]," *Family System Medicine* (July 1990).

[14]These include the Cues for Tension and Anxiety Survey Schedule in M. Hersen and A. S. Bellack, eds., *Behavioral Assessment: A Practical Handbook*, 2d ed. (New York: Pergamon Press, 1981); and the Allen and Hyde Symptom Checklist in R. J. Allen and D. Hyde, *Investigations in Stress Control* (Minneapolis: Burgess, 1980).

[15]These include measures such as the Automatic Thoughts Questionnaire of S. D. Hollon and K. M. Bemis, "Self Report and the Assessment of Cognitive Functions." In M. Hersen and A. S. Bellack, eds., *Behavioral Assessment: A Practice Handbook*, 2d ed., 125–74.

[16]Paper-and-pencil measures include The Assertive Behavior Survey Schedule in M. Hersen and A. S. Bellack, eds., *Behavioral Assessment: A Practical Handbook* (New York: Pergamon Press, 1976); and the Assertion Inventory in E. D. Gambrill and C. A. Richey, "An Assertion Inventory for Use in Assessment and Research," *Behavior Therapy* 6 (1975): 550–61.

[17]L. R. Derogatis, R. S. Lipman, K. Rickels, E. H. Uhlenhuth, and L. Covi, "The Hopkins Symtom Checklist (HSCL): A Self-Report Symptom Inventory," *Behavioral Science* 19 (1974): 1–15.

[18]This material is adapted slightly from Dorothy H. G. Cotton, *Stress Management*, 112.

[19]Ibid., 112.

[20]D. Sinyor, S. G. Schwartz, F. Peronnet, G. Brisson, and P. Seraganian, "Aerobic Fitness Level and Reactivity to Psychosocial Stress: Physiological, Biochemical and Subjective Measures," *Psychosomatic Medicine* 45 (1983): 205–17.

[21]S. C. Kobasa, S. R. Maddi, and M. L. Puccetti, "Personality and Exercise as Buffers in the Stress-Illness Relationship," *Journal of Behavioral Medicine* 5 (1982): 391–404.

[22]C. H. Folkins and W. E. Sime, "Physical Fitness Training and Mental Health," *American Psychologist* 36 (4), (1981): 373–89.

[23]Cotton, *Stress Management*, 172.

[24]D. A. Bernstein and T. D. Borkovec, *Progressive Relaxation Training: A Manual for the Helping Professions* (Champaign, Ill.: Research Press, 1973).

[25]See Nancy Norvell and Dale Belles, *Stress Management Training* (Sarasota, Fla.: Professional Resource Exchange, Inc., 1990), and Dorothy H. G. Cotton, *Stress Management*, for specific instructions.

[26]Norvell and Belles, *Stress Management Training*, 21.

[27]C. Samuel Verghese, *The Working People's Guide to Stress Management* (Cherry Hill, N.J.: National Stress Management and Biofeedback Institute/SVSMI Publishing, 1989), has detailed information on how to reduce stress, depression, and negative moods through nutrition.

[28]Donald Capps, *Reframing: A New Method in Pastoral Care* (Minneapolis: Fortress Press, 1990).

[29]Aaron T. Beck, *Cognitive Therapy and the Emotional Disorders* (New York: Times-Mirror, 1976), and Albert Ellis, *Reason and Emotion in Psychotherapy* (Secaucus, N.J.: Citadel Press, 1962) are the two most well-known proponents of challenge and change of underlying beliefs. Beck's approach is known as Cognitive Therapy, while Ellis's is called Rational-Emotive Therapy.

[30]Norvell and Belles, *Stress Management Training*, 23–28.

[31]Ibid., 24–25.

[32]Cotton, *Stress Management*, 231.

Conclusion

HEALING FOR THE CITY is based on several underlying principles that have served as the guiding substructure for the book. These principles are important in order for counseling to be effective in the urban context.

First, *cities impact people.* The urban environment in general, and specific sub-environments within the whole, significantly shape the physical, emotional, relational, cognitive, and spiritual functioning of urban dwellers. Although people's psychospiritual needs are the same regardless of life context, the ways in which they learn to address those needs vary with each person's particular setting. People learn to survive, physically, relationally, and emotionally in their immediate context. One of the key environmental realities of urban life is the intensification of stress. Stress demands the development of coping strategies. Much about the lifestyles and interaction patterns of urban dwellers reflects the attempt to positively cope with the stresses of city life.

Another reality of the urban setting that affects the functioning of urban dwellers is the diversity of the city. Cities are racially, culturally, economically, educationally, and spiritually pluralistic. As a result, individualism reigns. There is no compelling set of beliefs, mores, and norms that cohesively draws urban dwellers together in common purpose and behavior, unless it is the pursuit of financial success. The relativism that results makes it difficult for individuals to construct lives with any sense of healthy certainty. The results are a considerable amount of confusion about how to live life, and pain that comes from the tendency to reject the idea of any basic, God-given boundaries for living.

Second, *nonprofessional counselors can be agents of healing through counseling.* We have implied that there are four levels of helping available through the urban church. On the first level, the urban church can promote healing through *koinonia* or caring—Christian community. As believers implement the love of Christ, healing occurs. On a second level, healing is further encouraged through intensive discipling relationships. We have suggested that counseling and discipleship are compatible and complementary, at least in the urban setting. On a third level, carefully trained nonprofessional counselors (laity and pastors) can provide an even more finely tuned and knowledgeable form of intervention for specific problems a person or family may be experiencing. On the fourth level, professional counselors are available to deal with more complex and chronic problems that the nonprofessional counselors refer to them.

Third, *healing is multidimensional.* Because human beings are complex and integrated systems, healing cannot be approached from an exclusively biological, psychological, or spiritual angle. According to the Scriptures, human personality is unified but, in a reflection of the triune nature of the Godhead, also consists of the interrelated dimensions of body, soul, and spirit. In relation to a particular problem, singular intervention may be appropriate, but it is simply not wise to fragment people and approach their problems as being purely spiritual or purely psychological. The urban Christian worker must see psychospiritual counseling as a more comprehensive and adequate approach. As a result, counseling can be viewed appropriately as an ally of preaching, prayer, discipleship, and other forms of healing intervention, instead of as a threat.

Fourth, *counseling must be contextualized.* The enterprise of contemporary psychotherapy has been primarily built on a Western, middle-class value framework. It is geared toward those who are more highly educated and financially secure than are the majority of urban dwellers. It has a Euro-American cultural character. Christian counseling for the urban setting must be prepared to go beyond a monocultural structure. Because of the pluralistic, cross-cultural (or multitribal) nature of most major urban centers, counseling in the city must be anthropologically and sociologically sensitive. Urban counselors must be culturally and linguistically equipped to communicate with those coming to them from different cultural, economic, and racial backgrounds for counseling. They must also be able to train counselors from as many of those backgrounds as possible.

Healing for the City has provided some preliminary information that will be of help in dealing with African American, Asian, and Hispanic counselees, and has pointed out some considerations necessary for dealing with those of various economic classes. It is critical that the urban counselor be aware of his own contextual roots and be sensitive in his counseling to the realities of his counselees' existence.

Finally, *specific interventions are available for specific problems.* This implies that the counselor must become knowledgeable about the most likely problems she will face, and become aware of a number of appropriate interventions. Just being well-intentioned or spiritually sensitive are not enough. While God is definitely the source of wisdom, and sometimes gives a word of knowledge, urban counselors must learn as much as possible about issues if God is to fully use them as channels of his healing grace. The bibliographic and organizational resources listed at the end of the book are valuable in gaining needed knowledge.

Resources:
For Further Reading

† Denotes a particularly outstanding and helpful book for nonprofessional counselors

ADDICTIONS (NONCHEMICAL)

Backus, William. *Finding the Freedom of Self-Control*. Minneapolis: Bethany House, 1987.

Carnes, Patrick. *Out of the Shadows: Understanding Sexual Addiction*. Minneapolis: CompCare Publishers, 1983.

————. *Contrary to Love: Helping the Sexual Addict*. Minneapolis: CompCare Publishers, 1989.

Friends in Recovery. *The Twelve Steps for Christians from Addictive and Other Dysfunctional Families*. San Diego: Recovery Publications, 1988.†

May, Gerald G. *Addiction and Grace*. San Francisco: Harper & Row, 1988.†

Miller, J. Keith. *Sin: Overcoming the Ultimate Deadly Addiction*. San Francisco: Harper & Row, 1987.

Naphen, Craig. *The Addictive Personality: Roots, Rituals and Recovery*. Minneapolis: Hazelden Foundation, 1988.†

Walters, Richard P. *Counseling for Problems of Self-Control*. Resources for Christian Counseling Series. Waco, Tex.: Word, 1987.

ADULT CHILDREN OF ALCOHOLICS

Friel, John, and Linda Friel. *Adult Children: The Secrets of Dysfunctional Families*. Deerfield Beach, Fla.: Health Communications, Inc., 1988.

Friends in Recovery. *The Twelve Steps—A Spiritual Journey: A Working Guide for Adult Children from Addictive and Other Dysfunctional Families*. San Diego: Recovery Publications, 1988.

Marlin, Emily. *Hope: New Choices and Recovery Strategies for Adult Children of Alcoholics*. New York: Harper & Row, 1987.

Wilson, Sandra D. *Counseling Adult Children of Alcoholics*. Resources for Christian Counseling Series. Dallas: Word, 1989.†

AIDS

Albers, Gregg. *Counseling and AIDS*. Resources for Christian Counseling Series. Dallas: Word, 1990.

Hoffman, Wendell, and Stanley Grenz. *AIDS: Ministry in the Midst of an Epidemic*. Grand Rapids: Baker, 1990.

Kain, Craig, ed. *No Longer Immune: A Counselor's Guide to AIDS*. Alexandria, Va.: American Association for Counseling and Development, 1989.†

Kubler-Ross, Elisabeth. *AIDS: The Ultimate Challenge*. New York: Collier Books, 1987.

ASSERTIVENESS TRAINING

Alberti, Robert, and Michael Emmons. *Your Perfect Right.* 5th ed. San Luis Obispo, Calif.: Impact Publishers, 1976.

CHEMICAL ADDICTIONS

Arterburn, Stephen. *Drug-Proof Your Kids: A Prevention Guide and an Intervention Plan.* Pomona, Calif.: Focus on the Family, 1989.

Berger, Gilda. *Addictions: Its Causes, Problems and Treatment.* New York: Watts, 1982.

———. *Crack: The New Drug Epidemic.* New York: Watts, 1987.†

Clinebell, Howard. *Understanding and Counseling the Alcoholic.* Nashville: Abingdon, 1984.†

Edwards, Gabrielle. *Coping with Drug Abuse.* New York: Rosen Publishing Group, 1983.

Gorski, Terence T., and Merlene Miller. *Staying Sober: A Guide for Relapse Prevention.* Independence, Mo.: Independence Press, 1986.

Nace, Edgar P. *The Treatment of Alcoholism.* New York: Brunner/Mazel, 1987.

Van Cleave, Stephen, Walter Byrd, and Kathy Revell. *Counseling for Substance Abuse and Addiction.* Waco, Tex.: Word, 1987.†

CODEPENDENCE

Beattie, Melody. *Codependent No More.* Minneapolis: Hazelden Foundation, 1987.

———. *Beyond Codependency: And Getting Better All the Time.* San Francisco: Harper & Row/Hazelden Foundation, 1989.

Hemfelt, Robert, Frank Minirth, and Paul Meier. *Love is a Choice: Recovery for Codependent Relationships.* Nashville: Thomas Nelson, 1989.

Mellody, Pia, with Andrea Wells Miller and J. Keith Miller. *Facing Codependence: What It Is, Where It Comes From, How It Sabotages Our Lives.* San Francisco: Harper & Row, 1989.

Mellody, Pia, and Andrea Wells Miller. *Breaking Free: A Recovery Workbook for Facing Codependence.* San Francisco: Harper & Row, 1989.

CONFLICT RESOLUTION

Augsburger, David. *When Caring is Not Enough: Resolving Conflicts Through Fair Fighting.* Scottdale, Pa.: Herald, 1983.

Cosgrove, Mark P. *Counseling for Anger.* Resources for Christian Counseling Series. Dallas: Word, 1988.

COUNSELING AFRICAN AMERICANS

Background:

Angelou, Maya. *I Know Why the Caged Bird Sings.* New York: Bantam, 1971.

Wright, Richard. *Black Boy.* 1937. Reprint. New York: Harper & Row, 1966.

Counseling:

Boyd-Franklin, Nancy. *Black Families in Therapy: A Multi-Systems Approach.* New York: Guilford Press, 1989.†
Grier, William, and Price Cobbs. *Black Rage.* New York: Basic Books, 1968.
White, J., and T. Parham. *The Psychology of Blacks: An African American Perspective.* Englewood Cliffs, N.J.: Prentice-Hall, 1990.

COUNSELING ASIANS AND ASIAN AMERICANS

Background:

Shon, S. P., and D. Y. Ja. "Asian Families." In *Ethnicity and Family Therapy*, edited by M. McGoldrick, J. K. Pearce, and J. Giordano, 208–28. New York: Guilford, 1982.
Sue, S., and J. K. Morishima. *The Mental Health of Asian Americans: Contemporary Issues in Identifying and Treating Mental Problems.* San Francisco: Jossey-Bass, 1982.

Counseling:

Comas-Dias, L., and E. E. H. Griffith, eds. *Clinical Guidelines in Cross-Cultural Mental Health.* New York: Wiley, 1988.
Pedersen, P., J. Draguns, W. Lonner, and J. Trimble, eds. *Counseling Across Cultures.* Honolulu: University of Hawaii Press, 1989.
Sue, D. W., and D. Sue. *Counseling the Culturally Different.* (2d edition) New York: Wiley, 1990.

COUNSELING HISPANICS

Background:

Mirande, A., and E. Enriquez. *La Chicana.* Chicago: University Press, 1979.
Mirande, S. *The Chicano Experience.* Notre Dame: University Press, 1985.
Wagner, N. N., and M. J. Haug. *Chicanos: Social and Psychological Perspectives.* St. Louis: C. V. Mosby Co., 1971.

Counseling:

Acosta, F. X., J. Yamamoto, and L. A. Evans. *Effective Psychotherapy for Low-Income and Minority Patients.* New York: Plenum Press, 1982.
Jones, E. E., and S. J. Korchin, eds. *Minority Mental Health.* New York: Praeger Publishers, 1982.
LeVine, E. S., and A. A. Padilla. *Crossing Cultures in Therapy: Pluralistic Counseling for the Hispanic.* Belmont, Calif.: Brooks/Cole Publ.Co., 1980.

CRISIS COUNSELIN

Hoff, Lee Ann. *People in Crisis: Understanding and Helping.* (3d ed.) New York: Addison-Wesley, 1989.
Kennedy, Eugene. *Crisis Counseling: The Essential Guide for Non-Professional Counselors.* New York: Continuum, 1984.

Swihart, Judd, and G. Richardson. *Counseling in Times of Crisis.* Resources for Christian Counseling Series. Waco, Tex.: Word, 1987.†
Van Ornum, William, and John B. Mordock. *Crisis Counseling with Children and Adolescents: A Guide for Non-Professional Counselors.* New York: Continuum, 1987.
Wright, H. Norman. *Crisis Counseling: Helping People in Crisis and Stress.* San Bernardino, Calif.: Here's Life Publishers, 1987.

CRISIS PREGNANCIES

Jones, Nola M. *A Therapy Model of Crisis Intervention for Post-Abortion Syndrome.* Vacaville, Calif.: Victims of Choice, 1988.
Mall, David, and Walter Watts, eds. *The Psychological Aspects of Abortion.* Washington, D.C.: University Publications of America, 1979.
Stanford, Susan. *Will I Cry Tomorrow? Healing Post-Abortion Trauma.* Old Tappan, N.J.: Revell, 1986.†
Worthington, Everett L., Jr. *Counseling for Unplanned Pregnancy and Infertility.* Resources for Christian Counseling Series. Waco, Tex.: Word, 1987.

CROSS-CULTURAL COUNSELING

Augsburger, David. *Pastoral Counseling Across Cultures.* Philadelphia: Westminster, 1986.
McGoldrick, Monica, J. Pearce, and J. Giordano. *Ethnicity and Family Therapy.* New York: Guilford Press, 1982.
Sue, D. W. *Counseling the Culturally Different.* New York: Wiley, 1981.

DEATH AND DYING

Kopp, R. *When Someone You Love is Dying: A Handbook for Counselors and Those Who Care.* Grand Rapids: Zondervan, 1980.†
Rando, Therese. *Parental Loss of a Child.* Champaign, Ill.: Research Press, 1986.

DEPRESSION

Brandt, Frans M. J. *Victory Over Depression.* Grand Rapids: Baker, 1988.
Cleve, Jay. *Out of the Blues: Strategies That Work to Get You Through the Down Times.* Minneapolis: CompCare Publishers, 1989.
Hart, Archibald D. *Counseling the Depressed.* Resources for Christian Counseling Series. Waco, Tex.: Word, 1987.†

DIVORCE RECOVERY

Brock, Anita. *Divorce Recovery: Piecing Together Your Broken Dreams.* Fort Worth: Worthy Publishing Co., 1988.
Burns, Bob. *Through the Whirlwind: A Proven Path to Recovery from the Devastation of Divorce.* Nashville: Oliver Nelson Books, 1989.
Marshall, Sharon. *Separation and Divorce: How to Keep Going When You Really Don't Want To.* Grand Rapids: Baker, 1988.
Richards, Sue, and Stanley Hagemeyer. *Ministry to the Divorced: A*

Handbook for Churches to Promote Healing. Grand Rapids: Zondervan, 1986.†

Streeter, Carole S. *Finding Your Place After Divorce: How Women Can Find Healing*. Grand Rapids: Zondervan, 1986.

Weiss, Robert. *Marital Separation: Coping with the End of a Marriage and the Transition to Being Single Again*. New York: Basic Books, 1975.

DOMESTIC ABUSE

Besharov, Douglas J. *Recognizing Child Abuse: A Guide for the Concerned*. New York: The Free Press, 1990.

Martin, Grant L. *Counseling for Family Violence and Abuse*. Resources for Christian Counseling Series. Dallas: Word, 1987.

Neidig, P., and D. Friedman. *Spouse Abuse: A Treatment Program for Couples*. Champaign, Ill.: Research Press, 1984.

Sonkin, D., D. Martin, and L. Walker. *The Male Batterer: A Treatment Approach*. New York: Springer, 1985.

FORGIVENESS

Augsburger, David. *Caring Enough to Forgive/Caring Enough Not to Forgive*. Ventura, Calif.: Regal, 1981.

Smedes, Lewis. *Forgive and Forget: Healing the Hurts We Don't Deserve*. San Francisco: Harper & Row, 1984.†

Walters, Richard. *Forgive and Be Free: Healing the Wounds of the Past and Present*. Grand Rapids: Zondervan, 1983.

GRIEF

Worden, J. *Grief Counseling and Grief Therapy: A Handbook for the Mental Healthy Practitioner*. New York: Springer, 1982.

HOMOSEXUALITY

Saia, Michael R. *Counseling the Homosexual*. Minneapolis: Bethany, 1988.

Wilson, Earl D. *Counseling and Homosexuality*. Dallas: Word, 1988.

Worthen, Frank. *Steps Out of Homosexuality*. San Rafael, Calif.: Love in Action, 1984.

MARITAL COMMUNICATION

Beck, Aaron T. *Love is Never Enough*. New York: Harper & Row, 1988.†

Galvin, K. M., and B. B. Brommel. *Family Communication: Cohesion and Change*. (2d ed.) Glenview, Ill.: Scott Foresman, 1986.

Sieburg, Evelyn. *Family Communication: An Integrated Systems Approach*. New York: Gardner Press, 1985.

Smalley, Gary, and John Trent. *The Language of Love*. Pomona, Calif.: Focus on the Family, 1988.

MARITAL CONFLICT RESOLUTION

Augsburger, David. *When Caring is Not Enough: Resolving Conflicts Through Fair Fighting*. Scottdale, Pa.: Herald, 1983.

Guerin, Philip J., Leo F. Fay, Susan L. Burden, and Judith G. Kautto. *The Evaluation and Treatment of Marital Conflict*. New York: Basic Books, 1987.
Worthington, Everett L., Jr. *Marriage Counseling: A Christian Approach to Counseling Couples*. Downers Grove, Ill.: Inter-Varsity, 1989.†

PREJUDICE AND RACISM

Haselden, Kyle. *The Racial Problem in Christian Perspective*. New York: Harper & Row, 1964.
Ryan, William. *Blaming the Victim*. New York: Vantage Books, 1976.

RAPE

Bode, Janet. *Rape: Preventing It: Coping with the Legal, Medical and Emotional Aftermath*. New York: Watts Publishing, 1979.
Halpern, Susan. *Rape: Helping the Victim: A Treatment Manual*. Oradell, N.J.: Medical Economics Co., Book Division, 1978.
Hilberman, Elaine. *The Rape Victim: A Project of the Committee on Women of the American Psychiatric Association*. New York: Basic Books, 1976.
McCombie, Sharon. *The Rape Crisis Intervention Handbook: A Guide for Victim Care*. New York: Plenum Press, 1980.†

SELF-ESTEEM AND REJECTION

Ellison, Craig W., ed. *Your Better Self: Christianity, Psychology and Self-Esteem*. San Francisco: Harper & Row, 1983.
McGee, Robert S. *The Search for Significance*. Houston, Tex.: Rapha Publishing, 1990.
Narramore, S. Bruce. *You're Someone Special*. Grand Rapids: Zondervan, 1978.
Wagner, Maurice E. *The Sensation of Being Somebody: Building an Adequate Self-Concept*. Grand Rapids: Zondervan, 1975.

SEXUAL ABUSE

Barnard, George W., A. Kenneth Fuller, Lynn Robbins, and Theodore Shaw. *The Child Molester: An Integrated Approach to Evaluation and Treatment*. New York: Brunner/Mazel, 1989.
Courtois, Christine A. *Healing the Incest Wound: Adult Survivors in Therapy*. New York: W. W. Norton & Co., 1988.
Everstine, Diana Sullivan, and Louis Everstine. *Sexual Trauma in Children and Adolescents: Dynamics and Treatment*. New York: Brunner/Mazel, 1989.
Hancock, Maxine, and Karen Burton Mains. *Child Sexual Abuse: A Hope for Healing*. Wheaton, Ill.: Harold Shaw, 1987.
Ingersoll, Sandra L., and Susan O. Patton. *Treating Perpetrators of Sexual Abuse*. Lexington, Mass.: D.C. Heath & Co., 1990.
Stratford, Lauren. *Satan's Underground: The Extraordinary Story of One Woman's Escape*. Eugene, Ore.: Harvest House, 1988.
Vredvelt, Pamela, and Kathryn Rodriguez. *Healing the Hurts of Sexual Abuse*. Old Tappan, N.J.: Revell, 1987.

SHAME

Bradshaw, John. *Healing the Shame that Binds You.* Deerfield Beach, Fla.: Health Communications, Inc., 1988.
Fossum, Merle A., and Marilyn J. Mason. *Facing Shame: Families in Recovery.* New York: W. W. Norton, 1986.
Potter-Efron, Ronald, and Patricia Potter-Efron. *Letting Go Of Shame.* San Francisco: Harper & Row, 1989.

SINGLE PARENTING

Bustanoby, Andre. *Being a Single Parent.* New York: Ballantine Books, 1985.
Dodson, Fitzhugh. *How to Single Parent.* New York: Harper and Row, 1987.
Kalter, Neil. *Growing Up with Divorce: Helping Your Child Avoid Immediate and Later Emotional Problems.* New York: The Free Press, 1990.†
Lindblad-Goldberg, Marion, ed. *Clinical Issues in Single-Parent Households.* Rockville, Md.: Aspen Publishers, 1987.
McCoy, Kathleen. *Solo Parenting: Your Essential Guide.* New York: New American Library, 1987.
Morawetz, Anita, and Gillian Walker. *Brief Therapy with Single-Parent Families.* New York: Brunner/Mazel, 1984.

STEPFAMILIES

Visher, Emily B., and John S. Visher. *Step-Families: A Guide to Working with Stepparents and Stepchildren.* New York: Brunner/Mazel, 1979.
————. *Old Loyalties, New Ties: Therapeutic Strategies with Stepfamilies.* New York: Brunner/Mazel, 1988.

STRESS

Cotton, Dorothy H. G. *Stress Management: An Integrated Approach to Therapy.* New York: Brunner/Mazel, 1990.†
Ellison, Craig W. *Finding Shalom: Counseling and the Stress of Life.* Dallas: Word, forthcoming (1992).
Figley, Charles R. *Treating Stress in Families.* New York: Brunner/Mazel, 1989.

SUICIDE

Alvarez, Alfred. *The Savage God: A Study of Suicide.* New York: Random House, 1970.
Brenner, Francis. *Suicide: A Preventable Tragedy.* New York: Lodestone Books/Dutton, 1989.
Gardner, Sandra. *Teenage Suicide.* New York: Messner, 1985.
Grollman, Earl. *Suicide: Prevention, Intervention, Postvention.* Boston: Beacon Press, 1971.

Resources:
General Christian Counseling

Contemporary Christian Counseling Series
Word, Inc.
Gary Collins, Series Editor
Sequel to Resources for Christian Counseling Series, beginning in 1991.

Journal of Psychology and Christianity
P.O. Box 628
Blue Jay, CA 92317
Quarterly journal which emphasizes theoretical and practical articles of particular interest to Christian counselors. Also includes more general theory and research articles pertaining to Christianity and psychology.

Journal of Psychology and Theology
Rosemead Graduate School of Psychology
Biola University
13800 Biola Avenue
La Mirada, CA 90639
Quarterly publication which examines a wide variety of issues pertaining to the integration of Christianity and psychology from an evangelical viewpoint, including articles of relevance to counseling.

Resources for Christian Counseling Series
Word, Inc.
Gary Collins, Series Editor
Thirty-volume series dealing with a wide variety of counseling issues from a practical, evangelical perspective.

Urban Ministry Resource Series
Zondervan Publishing House
Craig W. Ellison, Series Editor
Projected fourteen-volume series on various aspects of ministry in major urban centers of the United States and the world. Publication is due to begin in 1992.

Resources: Organizations and Self-Help Groups

GENERAL INFORMATION SOURCE

National Self-Help Clearinghouse
33 West 42nd Street
New York, NY 10036
(212) 642-2944

ADDICTIONS (NONCHEMICAL)

Debtors Anonymous
314 W. 53rd Street
New York, NY 10159
(212) 969-0710

Friends in Recovery
1201 Knoxville Street
San Diego, CA 92110
(619) 275-1350
Christian group that sponsors Recovery Publications (same address).

Gamblers Anonymous
P.O. Box 17173
Los Angeles, CA 90017
(213) 386-8789

Overeaters Anonymous
World Service Office
2190 190th Street
Torrance, CA 90504
(213) 542-8363

The National Association for Christian Recovery
P.O. Box 11095
Whittier, CA 90603
Evangelical self-help organization with quarterly newsletter and information about local recovery groups for a wide variety of nonchemical addictions.

Sex Addicts Anonymous
P.O. Box 3038
Minneapolis, MN 55403

Sexaholics Anonymous
P.O. Box 300
Simi Valley, CA 93062

Turning Point
P.O. Box 8936
Chattanooga, TN 37411
(615) 698-2872
Evangelical self-help organization for life-controlling problems. Local groups in churches throughout the U.S.

Workaholics Anonymous
Westchester Self-Help Clearinghouse
Westchester Community College
75 Grasslands Road
Vahalla, NY 10959

ADULT CHILDREN OF ALCOHOLICS

Adult Children of Alcoholics
Central Service Board
P.O. Box 35623
Los Angeles, CA 90035
(213) 464-4423

Al-Anon/Alateen Family Group Headquarters, Inc.
Madison Square Station
New York, NY 10010
(212) 686-1100

Children of Alcoholics Foundation, Inc.
540 Madison Avenue, 23rd Floor
New York, NY 10022
(212) 351-2680

Co-Dependents Anonymous
P.O. Box 33577
Phoenix, AZ 85067-3577
(602) 944-0141

Overcomers Outreach, Inc.
2290 West Whittier Boulevard
La Habra, CA 90631
(213) 697-3994

National Association for Children of Alcoholics (NACOA)
31582 Coast Highway, Suite B
South Laguna, CA 92677
(714) 499-3889

AIDS

AIDS Action Council (AAC)
2033 M Street, 8th Floor
Washington, D.C. 20036
(202) 547-3101

National AIDS Network (NAN)
2033 M Street, Suite 800
Washington, D.C. 20036
(202) 293-2437

National Association of People With AIDS (NAPWA)
2025 I Street, N.W., Suite 415
Washington, D.C. 20036
(202) 429-2856

National Minority AIDS Council (NMAC)
714 G Street, S.E.
Washington, D.C. 20003
(202) 544-1076

ALCOHOL AND DRUG ABUSE

Alcoholics Anonymous World Services, Inc.
468 Park Avenue South
New York, NY 10016
(212) 686-1100

Alcoholics for Christ
1316 North Campbell Road
Royal Oak, MI 48067
(419) 782-1684

Narcotics Anonymous World Services Office, Inc.
P.O. Box 622
Sun Valley, CA 91352
(818) 780-3951

National Council on Alcoholism
12 West 21st Street, 8th Floor
New York, NY 10010
(212) 206-6770

National Clearinghouse for Alcohol Information
P.O. Box 1908
Rockville, MD 20850
(301) 468-2600

National Institute on Alcohol Abuse and Alcoholism
5600 Fishers Lane
Rockville, MD 20857
(301) 443-2403

National Clearinghouse for Drug Abuse Information
The National Institute on Drug Abuse (NIDA)
Room 10A56, Parklawn Building
5600 Fishers Lane
Rockville, MD 20857
(301) 443-6500

National Cocaine Hotline
(800) COC-AINE

Rapha
Box 580355
Houston, TX 77258
(800) 227-2657
Christ-centered in-hospital care units for substance abuse problems in
several states.
Substance Abusers Victorious
One Cascade Plaza
Akron, OH 44308
(216) 253-5444
Teen Challenge
444 Clinton Avenue
Brooklyn, NY 11238-1602
(718) 789-1414
Charismatic evangelical drug rehabilitation programs, nationwide, for
teen and young adult drug abusers.
Toughlove
P.O. Box 1069
Doylestown, PA 18901
(215) 348-7090

CRISIS PREGNANCIES

Christian Action Council
701 W. Broad Street
Falls Church, VA 22046
Crisis Pregnancies National Helpline
(800) 238-4269
Victims of Choice
124 Shefield Drive
Vacaville, CA 95687

DOMESTIC ABUSE

American Association for Protecting Children
9725 East Hampden Ave.
Denver, CO 80231
(303) 695-0811
Batterers Anonymous
P.O. Box 29
Redlands, CA 92373
(714) 383-3643
Child Abusers Anonymous
Center for the Prevention of Sexual and Domestic Violence
1914 North Thirty-fourth Street, Suite 105
Seattle, WA 98103
(206) 634-1903
Childhelp, U.S.A.
6463 Independence Ave.
Woodland Hills, CA 91367
(800) 422-4453

National Center on Child Abuse and Neglect
Clearinghouse
P.O. Box 1182
Washington, D.C. 22013
(301) 251-5157

National Child Abuse Hotline
(800) 422-4453

National Clearinghouse on Domestic Violence
P.O. Box 2309
Rockville, MD 20852

National Coalition Against Domestic Violence
1500 Massachusetts Ave., N.W.
Suite 35
Washington, D.C. 20005

GRIEF RECOVERY

Grief Recovery Institute
8306 Wilshire Blvd., 21-A
Los Angeles, CA 90211
(213) 650-1234
Not an organization as such, but it offers workshops around the United States.

Grief Recovery Helpline
1-800-445-4800
Not an organization, but counseling is provided over the telephone.

National SIDS Foundation
(800) 221-SIDS
(301) 964-8000 in Maryland

HOMOSEXUALITY

Exodus International
P.O. Box 2121
San Rafael, CA 34312
Umbrella association of Christian organizations working to help those wishing to be freed of homosexual lifestyles.

Love in Action
P.O. Box 2655
San Rafael, CA 34312
(415) 454-0960
One of the oldest Christian organizations working with those leaving homosexual lifestyles.

SEXUAL ABUSE

Incest Survivors Anonymous
P.O. Box 5613
Long Beach, CA 90800

84601

Parents United/Daughters & Sons United
Adults Molested as Children United
P.O. Box 952
San Jose, CA 95108
(408) 280-5055

Sexual Assault Center
Harborview Medical Center
325 9th Ave.
Seattle, WA 98104

SINGLE PARENTING

Big Brothers/Big Sisters
117 South 17th Street, Suite 1200
Philadelphia, PA 19103
(215) 567-2748

International Youth Council
c/o Parents Without Partners
7910 Woodmont Avenue, Suite 100
Bethesda, MD 20814
(800) 638-8078

National Institute for Latchkey Children
P.O. Box 682
Glen Echo, MD 20812
(301) 229-6126

Parents Anonymous
National Office
2230 Hawthorne Blvd., Suite 208
Torrance, CA 90505
(800) 421-0353
(800) 352-0386 in California

Toughlove
P.O. Box 70
Sellersville, PA 18960
(215) 257-0421

STEPFAMILIES

The Stepfamily Foundation
(212) 877-3244
(800) 759-STEP

SUICIDE

Contact
(717) 232-3501